AWESOME ALMANAC™

MICHIGAN

Created by
Jean F. Blashfield

Compiled and Written by
Annette Newcomb

B&B Publishing, Inc.

B & B Publishing, Inc.
P. O. Box 393
Fontana, Wisconsin 53125

Additional Materials by **Margie Benson** and **Nancy Jacobson**

Editor – **Jean B. Black**

Layout and Design – **Nancy Jacobson**

Photo Researcher – **Margie Benson**

Computer Design and Production Manager – **Dave Conant**

Computer Specialist and Indexer – **Marilyn Magowan**

Cover Design – **Gary Hurst**

Publisher's Cataloging in Publication

Blashfield, Jean F.
    Awesome almanac—Michigan / Jean F. Blashfield.
    p. cm.
    Includes index.
    Preassigned LCCN: 92-074709
    ISBN 1-880190-06-0

1. Michigan—Miscellanea. 2. Michigan—History. 3. Almanacs, American—Michigan. I. Title.

F564.B53 1993

                             977.4'003
                             QBI93-446

Printed in the United States of America

93 94 95 96 97   5 4 3 2 1

AWESOME ALMANAC is a trademark of B&B Publishing, Inc.

———————————————

ATTENTION SCHOOLS AND BUSINESSES:
This book is available at quantity discounts with bulk purchases for educational, business, or sales promotional use. For information, please write to B&B Publishing, Inc., P.O. Box 393, Fontana, WI 53125

TABLE OF CONTENTS

Capitol building in Lansing

THE WOLVERINE STATE

It's hard to understand how Michigan became known as the Wolverine State when, as far as experts can tell, the feisty animal never even lived their! However, legend has it that settlers heading west between Dearborn and Ypsilanti traveled the Great Sauk Trail. Today it's known as Michigan Avenue. It was there that Conrad "Old Coon" Ten Eyck's Tavern stood. Legend says the state's nickname was born there.

As tired settlers arrived at the tavern, Old Coon would greet them in person, then shout to his wife, "Sally, put on some more wolf steaks!" The wolf steaks may have been more of a joke than anything else—a way for Old Coon to give the greenhorns a hard time. One day a young guest asked if she had really just eaten wolf steak. Old Coon assured her she had, and the young guest asked, "Then I suppose I am a wolverine?" Old Coon said she was and would be from that day forward. The name stuck and settlers began calling themselves Wolverines!

As you will see on this awesome journey, Michigan is a state of many faces and places. There's not much you can't find in Michigan. You can even get a great deal on a car!

- The Wolverine Facts
- The State Takes Shape
- The Government
- Capital and Capitol
- The People
- Michigan County Almanac
- Flags, Symbols & Songs

THE WOLVERINE FACTS

Michigama: The Great Water state

The name "Michigan" is derived from the Ojibwa (Chippewa) word *Michigama,* meaning "Great Water." Lake Michigan was named before the territory.

The primary state nickname is Wolverine State, but Michigan has also been called the Lake State, the Auto State, the Great Lake State, the Water Wonderland, and the Lady of the Lake.

UP or down

Michigan is the only state divided into two completely separate sections, each of which is attached to another state. The northern section, the Upper Peninsula, is usually called the UP, but the southern section, the Lower Peninsula, is rarely referred to as the LP. For well over a hundred years the only way to get from one peninsula to the other was by ferryboat across the Straits of Mackinac, which is where Lakes Michigan and Huron meet, or by a long drive through Wisconsin and around Lake Michigan.

Water everywhere

Four of the five Great Lakes surround Michigan's two peninsulas with 3,200 miles of shoreline, which is more than the entire Atlantic seaboard of the United States—more freshwater coast than any other state and more coastline than any state except Alaska. On the Michigan shore there are 378 beaches that draw visitors. Dotting the state are 11,000 inland lakes as well as 36,000 miles of rivers and streams.

The Land

Land area - 58,527 square miles (23rd largest state; largest state east of the Mississippi)

Highest point - Mt. Curwood at 1,980 feet

Lowest point - Lake Erie in Monroe County at 571 feet

Average elevation - 900 feet

Longest distance from north to south - 490 miles (only 286 miles of it is in one chunk of land, the Lower Peninsula)

Longest width from east to west - 334 miles in the Upper Peninsula, and 200 miles in the Lower

Geographic center - Wexford, 5 miles north-northwest of Cadillac

Largest inland lake - Houghton Lake, at 30.8 square miles

Mighty Mac: An awesome bridge

It takes an awesome bridge to connect the two awesome halves of Michigan across the Straits of Mackinac. The Mackinac Bridge is the world's longest suspension bridge, although its main span is only the fifth longest (or will be when Japan finishes its Akashi Strait bridge). The total bridge system is five miles (26,444 feet) across, and connects Michigan's Upper and Lower peninsulas.

Construction began in 1954 and the bridge was opened to traffic on November 1, 1957. The main towers soar 552 feet above water and start

210 feet below the water's surface. An incredible 42,000 miles of cable were used on the bridge. Maximum tension on each cable is 16,000 tons! The weight of the cables alone is 11,840 tons. The main cables are $24\frac{1}{2}$ inches in diameter. The bridge's main span is 3,800 feet. Designed by D.B. Steinman, the bridge is made to withstand many times the estimated tension from ice, wind, and gravity.

Working on the Mighty Mac

The Ambassador Bridge spanning 1,850 feet between Detroit and Windsor, Ontario, was dedicated November 11, 1929. The bridge, constructed at a cost of $20 million, linked the United States and Canada. It was the first bridge to connect two countries.

First bridge to link U.S. with another country

THE STATE TAKES SHAPE

The Quebec Act, proclaimed by the British in 1774, made Michigan part of Quebec which was extended southward to the Ohio River and westward to the Mississippi. It later became part of the Northwest Territory. Michigan was known as Quebequoise for a while. The British, having decided not to deport the French, granted them two legal systems—French civil law and British criminal law. They also granted the Catholics religious freedom, which they did not have in the Puritan New England colonies. However, those colonies insisted that their charters granted the lands west of them. Michigan became a bone of contention contributing to the Declaration of Independence.

When Michigan was Quebec

**When Michigan
was still British**

After the American Revolution had ended, Michigan was still under the control of the British. The politicians' first inclination after the war was to allow each nation to keep what it possessed when the war ended. If that had been the case, Michigan would still be part of Canada. However, negotiations that went on in Europe also involved Spain which wanted some of the New World. The British, determined to keep Spain out of North America, solved the problem by letting the United States have all of the Northwest Territory, north of the Ohio River and east of the Mississippi. In the final negotiations, Benjamin Franklin attempted to set the boundary between the United States and Canada at the 45th parallel. If the U.S. had included southern Ontario, Michigan would have lost the northern part of the Lower Peninsula and all of the Upper Peninsula.

**Michigan was almost
in Wisconsin**

When the Old Northwest was being split up into future states, Thomas Jefferson suggested names for several, including Pelisipia, Polypotamia, and Michigania, but his Michigania was in the territory of what later became Wisconsin. What is now Michigan was split among Cherronesus, Metropotamia, and Sylvania. It's probably just as well that his plan didn't go into effect—think of the spelling problems.

TOPSY-TURVY BOUNDARIES

1800	Territory of Indiana was created January 4, splitting the land that would eventually become Michigan between the Indiana Territory and the Northwest Territory along a line extending northward from the Ohio-Indiana border.
1803	Ohio was created with boundary descriptions to include land from the southern tip of Lake Michigan extending at an angle to the northern edge of Maumee Bay. That part of Michigan in the Northwest Territory was added to the Indiana Territory.
1805	Territory of Michigan, which included the eastern tip of the UP, was separated on January 11 from the Indiana Territory. The description of the southern border included the mouth of the Maumee River.
1816	Indiana was made a state with its northern boundary 10 miles north of the original line so that Indiana could have some Great Lakes coast.
1818	Illinois was made a state. All remaining land in the Northwest Territory was attached to Michigan including Wisconsin and part of Minnesota. Indian claims were cleared and a government land office was finally opened, allowing the sale of land outside the areas near Detroit and Mackinac.
1834	The western boundary was moved from the Mississippi River to the Missouri River.
1835	Michigan began to operate as a state (though Congress had not approved such a move). Ohio claimed a 10-mile strip in Maumee Bay, setting up what is now called the "Toledo War"—although Toledo did not even exist at that time, and delaying statehood.
1836	Wisconsin Territory was separated from Michigan, taking all of the western lands with it. Borders were rather vague.
1837	Michigan became the 26th state when it was admitted to the Union January 26. Its boundaries included the UP in exchange for giving up the Toledo Strip.

THE GOVERNMENT

The chief executives of the state are the governor and the lieutenant governor, both of whom are elected for four-year terms.

The executive

The present constitution was adopted on April 1, 1963, and went into effect on January 1, 1964.

The constitution

The state legislature consists of an upper house, the **Senate**, which has 38 members serving four-year terms, and the lower house, the **House of Representatives**, which has 110 members serving two-year terms.

The legislature

Because so much of Michigan's population is concentrated in four counties (Wayne, Genesee, Macomb, and Oakland), there has always been a major fight between populous and little-populated regions about the apportionment of legislative seats. From the time statehood was achieved until 1964, the people of the state never had equal representation in the legislature. Finally, in 1964, the federal courts required equal representation. When state legislators were unable to agree on an apportionment plan, the state Supreme Court stepped in and developed a new map of legislative districts.

Michigan has two U.S. Senators and 16 U.S. Representatives in Washington, D.C. (down 2 from the previous census), adding up to 18 electoral votes.

Currently in office

The following top elected officials are in office until January 1995:

Governor: John M. Engler, Republican

Lieutenant Governor: Connie Binsfeld, Republican

Secretary of State: Richard H. Austin, Democrat

Attorney General: Frank J. Kelley, Democrat

The Michigan Supreme Court consists of seven judges who are elected for eight-year terms, with two elected every other year. Lower courts include a court of appeals, circuit courts, and probate courts.

The court system

CAPITAL AND CAPITOL

In 1805, Congress organized the Territory of Michigan, naming Detroit as capital. General William Hull was named the first governor and when he arrived in Detroit to attend his inauguration in July, he found the fort and village in ruins. A month earlier, the settlement, the fort, and 200 wooden structures had burned to the ground. All 2,200 residents survived.

First governor finds capitol in ashes

Territorial Judge Augustus B. Woodward was given the job of redesigning the lost city. Ten thousand acres were allocated for it. Woodward chose to follow L'Enfant's design of Washington, D.C., a hexagon with a park in the middle and with streets radiating outward, in a hub-and-spoke pattern. As the city grew, the original pattern was repeated. City officials required that sidewalks be in place by 1827 and street names on corners by 1836. By 1837, Detroit's population hit 10,000. The population doubled every decade from 1830 to 1860.

State Capitol Building

It started as a joke

Lansing became the state capital more as part of a legislative prank than by way of a well-thought-out political move. Detroit was temporarily proclaimed the state capital in the constitution of 1835, which required that by 1847 a permanent capital would be selected. After much debate and argument (what a surprise), someone suggested a remote area in Ingham County. Laughter resounded—at that time the future Lansing consisted of one log house and a sawmill. But the laughter died down. Most legislators accepted the fact that at least the town was in a central location. Naming the capital was another problem. Originally it was to be Michigan, but the House somehow approved Aloda. Finally, they chose Lansing at the suggestion of the residents.

Small as it was, the future capital had already been the site of a scandal. It seems that two speculators had sold some New York families lots in a "city" in the central Lower Peninsula. Of course, they were appalled and angry when they found no city and a township that was little more than a bump in the road. A few hearty souls stayed and named the area after their home of Lansing, New York.

And the winner — The Capitol Building!

In 1847, legislators began functioning in Lansing out of a small, hastily built wooden building. It was replaced by a more substantial brick structure in 1854. As the state grew, they realized that a building more permanent and grand was needed. Word went out in 1872 that a contest was being held to design a new capitol building to cost $1.2 million. The winner was Elijah Myers, an architect from Springfield, Illinois, where he had been ignored when Illinois was building a new capitol. Michigan's building is cross-shaped, 420 feet long, 274 feet wide, and 267 feet high.

A fire erupted in the State Office Building in Lansing on February 8, 1951. The blaze burned for two days, destroying the top two floors. Unfortunately hundreds of records were stored on these levels. The remaining five floors received smoke and water damage.

Fire destroys state records

Michigan's first governor was a mere boy when he went into politics. At 19 years old, Stevens Thomson Mason was appointed secretary of Michigan Territory. That position placed him in the role of acting territorial governor following the death of Governor George Porter. Mason fought hard for Michigan's statehood, as well as the boundary dispute with Ohio over the "Toledo Strip." The young man was elected governor of Michigan in 1837. To his constituents he was a brave and confident leader, but his youth and lack of experience also brought criticism. He had made some errors of judgment, especially during the 1837 panic in Michigan. Mason served two terms, then moved to New York City where he practiced law. The "boy governor" died at age 31 and is buried in Capitol Square Park, Detroit.

Boy governor of Michigan

THE PEOPLE

The total population of Michigan in the 1990 census was 9,295,297, making it the eighth largest state. The breakdown of the census shows 4,512,781 males and 4,782,516 females living in the Wolverine State. A further breakdown by race is 7,756,086 (83.4%) Caucasians; 1,291,706 (13.9%) African-Americans; 201,596 (2.2%) Hispanics; 104,983 (1.1%) Asian or Pacific Islanders; 55,638 (0.6%) American Indian, Eskimo, or Aleutians; and 86,884 (0.9%) other races. The median age of Michiganders is 32.6 with 26.5 percent under age 18 and 11.9 percent 65 and older.

The 1990 census

POPULATION GROWTH

Census Year	Michigan	United States
1990	9,295,297	248,709,873
1980	9,262,044	226,542,203
1970	8,881,826	203,302,031
1960	7,823,194	179,323,175
1950	6,371,766	151,325,798
1940	5,256,106	132,164,569
1930	4,842,325	123,202,624
1920	3,668,412	106,021,537
1910	2,810,173	92,228,496
1900	2,420,982	76,212,168
1890	2,093,890	62,979,766
1880	1,636,937	50,189,209
1870	1,184,059	38,558,371
1860	749,113	31,443,321
1850	397,654	23,191,876
1840	212,267	17,063,353
1830	31,369	12,860,702
1820	8,896	9,638,453
1810	4,762	7,240,000

Graph shows the population of Michigan as a percentage of the United State population.

MICHIGAN COUNTY ALMANAC

Michigan has 83 counties. Two of them are among the 30 counties in the United States with a population of more than 1 million, according to the 1990 census: Wayne County is the eighth largest and Oakland is the twenty-eighth. The smallest county in population is Keweenaw. The smallest in area is Benzie; the largest is Chippewa. Dickinson was the last county to be created.

MICHIGAN COUNTIES

COUNTY	1990 POP.	COUNTY SEAT	SQ. MILES	FOUNDED	NAMED AFTER
Alcona	10,145	Harrisville	679	4/1/1840	Indian word for "a fine or excellent plain"
Alger	8,972	Munising	912	3/17/1885	Gov. Russell A. Alger
Allegan	90,509	Allegan	832	3/2/1831	Indian tribe Allegami or Allegans
Alpena	30,695	Alpena	567	4/1/1840	Indian meaning "a good partridge country"
Antrim	18,185	Bellaire	480	4/1/1840	County Antrim, Northern Ireland
Arenac	14,931	Standish	367	3/2/1831	Latin: arena, plus Indian for "sandy place"
Baraga	7,954	L'Anse	901	2/19/1875	Missionary Father Baraga
Barry	50,057	Hastings	560	10/29/1829	Gov. John S. Barry
Bay	111,723	Bay City	447	4/20/1857	Location along Saginaw Bay
Benzie	12,200	Beulah	322	2/27/1863	From French Aux-Bec-Scies, applied to the Betsie River
Berrien	161,378	St. Joseph	576	10/29/1829	Atty. Gen. John M. Berrien
Branch	41,502	Coldwater	508	10/29/1829	Sec. of Navy John Branch
Calhoun	135,982	Marshall	712	10/29/1829	Vice President John C. Calhoun
Cass	49,477	Cassopolis	496	10/29/1829	Territorial Gov. Lewis Cass
Charlevoix	21,468	Charlevoix	421	4/1/1840	Missionary Pierre F. de Charlevoix
Cheboygan	21,398	Cheboygan	720	4/1/1840	Indian word for "river that comes from the ground"
Chippewa	34,604	Sault Ste. Marie	1,590	12/22/1826	Chippewa tribe
Clare	24,952	Harrison	570	4/1/1840	County Clare, Ireland
Clinton	57,883	St. Johns	573	3/2/1831	New York gov. De Witt Clinton
Crawford	12,260	Grayling	559	4/1/1840	Am. Rev. officer William Crawford

COUNTY	1990 POP.	COUNTY SEAT	SQ. MILES	FOUNDED	NAMED AFTER
Marquette	70,887	Marquette	1,821	3/9/1843	Jesuit missionary Jacques Marquette
Mason	25,537	Ludington	494	4/1/1840	First governor, Stevens T. Mason
Mecosta	37,308	Big Rapids	560	4/1/1840	Chief Mecosta
Menominee	24,920	Menominee	1,045	3/15/1861	Menominee tribe
Midland	75,651	Midland	525	3/2/1831	Located near center of Lower Peninsula
Missaukee	12,147	Lake City	565	4/1/1840	Chief Mesaukee
Monroe	133,600	Monroe	557	7/14/1817	President James Monroe
Montcalm	53,059	Stanton	713	3/2/1831	French General Marquis Louis Joseph de Montcalm de Saint Veran
Montmorency	8,936	Atlanta	550	4/1/1840	Count Morenci, aided colonies in Am. Rev.
Muskegon	158,983	Muskegon	507	2/4/1859	Indian word for "river with marshes"
Newaygo	38,202	White Cloud	847	4/1/1840	Chippewa Chief Newaygo
Oakland	1,083,592	Pontiac	875	3/28/1820	Abundance of oak trees
Oceana	22,454	Hart	541	3/2/1831	Name of a 17th-century book by James Harrington
Ogemaw	18,681	West Branch	570	4/1/1840	Ogemaw tribe
Ontonagon	8,854	Ontonagon	1,311	3/9/1843	Indian word for "hunting river"
Osceola	20,146	Reed City	569	4/1/1840	Seminole Chief Osceola
Oscoda	7,842	Mio	568	4/1/1840	Indian word for "pebbly prairie"
Otsego	17,957	Gaylord	516	4/1/1840	Otsego tribe
Ottawa	187,786	Grand Haven	567	3/2/1831	Ottawa tribe
Presque Isle	13,743	Rogers City	656	4/1/1840	French word for "narrow peninsula"
Roscommon	19,776	Roscommon	528	4/1/1840	County Roscommon, Ireland
Saginaw	211,946	Saginaw	815	9/10/1822	Chippewa word for "Land of the Sacs"
St. Clair	145,607	Port Huron	734	3/28/1820	Gov. Arthur St. Clair
St. Joseph	58,913	Centreville	503	10/29/1829	Patron saint of France
Sanilac	39,928	Sandusky	964	9/10/1822	Chief Sanilac
Schoolcraft	8,302	Manistique	1,173	3/9/1843	Prominent figure, Henry R. Schoolcraft
Shiawassee	69,770	Corunna	540	9/10/1822	Indian word for "river that twists about"
Tuscola	55,498	Caro	812	4/1/1840	Indian word for "level place"
Van Buren	70,060	Paw Paw	611	10/29/1829	Sec. of State Martin Van Buren
Washtenaw	282,937	Ann Arbor	710	9/10/1822	Indian word for "at or on the river"
Wayne	2,111,687	Detroit	615	11/21/181	"Mad" Anthony Wayne
Wexford	23,360	Cadillac	586	4/1/1840	County Wexford, Ireland

COUNTY	1990 POP.	COUNTY SEAT	SQ. MILES	FOUNDED	NAMED AFTER
Delta	37,780	Escanaba	1,173	3/9/1843	Greek letter delta, meaning "triangular"
Dickinson	26,831	Iron Mountain	770	5/21/1891	Postmaster General Donald M. Dickinson
Eaton	92,879	Charlotte	579	10/29/1829	Sec. of War John M. Eaton
Emmet	25,040	Petoskey	468	4/1/1840	Irish patriot and fighter Robert Emmet
Genesee	430,459	Flint	642	3/28/1835	Genesee County, NY
Gladwin	21,896	Gladwin	505	3/2/1831	British commander of Detroit Henry Gladwin
Gogebic	18,052	Bessemer	1,105	2/7/1887	Lake Agogebic
Grand Traverse	64,273	Traverse City	466	4/7/1851	French words meaning "long crossing"
Gratiot	38,982	Ithaca	570	3/2/1831	Army officer Charles Gratiot
Hillsdale	43,431	Hillsdale	603	10/29/1829	Refers to the landscape
Houghton	35,446	Houghton	1,014	3/19/1845	State geologist Douglas Houghton
Huron	34,951	Bad Axe	830	4/1/1840	Huron tribe
Ingham	281,912	Mason	560	10/29/1829	Sec. of Treas. Samuel D. Ingham
Ionia	57,024	Ionia	577	3/2/1831	Grecian province
Iosco	30,209	Tawas City	546	4/1/1840	Indian word for "water of light"
Iron	13,175	Crystal Falls	1,163	4/3/1885	Iron ore found in county
Isabella	54,624	Mt. Pleasant	577	3/2/1831	Spanish Queen Isabella
Jackson	149,756	Jackson	705	10/29/1829	President Andrew Jackson
Kalamazoo	223,411	Kalamazoo	562	10/29/1829	Indian word for "mirage or reflecting river"
Kalkaska	13,497	Kalkaska	563	4/1/1840	Chippewa word for "burned over"
Kent	500,631	Grand Rapids	862	3/2/1831	NY Judge James Kent
Keweenaw	1,701	Eagle River	543	3/11/1861	Indian word for "carrying place" or "portage"
Lake	8,583	Baldwin	568	4/1/1840	Location on water
Lapeer	74,768	Lapeer	658	9/10/1822	French word for "stone"
Leelanau	16,527	Leland	341	4/1/1840	Chippewa word for "delight of life"
Lenawee	91,476	Adrian	753	9/10/1822	Indian word for "man or male"
Livingston	115,645	Howell	574	3/21/1833	Sec. of State Edward Livingston
Luce	5,763	Newberry	904	3/1/1887	Governor Cyrus G. Luce
Mackinac	10,674	St. Ignace	1,025	3/1/1887	Part of Indian term for "green turtle"
Macomb	717,400	Mt. Clemens	482	1/15/1818	Brig. Gen. Alexander Macomb
Manistee	21,285	Manistee	543	4/1/1840	Indian word for "lost river"

FLAGS, SYMBOLS & SONGS

The wordy state seal

The State Seal, which is also on the State Flag, contains three different Latin phrases. The word in the center (see the flag below), *Tuebor,* means "I will defend." Below the elk and moose is the state motto—*Si Quaeris Peninsulam Amoenam Circumspice,* which means "If you seek a pleasant peninsula, look about you." (Fortunately, that holds true whether you are in the Lower Peninsula or the Upper Peninsula.) The third phrase, located at the top, *E Pluribus Unum,* is, of course, the motto of the United States, "From many, one."

State symbols

The State Flag bears the central part of the State Seal on a blue background.

State Flower – Apple blossom (adopted 1897)
State Bird – Robin (adopted 1931)
State Fish – Trout (adopted 1965), made more specific in 1988: Brook trout
State Gem – Isle Royale greenstone (a.k.a.: chlorastrolite) (adopted 1972)
State Stone – Petoskey stone (adopted 1965)

Michigan, My Michigan

A song to thee, fair State of mine,
Michigan, my Michigan,
But greater song than this is thine,
Michigan, my Michigan,
The whisper of the forest tree,
The thunder of the inland sea;
Unite in one grand symphony
Of Michigan, my Michigan.

I sing a State of all the best,
Michigan, my Michigan;
I sing a State with riches bless'd,
Michigan, my Michigan;
Thy mines unmask a hidden store,
But richer thy historic lore,
More great the love thy builders bore,
O Michigan, my Michigan.

The State Song

Michigan has no official state song, but one song, "Michigan, My Michigan," is frequently used. The words to the first version were written in 1863 by Winifred Lee Brent using the melody of the Christmas song "O Tannenbaum." Then in 1902 a second version was written by Douglas M. Malloch. His words are generally used—but not all of the dozen or more verses he wrote.

WOLVERINE NATURAL WONDERS

Michigan is truly a state that has it all. Surrounded by three of the Great Lakes, the state has within its borders 40,000 square miles of lakes, and residents enthusiastically take advantage of this natural wonder. At last count, 600,000 pleasure boaters and 500 fishing charters were registered with the state. That's good news, because wherever you are, you're within 85 miles of Great Lakes' water and within six miles of one of the state's 11,000 inland lakes. And don't forget the 36,000 miles of rivers and streams. Of course, the state's 149 native fish love it, too!

There's 65 species of animals thriving in 18.4 million acres of timberland, along with 300 different kinds of birds. Michigan is also home to a rare songbird, the Kirtland's warbler. Coyote, bobcat, red fox, beaver, muskrat, otter, and mink call the state forests home.

Michigan is indeed filled with awesome natural resources.

- Natural Phenomena
- Endangered in Michigan
- Majestic Timbers
- Hazardous to Our Health
- Parks and Wildlife Refuges
- Where a River Flows
- Underwater Michigan
- Weather Notes

NATURAL PHENOMENA

Leaf me alone!

A deer hunter from White Pine, Jim Harter, found a very unusual pair of trees. It seems they have a four-foot branch in common. Heavy snow probably caused one tree to grow sideways behind the other and when it began growing vertically again, a right angle was formed. As a new limb grew, it attached itself to the other tree. Harter won't say exactly where the odd trees are located because they are on his best hunting ground! He will admit that the trees are somewhere in western Ontonagon County close to Porcupine Mountains Wilderness State Park.

Talkin' turkey

Before the white settlers arrived, about 94,000 wild turkeys had the run of the Lower Peninsula from Bay City to Muskegon. Some Indians thought turkey meat was unfit to eat and used only the feathers. When the settlers arrived, most of the wild turkeys' forest habitat was cleared away and by 1900 the birds had disappeared. The last turkey was shot in Van Buren County in 1897.

Between 1954 and 1963 the Department of Conservation released 882 wild turkeys. To the delight of hunters today there are about 74,000 wild turkeys in 75 of the state's 83 counties. This reintroduction wasn't cheap. In 1990, Michigan received 45 more wild turkeys for transfer to the wild from Wisconsin at a cost of $500 per turkey. The bill came to a grand sum of $22,500!

The "humongous fungus"

It's creepy, it's clammy, it covers 37 acres and weighs 1,000 tons! No, it's not a Steven Spielberg movie gone mad, it's a humongous fungus growing on the Michigan-Wisconsin border. Scientists refer to their little discovery as *Armillaria bulbosa*, and describe it as a mass of subterranean cytoplasm which is sprouting a plague of mushrooms.

The mushrooms are really like little antennas from the mother ship which grows just below the surface. Scientists estimate that the monster is about 1,500 years old and it's so big they're not sure if they've found it all. At its present rate of growth, it could creep south and reach Milwaukee, Wisconsin, in 1.6 million years.

A "Twainian" getaway

If in your deepest yearnings you're really Tom Sawyer, Michigan has the cave for you. Bear Cave is located about four miles from Buchanan and has all the makings of a setting for a Twain story. The 150-foot-long tufa rock cave is accessible only by a 40-foot climb down winding stairs. There are many things to see, including lots of flapping bats. The major point of interest is the 250,000-year-old Kansan Boulder. The cave is a clammy 58° Fahrenheit year-round and the pathways are described as "narrow."

Life's a beach!

The Lake Michigan dune system starts in Indiana and extends all the way up the coast almost to the Straits of Mackinac, covering 275,000 acres. Constantly being moved by the wind, it is the largest system of freshwater dunes in the world. However, these fragile dunes are now in danger of being destroyed due to careless misuse.

In 1989, the legislature passed a law to protect 70,000 acres of the most sensitive dunes on Lake Michigan and Lake Superior. Only 40 percent of the coastline dunes are under federal or state protection; the remaining dunes are on unprotected private property. The map shows the location of Michigan coastal dunes.

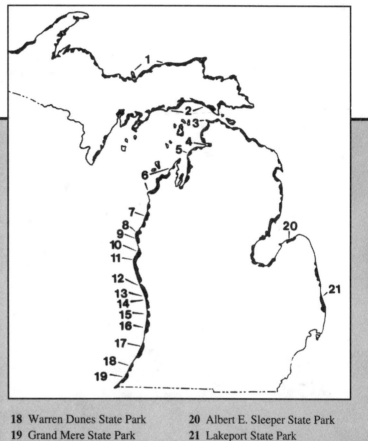

  1 Pictured Rocks National Lakeshore
  2 Hiawatha National Forest
  3 Wilderness State Park
  4 Petoskey State Park
  5 Fisherman's Island State Park
  6 Sleeping Bear Dunes National Lakeshore
  7 Orchard Beach State Park
  8 Ludington State Park
  9 Nordhouse Dunes
 10 Mears State Park
 11 Silver Lake State Park
 12 Muskegon State Park
 13 P.J. Hoffmaster State Park
 14 Grand Haven State Park
 15 Holland State Park
 16 Saugatuck State Park
 17 Van Buren State Park
 18 Warren Dunes State Park
 19 Grand Mere State Park
 20 Albert E. Sleeper State Park
 21 Lakeport State Park

A Chippewa legend tells of a mother bear and her cubs fleeing a huge Wisconsin forest fire by swimming across Lake Michigan. Once mother bear made it to shore, she climbed up a large bluff to watch for her cubs, but they never arrived. The mother bear waited on the bluff for them until she died.

The Chippewa say she still waits. They believe that Manitou, the Great Spirit, placed a mound of sand where she died, a mound the Indians call Sleeping Bear Dune. The North and South Manitou Islands are located where the cubs perished.

Sleeping Bear Dunes National Lakeshore runs 33 miles along the Lower Peninsula's northwestern shore with sand bluffs rising as high as 480 feet above Lake Michigan. As nature shifts the dunes' shape and location, "ghost forests" are revealed.

A mother's love

Oh, Pierre, you devil!

Discovered in 1658, Grand Portal used to be one of the most impressive sights along Lake Superior's rocky coast. A wide stone archway was once the entrance to a six-acre cave. The Indians thought the rock formation looked like an evil face so they called it *Nanitoucksinago,* which means "likeness of an evil spirit."

Pierre Radisson, the first white man to see the archway, named it Grand Portal or "St. Peter." Today the area is called Pictured Rocks National Lakeshore. Weakened by tremors and erosion over hundreds of years, part of the Portal's roof collapsed in 1906. Eventually the entire cave was closed, becoming home to thousands of sea gulls.

ENDANGERED IN MICHIGAN

Population explosion

By 1877, the once common eastern elk had vanished from the Lower Peninsula. Realizing their loss, the state officials placed seven hardy (and prolific) Rocky Mountain elk in Cheboygan County in 1918. There are approximately 1,100 elk in the northern Lower Peninsula today. The largest elk herd east of the Mississippi now covers a range of 600 square miles in four counties with the largest concentration in Pigeon River Country State Forest.

In September the bulls start looking for love in all the right places. These 700- to 900-pound animals not only attract the opposite sex, but also draw humans who gather to watch the bulls enchant their moose cow harems with high-pitched, whistle-like sounds, called bugling.

Heard but not seen

The entire population (such as it is) of Michigan's most famous songbird—the blue-gray and yellow Kirtland's warbler—nests in the northern Lower Peninsula's jack pine forests. Each winter the flock makes the 1,400-mile flight to its winter home in the Bahamas and then returns each spring.

Counting the male population is easy, because the boys never stop singing! In 1992, 393 singing males were counted in Michigan and one lone male in Wisconsin. The count was the largest in 30 years for this bird which appears on the Federal Endangered Species list. In 1992 alone, 2.5 million trees were planted on government lands to ensure them a habitat. Today one-fourth of all Kirtland warblers live there.

A message arrives too late

The sky used to be pitch-black when migrating passenger pigeons flew over Shelby. In fact, Shelby was a famous place to watch the birds' yearly trek. Unfortunately, as with the state forests, no one thought the supply would run out, and in one year alone over 700,000 birds were slaughtered by hunters. This nationwide practice eventually led to the extermination of the passenger pigeon in the entire country. The last known bird died in an Ohio zoo in 1914.

Protecting endangered species

Black bear and white-tailed deer were plentiful in Michigan when early settlers arrived, and their descendants can still be found in the state today. However, the wolverine, the animal for which Michigan is nicknamed, is not among the present wildlife population. In fact, some zoologists believe it never inhabited the region at all. Caribou once lived in Michigan, but they're gone forever. The same thing can happen to other native species. The following animals are protected in the state of Michigan (there are also 197 species of plants on the list). Those with an asterisk (*) next to their name are on the Federal Endangered Species List.

Mussels
Purple lilliput
Catspaw
Northern riffleshell
Round hickorynut
Clubshell
Salamander mussel
Bean villosa

Snails
Petoskey pondsnail

Mammals
Gray wolf
Cougar*
Lynx
Indiana bat*

Birds
Short-eared owl
Piping plover*
Kirtland's warbler*
Peregrine falcon*
Loggerhead shrike
King rail
Barn owl

Amphibians and Reptiles
Smallmouth salamander
Kirtland's snake
Copperbelly watersnake

Fish
Shortnose cisco

Bigeye chub
Ironcolor shiner
Weed shiner
Northern madtom
River darter

Insects
Hungerford's crawling water
    beetle
Three-staff underwing
Mitchell's satyr butterfly*
American burying beetle*
Phlox moth
Leadplant moth
Regal fritillary

Moving white "rocks"

French explorer Antoine Laurent Cadillac was probably surprised when he approached the shore at the future site of Detroit. Huge white rocks that dotted the shoreline seemed to be moving. What he was seeing were, in fact, flocks of white trumpeter swans.

The need for quill pens marked the end of the trumpeter swan. By the early 1930s, there were fewer than 100 trumpeters left in the nation. In 1992, wildlife officials were thrilled with the birth of six trumpeter cygnets. It was the first time in over 100 years that successful nesting had occurred in the state. Two cygnets were hatched in Cass County and four in the Seney National Wildlife Refuge. Officials believe these are the offspring of swans released in 1989 or 1990.

Moose fly the friendly skies

Van Ripper State Park on Lake Michigamme is moose watchers' heaven. The Park Service even provides a locator guide for the truly enthusiastic. During 1985 and 1987, a total of 59 moose were airlifted to the park to ensure their survival in the area. An extensive study of the moose population is made each year, including a study of causes of moose death.

The cycles of nature continue and only the fit survive. As of January 1992, the parks had tallied 74 moose deaths from various causes, including falling down a steep slope and exhaustion from being stuck in the mud. The total moose population by 1993 was 218.

Michigan's mastodons make tracks

Mastodons roamed Michigan about 10,000 years ago. In 1992, some of the oldest preserved mastodon tracks were found in a pasture near Saline. The prints are so clear that scientists can tell exactly where the huge mastodon stumbled and tripped over a log.

The 20 footprints and some mastodon bones were accidentally discovered by Harry Brannon while he was excavating for a pond. He surrendered the find to the scientific community. Copies of the footprints were made and sent to the University of Michigan for further study.

Worming her way to success

Twenty-years-ago, Mary Appelhof of Kalamazoo spent $32 to purchase two pounds of red worms through an organic gardening catalog.

Hoping to make big money by raising the worms for bait, she put them in a bin in her basement with manure and peat moss. Soon afterward, Appelhof got interested in a booklet entitled *Let an Earthworm Be Your Garbage Man.* The booklet gave her the idea of burying her garbage in a worm bed and letting the worms dispose of it the natural way.

To Appelhof's surprise, the experiment worked. The worms devoured the garbage and left behind usable fertilizer. The first year of the experiment she fertilized one-third acre of broccoli with the recycled garbage. In 1973, Appelhof published her first book, *Basement Worm Bins—Reduce Garbage and Produce Potting Soil.* It's not a best-seller yet, but she has sold over 37,000 copies.

Appelhof, who holds master's degrees in education and biology, received a patent for her worm bin, Worm-A-way®, in 1992. She has since quit her part-time job as a file clerk at Upjohn, and if things go the way she hopes, soon everyone will have worms in their basements!

MAJESTIC TIMBERS

The giant Estivant pines have been growing near the Montreal River near Isle Royale National Park for hundreds of years. In fact some have been traced back 500 years to 1492 which means they began growing before Columbus even discovered America! The largest white pine on record, "The Leaning Giant," measures 23 feet in circumference. It finally leaned to the point of no return and now lies on the ground.

Land of the giants

A touch of paradise . . . on national land

Hiawatha would be proud. His namesake in the UP, the Hiawatha National Forest, has swallowed up 880,000 acres. The forest is bordered by three Great Lakes—Huron, Michigan, and Superior. To make this the ultimate Shangri-la, the forest also takes in two uninhabited and unspoiled islands—Round Island and Government Island. The headquarters of the forest are at Escanaba.

Two other national forests cover a large portion of Michigan:

Huron-Manistee National Forest—915,000 acres, headquartered in Cadillac.

Ottawa National Forest—1,522,000 acres, headquartered in Ironwood.

Standing tall

The most forested counties in the state are Baraga (89 percent), Gogebic (88 percent), and Iron (87 percent), all in the northwest UP.

There are six Michigan state forests—

In the northern Lower Peninsula:
Au Sable
Mackinaw
Pere Marquette

In the Upper Peninsula:
Copper Country
Escanaba River
Lake Superior

Adoption by the acre

Similar to the Adopt-a-Road programs, Michigan has an Adopt-a-Forest program. Established in 1991, the program has matched 105,000 forested acres with concerned organizations and individuals dedicated to maintaining clean and safe forest lands. The state hopes this program in which people voluntarily collect the trash in forests will help meet its goal of reducing waste—especially waste that won't degrade—50 percent by the year 2005.

The program has made significant progress in the war against garbage. Each person in Michigan creates 1.27 tons of trash a year, eighth highest in the nation. And a lot of it gets dumped on state forest lands illegally. Almost 200,000 cubic yards of junk, enough to fill an 18-story building, has been dumped on just 5,000 square acres of the northern Lower Peninsula public forestlands alone!

The biggest and the best

Almost eleven percent (85) of the nation's biggest trees on the National Register of Big Trees are in Michigan. A black willow in Grand Traverse County has the biggest circumference at 379 inches. A crack willow in Beverly Hills has the largest crown at 153 feet. And an eastern white pine in Marquette is the tallest, measuring in at 210 feet.

Crown has a priceless jewel

One section of Michigan's 17 million-plus acres covers 30 percent of the western Upper Peninsula. It is often referred to as "Michigan's Crown."

A former mining area, Keweenaw is in the heart of the crown. Covering 2,300 square miles is a forest of the whitest hard maple in the world, as well as rare birds-eye maple. Foreign businessmen travel here to purchase the best money can by—and it takes money! At last report, one log of the rare birds-eye maple sold for $3,000!

The birds-eye maple is among the rarest woods in the world. Tiny knots give the sanded wood an abundance of swirls and circles in the grain. And no one knows how or why they are formed. All we know is that planting a birds-eye seed does not guarantee a birds-eye maple. Nature has the final say. One in a thousand maple trees is a birds-eye, making it a rare bird—or log—indeed.

HAZARDOUS TO OUR HEALTH

Environmental WRAP

In 1986, Dow Chemical in Midland began a waste reduction program called WRAP, "Waste Reduction Always Pays." It's now the cornerstone of its waste-management policy. The chemical company implemented the program by having each plant inventory impact of its waste streams on land, water, and air. Ideas generated from employees have allowed Dow to cut harmful air emissions by more than 85 percent. Dow plants compete to stay off the company's "Top Ten Waste Generators" list.

Poisoned food chain

Michigan farmers were at the center of a chemical poisoning disaster in the mid-1970s which affected millions of people and livestock. The poisonous chemical PBB (polybrominated biphenyl) was accidentally mixed into a large supply of livestock feed. The feed was consumed by thousands of cattle, which eventually had to be destroyed.

Many of the animals had already been sent to market where the meat was sold in supermarkets around the state. Land, milk, eggs, and cheese were contaminated. An estimated eight million Michiganders ate the tainted food and are to some degree contaminated with PBB.

Paper mills and PCBs

One of the most dangerous places in the nation where hazardous waste has entered the environment is Kalamazoo County. Most of the damage was caused by paper mills and the polychlorinated biphenyls (PCBs) they released. (PCBs are synthetic compounds used to insulate electrical equipment. For almost 20 years, PCBs have been known to cause cancer.) An 80-mile portion of the Kalamazoo River, a three-mile stretch of Portage Creek, and hundreds of acres of wetlands are contaminated with over 300,000 pounds of the chemical. Every time it rains or natural erosion occurs along the waterways, more of the cancer-causing chemical flows into the water, on into Lake Michigan, and into the food chain. The uncontained disposal ponds belonging to paper mills are a major problem.

The Bryant Mill Pond covers 70 acres alone and PCB concentrations are so exposed in its sediment that even touching the soil or inhaling a dry particle is a health risk. A fence has been erected to keep people out. Despite numerous warnings and a fish consumption advisory for the Kalamazoo River in effect since 1977, people are still catching and eating the fish. Work plans for cleanup were finally completed in 1993 with final cleanup scheduled for 1998.

Michigan's Superfund Sites

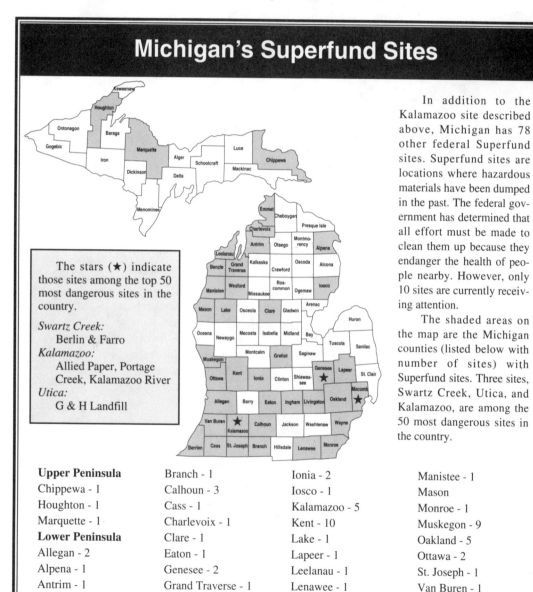

The stars (★) indicate those sites among the top 50 most dangerous sites in the country.

Swartz Creek:
   Berlin & Farro
Kalamazoo:
   Allied Paper, Portage Creek, Kalamazoo River
Utica:
   G & H Landfill

In addition to the Kalamazoo site described above, Michigan has 78 other federal Superfund sites. Superfund sites are locations where hazardous materials have been dumped in the past. The federal government has determined that all effort must be made to clean them up because they endanger the health of people nearby. However, only 10 sites are currently receiving attention.

The shaded areas on the map are the Michigan counties (listed below with number of sites) with Superfund sites. Three sites, Swartz Creek, Utica, and Kalamazoo, are among the 50 most dangerous sites in the country.

Upper Peninsula	Branch - 1	Ionia - 2	Manistee - 1
Chippewa - 1	Calhoun - 3	Iosco - 1	Mason
Houghton - 1	Cass - 1	Kalamazoo - 5	Monroe - 1
Marquette - 1	Charlevoix - 1	Kent - 10	Muskegon - 9
Lower Peninsula	Clare - 1	Lake - 1	Oakland - 5
Allegan - 2	Eaton - 1	Lapeer - 1	Ottawa - 2
Alpena - 1	Genesee - 2	Leelanau - 1	St. Joseph - 1
Antrim - 1	Grand Traverse - 1	Lenawee - 1	Van Buren - 1
Benzie - 1	Ingham - 3	Livingston - 3	Wayne - 1
Berrien - 2	Gratiot - 3	Macomb - 3	Wexford - 2

Fish blasted by tanker explosion

At 8:30 A.M. on September 16, 1990, the *Jupiter*, a gasoline tanker moored in the Saginaw River at Bay City, exploded, pouring 1.5 million gallons of unleaded gasoline into the water. A fire raged for almost two days. Miraculously, only one crewman was killed, but the fish weren't so lucky. According to state wildlife officials, the impact of the explosion caused the death of thousands of fish which floated downstream for several days after the accident. By September 19, most of the soot and gasoline had either evaporated or been vacuumed up. Long-term impacts have not been determined.

Park it!

In Michigan three national parks and 94 state parks cover 878,000 acres of the land, making Michigan the 10th largest park state in the nation.

The one, lone state park on Lake Erie is Sterling State Park.

PARKS AND WILDLIFE REFUGES

Almost a national park

Porcupine Mountains Wilderness State Park, affectionately known as "Porkies," is Michigan's largest state park. It covers 58,000 acres of undeveloped land. The Indians named the mountains because their rough ridges looked like crouching porcupines. The park is the one area of Michigan that loggers weren't able to spoil—it was just too rugged.

Prior to World War II, Porkies was to be designated a national park, but the war broke out and the whole idea was tabled. Following the war, in the early 1950s, there was pressure to log the area, but the state moved quickly to preserve its rugged beauty as a wilderness state park.

Island paradise

Ninety-five percent of Mackinac Island was named a state park in 1895. Eighty percent of the island's forested lands have been preserved along with unique rock formations such as Lover's Leap, Devil's Kitchen, and Arch Rock. From some vantage points, Arch Rock, 149 feet above water with a 50-foot span, looks as if it's suspended in air. The Indians say giant fairies built Arch Rock as the gateway to the island. The island has no lakes or rivers. Instead, natural springs such as Wishen Springs gush up from deep in the rock.

A spring, a falls, and a rock give fame to Michigan parks

The largest spring in the state, **Kitchi-iti-kipi** (Big Spring), is located in Palms-Book State Park. Gushing 10,000 gallons of water a minute from a gap in the limestone, the spring is 405 feet deep and 200 feet in diameter. Through the crystal-clear water, limestone-encased trees and branches can be seen at the bottom. Kitchi-iti-kipi is associated with the Hiawatha legends.

The most famous waterfall in the state is located in Tahquamenon Falls State Park. **Upper Tahquamenon Falls** is the second largest falls east of the Mississippi. It is 200 feet across and 50 feet high. Longfellow was so impressed with its beauty that he included Upper Tahquamenon Falls in his "Song of Hiawatha."

One of the best places to find **Petoskey stones** is at Fisherman's Island State Park. The beautiful rocks, now made into jewelry, are remnants of coral reefs formed in the warm sea that existed from Alpena to Charlevoix over 300 million years ago. The stones, named for the Petoskey area, are the official State Stone.

Petroglyph Park and Nature Trail in Sanilac County has the only Indian rock carvings in the entire state. The carvings are on a single sandstone rock in an area where Indian chiefs used to meet. They might never have been discovered if the area hadn't been damaged by forest fires in the late 1800s which thinned out the timberland.

Near the mouth of Lake St. Clair in the Detroit River lies Belle Isle, formerly named Swan Island, Rattlesnake Island, Hog Island, and who knows what else. Three miles long and less than half a mile from shore, it was called Swan (Wah-na-be-zee) Island and Rattlesnake Island by the Chippewa and Ottawa because of the snakes and beautiful migrating swans that stopped there. Detroit's founder, Cadillac, came along and changed the name to Isle La Margerite for his daughter. Cadillac decided the island was fit only for grazing and wanted it "free from the mischievous savages and depredations of wild animals." The name Isle Au Cochons (Hog Island) appeared when the French used swine to rid the island of snakes.

Everything changed in 1845 when the island received its present name, Belle Isle, in honor of Lewis Cass's daughter. The city of Detroit bought the 1,000-acre island in 1879, made the name official in 1881, and created one of the first parks of its kind. The park has an aquarium which was built in 1904, making it the oldest aquarium in North America.

In the eye of the beholder

Nature's scrapbook

Pictured Rocks, a series of cliffs reaching a height of 200 feet and stretching 27 miles from South Bay near Munising to Grand Sable Banks, were carved by nature's elements. The soluble oxide deposits in the sandstone stained the cliffs with a variety of colors. Indian Head, Miner's Castle, Battleship Rock, the Colored Caves, and Chapel Rock make this a visual paradise.

Camping in Pictured Rocks each summer, the Chippewa believed the gods of thunder and lightning lived in the caverns. Hiawatha, their warrior-hero, hunted in these woods and stalked game along the cliffs. In 1966, Pictured Rocks was designated the first national lakeshore.

The mistake in the lake

You won't run into too many people on Lake Superior's largest island, Isle Royale, located 50 miles northwest of the Keweenaw Peninsula. The island is U.S. territory, thanks to inaccurate British maps, which placed the island much farther south than it really is. After

the Revolutionary War, negotiators decided the island was part of the UP. If they had used the more accurate maps prepared by French explorers, things would have been different.

In 1931, Isle Royale was made a national park and in 1976, wilderness legislation was passed to ensure its continuing survival. Today, almost 99 percent of the park is wilderness—nothing but beautiful, rugged, dense overgrowth and an abundance of wildflowers. Beaver, loon, mink, moose, red fox, wolf, and snowshoe hare are some of the year-round residents. As the country's only island national park, Isle Royale is the least visited, which is probably a blessing. In 1980, the United Nations' "Man and The Biosphere" program designated the island as an International Biosphere Reserve.

From wasteland to wonderland

The area now known as the Seney National Wildlife Refuge and the Great Manistique Swamp was ravaged in the 1870s by loggers. Trees were stripped away and fires intentionally started to remove unwanted debris for logging operations. The camps moved on and in 1911 land developers moved in to drain away the great swamp and sell it to unsuspecting farmers.

The farmers soon realized they'd been cheated. The land was too poor to grow much of anything. This "wasteland" sat until 1935 when the U.S. Fish and Wildlife Service purchased it to provide habitat for wildlife, primarily waterfowl migrating to nesting grounds in Canada.

Civilian Conservation Corps workers constructed dikes, creating 7,000 acres of water in 21 major ponds, and miraculously restored the swamp. It became an "official" wildlife habitat when 332 Canada geese were released in 1936. Today the refuge covers 95,433 acres and is the largest national wildlife refuge east of the Mississippi. Over 200 species of birds, including bald eagles, and the largest number of nesting loons in the state make the refuge and swamp their home.

Michigan has seven national wildlife refuges:

Harbor Island - a single island (695 acres) north of Drummond Island in Lake Huron.

Huron Islands - composed of eight islands (147 acres) located three miles off the south shore of Lake Superior near Houghton.

Michigan Islands - consists of five small islands (as small as 2 acres), three in northern Lake Michigan and two off Thunder Bay in Lake Huron. Provides breeding places for migratory birds such as gulls, terns, cormorants, and herons.

Thunder Bay Island - has an old growth forest of American yew.

Seney - bogs and woods; some closed to people in summer.

Shiawassee - 8,900 acres where six rivers which drain 4,000,000 acres meet. Established in 1953 mainly for migrating Canada geese; also motel to whistling swans during spring migration.

Wyandotte - Two small islands, Grassy and Mammajuda, located in the Detroit River. A grassy breeding area for migratory birds.

WHERE A RIVER FLOWS

Michigan's 120 major rivers were formed when the glaciers retreated over 10,000 years ago. Forty percent of the rivers flow into Lake Superior, 35 percent into Lake Michigan, and the rest into Lakes Erie and Huron. Of the state's six largest rivers—the Saginaw, St. Joseph, Muskegon, Au Sable, Menominee, and Grand—Saginaw has the largest drainage area, 6,270 square miles in 21 counties.

The Sturgeon River Gorge waterfall is the largest and deepest in the Great Lakes states, plunging more than 400 feet deep in some areas. Almost all of the more than 150 waterfalls in the state are in the UP, with 11 on the Black River.

Michigan's rivers: Wild, scenic, and natural

In 1992, President George Bush signed the Michigan Scenic Rivers Act, the most comprehensive national river protection bill for any state east of the Rocky Mountains. Fourteen rivers are designated as "wild and scenic rivers" with nine more under study. Such a designation protects a river, or parts of a river, from development that might destroy its character.

Federal wild and scenic rivers:

Presque Isle	Whitefish
Ontonagon	Indian
Paint	Tahquamenon
Black	Carp
Sturgeon (Baraga County)	Manistee
Yellow Dog	Pine
Sturgeon (Cheboygan County)	Bear Creek

The state of Michigan thinks its Natural Rivers Program, created in 1970 by the state legislature, is the best in the nation. In the program, tributaries are considered as part of a river, while the federal program leaves them out.

The state's natural rivers:

Jordan	Flat Rifle
Two Hearted	Lower Kalamazoo
White	Pigeon
Boardman	Au Sable
Huron	Fox
Pere Marquette	Rogue

UNDERWATER MICHIGAN

Underwater preserves

You must be a diver to enjoy these historic sites, but Michigan's nine preserves are worth the effort. Established to protect the Great Lakes' underwater history, the preserves are graveyards for some of the worst shipwrecks on Lakes Superior, Michigan, and Huron. They also provide a view of nature's underwater landscape. However, artifacts are protected and violators will be prosecuted.

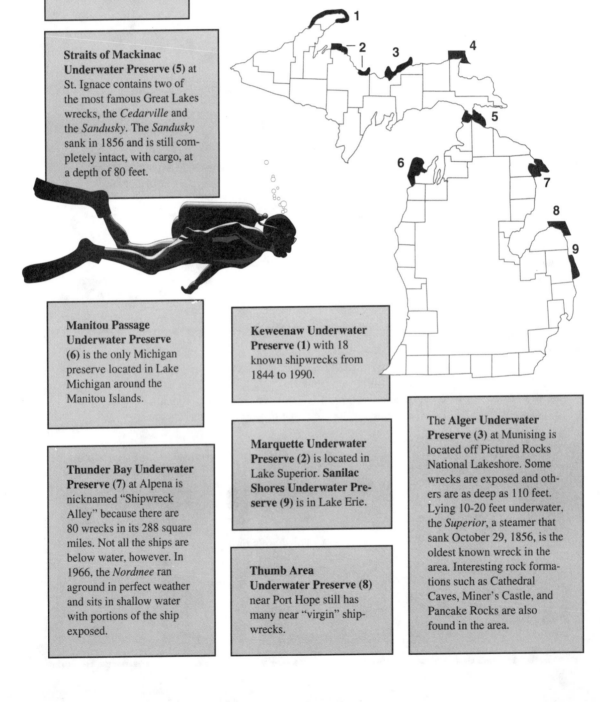

Whitefish Point Underwater Preserve (4) at Paradise is located along some of the most dangerous waters in Lake Superior.

Straits of Mackinac Underwater Preserve (5) at St. Ignace contains two of the most famous Great Lakes wrecks, the *Cedarville* and the *Sandusky*. The *Sandusky* sank in 1856 and is still completely intact, with cargo, at a depth of 80 feet.

Manitou Passage Underwater Preserve (6) is the only Michigan preserve located in Lake Michigan around the Manitou Islands.

Keweenaw Underwater Preserve (1) with 18 known shipwrecks from 1844 to 1990.

Thunder Bay Underwater Preserve (7) at Alpena is nicknamed "Shipwreck Alley" because there are 80 wrecks in its 288 square miles. Not all the ships are below water, however. In 1966, the *Nordmee* ran aground in perfect weather and sits in shallow water with portions of the ship exposed.

Marquette Underwater Preserve (2) is located in Lake Superior. **Sanilac Shores Underwater Preserve (9)** is in Lake Erie.

Thumb Area Underwater Preserve (8) near Port Hope still has many near "virgin" shipwrecks.

The **Alger Underwater Preserve (3)** at Munising is located off Pictured Rocks National Lakeshore. Some wrecks are exposed and others are as deep as 110 feet. Lying 10-20 feet underwater, the *Superior*, a steamer that sank October 29, 1856, is the oldest known wreck in the area. Interesting rock formations such as Cathedral Caves, Miner's Castle, and Pancake Rocks are also found in the area.

You don't need hiking boots to travel on Michigan's Island Explorer Water Trail! A windsurfing board will do just fine! Nicknamed "H_2O," the trail, limited to "energy independent" craft, will eventually hug the shores of Lake Superior for 3,000 miles, linking four national parks and lakeshores, 25 provincial and state parks, 7 national and state forests, 14 island groups, and numerous separate islands.

No hiking boots allowed!

Currently there is a generalized map that shows three present trail segments around the Keweenaw Peninsula, the islands in St. Mary's River, and Wisconsin's Apostle Islands.

The idea became a reality in 1987 when the Inland Sea Society, a nonprofit group with membership in all the Great Lakes states and Canada, and various state agencies in Michigan, Minnesota, and Wisconsin began working together to create a trail that would focus attention on the lake water as a valuable resource worth sustaining.

Ultimately, the trail will include the entire Great Lakes system which contains 20 percent of the world's fresh water. The hope is that this trail will give the traveler a close interaction with the water and a concerned interest in preserving the lakes.

WEATHER NOTES

When the big wind-driven schooners sailed the Great Lakes, sailors became adept at observing nature's weather warnings. To protect themselves and their vessels they studied such phenomena as the northern lights, actions of sea gulls, and changes in wind direction. A whole body of "weather" language developed through these observations, some of which had a sing-song rhythm to it: For example,

Nature predicted weather to sailors

> *Evening red and morning gray,*
> *will send the sailor on his way.*
> *But evening gray and morning red*
> *will bring rain down upon his head.*

Other weather beliefs included:
- The higher the clouds, the fairer the weather.
- A rainbow in the morning indicates bad weather; in the evening, good weather.
- Sea gulls flying high and out over the land indicate a gale of wind. When they fly far to seaward, moderate winds and fair weather may be expected.
- A bright yellow sunset indicates a strong wind.
- Rain before wind, take your topsails in. Wind before rain, hoist 'em up again.
- If the clouds seem scratched by a hen, better take your topsails in.

Freshwater Fury

The huge Great Lakes windstorm known as the "Freshwater Fury" struck November 9, 1913. Gale-force winds blew continually for 24 hours at Port Huron and 270 people lost their lives. Ten huge, heavy ore carriers sank in the lake.

Weather at a glance

Most of Michigan can expect the lowest temperatures to be between minus 10 and 20 degrees Fahrenheit during the winter months. The last frost happens between April 15 and June 15. A section of the northwest UP and inland northern Lower Michigan can expect to get hit with average minimum temperatures of 20 to 30 degrees below zero!

If you love warm weather, the last place you want to be is Marquette—only four days a year reach 90° F. The high temperature averages 32° F or below on 96 days each year and 37 of these days average a mighty cold 0° F. Since the area is populated by descendants of Finnish miners, they're right at home!

> **Did "ja" know?**
> • Hottest day: July 13, 1936, 112° F at Mio
> • Coldest day: -51° F, Feb. 9, 1934, at Vanderbilt
> • Most precipitation in a day: September 1, 1914, 9.78 inches of rain fell at Bloomingdale
> • Most precipitation in a month: September, 1986, 19.05 inches at Big Rapids
> • Record snowfall was 391.7 inches at Delaware during 1978-79

The big winds cometh

There are an average of 16 tornadoes each year in Michigan, resulting in an average of seven deaths annually.

In 1896 such a tornado struck at 6 P.M. on May 25. It cut a half-mile-wide path in Oakland County and moved eastward, destroying the villages of Thomas and Oakwood. Barely missing Detroit's suburbs, it killed 47 people by the time it dissipated.

Years later weather conditions were right again for the terror of the tornado. On June 8, 1953, deadly tornadoes swept across both Michigan and Ohio, leaving 142 dead. Four were killed near Erie, four at Tawas City, and one at Brown City. Flint suffered a total of 116 residents killed and 1,000 injured.

Destruction on Palm Sunday

On April 11, 1965, another 271 were killed as tornadoes plowed their way across Michigan, Illinois, Ohio, Indiana, and Wisconsin. History repeated itself almost to the day on April 21, 1967, when humid summer conditions spawned tornadoes that ripped through Illinois and Michigan, claiming 33 victims.

Kalamazoo targeted

A seemingly unending string of tornadoes hit Kalamazoo on May 13, 1980. When it was over, seven people were dead and hundreds more were injured. A total of 400 buildings were destroyed, mostly in the downtown area. About 1,200 people were left homeless.

LAND OF THE GREAT LAKES

The search for the great Northwest Passage, the waterway that would allow ships to sail through North America to the Orient, brought French explorers to Michigan.

Traditionally, explorer Samuel de Champlain has been called the first white man to visit Michigan, but many credit Étienne Brulé with that honor. In 1618 he explored the Great Lakes and landed at Sault Ste. Marie, which 15,000 Indians called home. Jean Nicolet passed through the Straits of Mackinac in 1634, also searching for the elusive passage. So confident was Nicolet of his success that he brought along a colorful silk robe to wear upon arrival in China. Instead, he landed at the future site of Green Bay, Wisconsin. The Indians were impressed by the colorful garment, although we can assume Nicolet was disappointed to find the Native Americans not speaking Chinese.

The door to the Michigan Territory was ajar. Those who followed, thirsty for a new life, kicked it wide open. The new land represented adventure for some, fame and fortune for others, and religious and political freedom for many more. Michigama, land of the great lakes, stood ready.

- Struggle for the New World
- Michigan Indians
- Wolverine Firsts
- We the People: Residents Serve
- They Came by Water
- Politics and Public Figures
- A Haven for Slaves
- Michigan and the Military
- Women Made a Difference

STRUGGLE FOR THE NEW WORLD

12 beaver pelts buy one gun

As the fur trade became more competitive, trappers relied on Indians to supply pelts. The Potawatomi were considered Michigan's most advanced farmers, but, enticed by the white man's goods, they abandoned their traditional way of life and replaced farming with hunting. Indian hunters could trade twelve beaver pelts for one flintlock gun. Soon the Indians were forced to rely on the white man even for the bare necessities.

Niles, city of four flags

Niles is called the City of Four Flags. The flags of France, England, Spain, and the United States have all flown over the region. Fort St. Joseph was located where Niles is today. It was surrendered to the British in 1761, then captured in 1763 by the Indians, thanks to Chief Pontiac's uprisings. The British regained control, only to lose it in 1780 to the French. The French then lost the fort to Spain. A Spanish commander arrived from St. Louis to demonstrate to his Indian allies that the Spanish were more powerful than the British. The day after they captured the fort and its soldiers, the Spanish left. Demonstration over . . . the fort was returned to the British!

War of 1812

⭐ War had been declared in 1812, but word had not reached the Americans at Fort Mackinac. Somehow the British knew and used the opportunity to reclaim the fort. They amassed a force of 1,000 soldiers, Indians, and trappers. Landing secretly at night, the British mounted two cannons above the American fort. Unprepared for the attack, Commander Sinclair realized his 57 men had no chance against 1,000 armed men and two cannons. Sinclair surrendered.

You can't judge a ship by its flag

⭐ Two years after the British captured Mackinac Island, the Americans attempted to reclaim it. They brought in two warships, the *Tigress* and the *Scorpion,* to serve as blockades on the island, choking off supplies. This worked well until one night about 70 very hungry British soldiers rowed to the *Tigress* and captured her. Two days later the *Tigress,* flying the American flag, drew alongside the *Scorpion* at daybreak and opened fire with heavy guns, demolishing the ship. The Treaty of Ghent, signed in 1814, signaled the end of the war. The English withdrew and the Americans reclaimed the fort for good.

Cass escorts Indians West

Lewis Cass served as governor of the Michigan Territory from 1813 to 1831. He negotiated treaties with the Indians and secured half the land in the Lower Peninsula for the U.S. He forced many tribes to head west with a military escort. It was the first time Indians were expelled in this manner. Cass was elected to the Senate in 1842 and was the Democratic nominee for president in 1848, losing to Zachary Taylor.

Nine novels of Michigan history

Fire on the Wind by David Garth (1951)—a look at the Upper Peninsula in the 1860s.

Hatchet in the Sky by Margaret Cooper Gay (1954)—the story of early Detroit, Chief Pontiac, and the life of the Ojibway Indians.

Gabriel's Search by Della Lutes (1940)—depicting daily life in the early 1800s in Michigan.

Mission to Mackinac by Myron David Orr (1956)—Mackinac Island and the English-French conflict before the War of 1812.

Laughing Whitefish by John Donaldson Voelker (1965)—an Indian girl sues the powerful Marquette mining company in 1873.

A Bashful Woman by Kenneth Horan (1944)—family life, the automobile industry, and a Michigan city. How they grew from the 1890s to World War II.

Once a Wilderness by Arthur Pound (1934)—a look at a Michigan farm family from 1890 to 1913.

The Original by Larry Smith (1972)—Michigan is the setting for this grim picture of life on a farm during the turn of the century.

Log Jam by Leslie Turner White (1959)—the days of lumber barons in Michigan's Lower Peninsula in the 1870s.

MICHIGAN INDIANS

Keepers of the land

The main Indian tribes living in Michigan when white men began to explore the area were the Chippewa (Ojibway), Ottawa, and Potawatomi, all members of the Three Fires Confederation. Others, such as the Menominee, lived in the UP, and the Miami and Wyandot (Huron) lived near the future city of Detroit.

The man with the preaching habit

The first known mission in Michigan was started by Père Marquette on St. Mary's River in 1668, but the more dramatic missionary work was done by Father Claude Allouez, primarily around St. Joseph. He supposedly gave religious instruction to at least 100,000 Indians and may have baptized more than 10,000.

Crafty Chief Minavavana

⭐ Chippewa chieftain Minavavana responded to Pontiac's plan to take white men's forts by attacking Fort Michilimackinac with a deadly ruse. Apparently befriending the commander of the fort, Minavavana organized a special game to be played in celebration of King George's birthday on June 2, 1763. The commander was warned that the game might be a trick, but he couldn't see past his own pride in having an Indian for a friend. The chief had his warriors play a game called "bagataway" (apparently lacrosse) in front of the fort. Interested in the game, the British opened the gates and came outside to watch. While they were engrossed in the game, the Chippewa women, wrapped in blankets that concealed weapons, moved closer to the gate. At a signal, warriors retrieved their weapons and massacred almost everyone. Four Englishmen escaped, hid in the surrounding forest, then fled to civilization where they told their story.

Pontiac's conspiracy

In the closing days of the French and Indian War, the Indians hoped for more respect from the British than they had received from the French, but to no avail. Ottawa Chief Pontiac urged rebellion among the tribes and organized attacks on all the forts. He himself took on Fort Detroit. Speaking to a French friend, Antoine Cuillerier, Pontiac said that he would get into the fort by arriving apparently ready to hold peace talks. When the moment was right he would signal for an ambush. But he didn't know that Cuillerier's daughter, Angelique, had overheard him and was concerned for the safety of her boyfriend, a merchant inside the fort. She warned her lover and he warned the commander, Major Gladwin. Pontiac, seeing the soldiers ready to fight when he arrived on May 7, 1763, called off the attack.

However, skirmishes in the surrounding area during the following days finally led to a full-fledged siege of Fort Detroit. There were about 150 men inside the fort, and perhaps 500 Indians outside. Oddly enough, it was not a total siege because supplies, and even men, could be brought into the fort from ships coming up the river. An additional 250 British soldiers arrived in July, many of whom were killed in the Battle of Bloody Run in trying to attack Pontiac's camp. Gradually the siege died away, and on October 31 Pontiac officially capitulated. He left for Illinois where he was later murdered. The Indian uprising in Michigan was over.

Hairs for furs

✪ The Europeans introduced steel knives (as well as tuberculosis) to the Indians. Although the Indians had made a practice of scalping their enemy, they had used crude stone knives which were not very effective. The practice of scalping became more widespread—and more efficient—when British Commander Henry Hamilton, known as "Hamilton the Hair Buyer," began putting a price on scalps of settlers to keep them out of the area in order to protect the fur trade.

Sacred ground in Muskegon

✪ An Indian burial ground dating back to 1750 was once considered a sacred spot by Muskegon residents. A large band of Algonquin were fighting their way through the area when the Potawatomi attacked the invaders. It was said, "When the war clubs clashed they made a sound like thunder in the air." The bodies of thousands of warriors from both tribes were scattered over a large area.

Apparently, skeletons lay on the ground for years afterward. In the 1920s businessmen tried to purchase the lakefront property for development, but Chicago lumberman Martin Ryerson, whose wife was a Chippewa, stopped it.

⭐ In the mid-1800s, 30 chiefs from different regional tribes gathered at Greensky Hill to create the Council Trees of the Ottawa. Each chief planted a tree and vowed as long as it grew and bore leaves, he would remain at peace. The saplings were bent and tied with basswood thongs so each tree grew with a right-angle bend.

Council Trees of the Ottawa

⭐ The unmarked grave of Potawatomi Chief Sawauquette is in Mendon. He sold the tribal lands for $10,000 in 1883. When he attempted to persuade his people to leave for the rich hunting grounds promised them in Kansas, they poisoned him. He was given a Christian funeral by settlers.

We won't go!

The Snowshoe Priest

For 35 years, Father Frederic Barga served as teacher, priest, and legal adviser to the Indians. He was known as the Snowshoe Priest because he traveled up to 300 miles at a time on snowshoes during the winter. Father Barga used his legal knowledge to stop government agents from swindling Indians out of their copper-rich land. He taught himself the Indian dialect, then wrote books in the language of the Chippewa and Ottawa. He died in 1868 and his crypt is in St. Peter Cathedral in Marquette. In L'Anse Indian Reservation stands a six-story statue of Barga with 26-foot-long snowshoes.

WOLVERINE FIRSTS

⭐ A massive forest fire spread across the UP in 1881 and left between 200 and 300 dead and at least two counties devastated. The American Red Cross, only a month old, was called into action at the Michigan fire. At the urging of Clara Barton, President Garfield had, just days before his assassination, recommended to Congress that the Red Cross be recognized. The organization was considered a wartime assistance group, but the activities of volunteers at the Great Fire showed it could help in all types of disaster.

First disaster handled by Red Cross

⭐ Detroiters were an independent lot and did as they pleased. In 1802, in a muddy frontier post, they held the first known town meeting, incorporated the city, and then gave women the right to vote—only to be taken away by the 15th Amendment!

Women get the vote in 1802 Detroit!

Madam President ⭐ Emma Augusta Stowell Fox was nominated for the presidency in 1940. Unfortunately, the nomination came during a mock Republican Convention staged by women. Fox had a flair for parliamentary procedure. She founded the Detroit Parliamentary Law Club in 1899 and directed it for the next 45 years. Although Fox never made it to the Oval Office, she was the second woman ever to serve on the Detroit Board of Education—from 1893-95.

First congresswoman from Michigan

Ruth Thompson of Whitehall, who had been a probate judge in Muskegon County for eighteen years, was elected to Congress in 1950, the first woman to be sent to Washington by the state. Thompson served three terms in Congress and became the first woman to sit on the House Judiciary Committee. She lost her seat when squabbles about the location of U.S. Air Force jet interceptor base became public and voters became resentful of her role in the fight.

Just sign on the dotted line ⭐ Lieutenant Colonel Mattie V. Parker was the first woman ever to assume command of a U.S. Army Recruiting Armed Forces Examining and Entrance Station. Parker assumed command in Detroit in 1975.

Female civil rights worker murdered ⭐ The first white female civil rights worker to be murdered was Viola Liuzzo of Detroit. In 1965, she was riding in a car with a black man traveling from Selma, Alabama, to Montgomery, when a group of men stopped the car and shot Liuzzo. Two days later, four Ku Klux Klan members were arrested for murder.

Mother of the ERA ⭐ Martha Wright Griffiths was elected to Congress in 1955, and she served 20 years, or 10 terms, in office. The Romeo resident (born in Missouri) guided the Equal Rights Amendment through both the House and the Senate. She was the first woman appointed to the House Ways and Means Committee. Seven years after retiring in 1976, she became the first woman elected lieutenant governor in Michigan's history, a post she held until 1990.

WE THE PEOPLE: RESIDENTS SERVE

The Republican Party is born under oaks

The town of Jackson gained its greatest fame on July 6, 1854, when it hosted a convention during which the Republican Party (Grand Old Party or GOP) was formed to oppose the Kansas-Nebraska Act which allowed new states to decide the issue of slavery for themselves. Over 5,000 delegates attended—so many the event had to move outdoors under "the green spreading oaks."

(The town of Ripon, Wisconsin, also claims to be the founding site of the Republican Party. The previous March, representatives from three parties had met there and decided to form a new party, but the official formation actually occurred in Jackson.)

⭐ Thomas E. Dewey was an Owosso-born lawyer who challenged Roosevelt's New Deal and gave Harry Truman a run for the White House. He was elected district attorney for New York County, New York, in 1935 and ran for governor, losing to Herbert Lehman in 1938. In 1940 Dewey lost the Republican presidential nomination to Wendell Willkie. He was finally elected governor in 1942 and re-elected for two additional terms.

He is best known for his strong opposition to President Roosevelt's New Deal. Dewey challenged Roosevelt in the 1944 presidential race and lost. In 1948 he selected California's Governor Earl Warren (later Supreme Court Justice) as his running mate, challenging Harry S. Truman for the president's office and again he lost. He retired from public life in 1955 but remained active in the Republican Party until his death.

Dewey was a winner!

Ford, the unique president

Gerald Ford was born Leslie Lynch King, Jr., in Omaha, Nebraska, in 1913, although people associate him with Grand Rapids. His parents divorced when he was young and his family moved to Michigan. His mother remarried, and she and her new husband changed her son's name to Gerald Rudolph Ford, Jr.

Ford was elected to the House of Representatives from Grand Rapids in 1948 and became the House minority leader in 1965. He was nominated by President Nixon in 1973 to take the place of Vice President Spiro Agnew, who had been forced to resign. This made Ford the first vice president to take office in the middle of an administration. In 1974, following Nixon's resignation, he became the 38th President of the United States. This made him the only president never to have been elected to that position or to the vice presidency. One of his first actions was to pardon President Richard Nixon.

Wouldn't mail Lady Chatterley's Lover

⭐ Arthur E. Summerfield of Pinconning was named U.S. Postmaster General in 1953. He is best known as the postmaster who refused to allow D. H. Lawrence's *Lady Chatterley's Lover* to go through the U.S. mails. That decision bumped the book up to best-seller status. However, Summerfield stood firm, saying, " . . . filth is filth."

Mitchell goes down with the ship

⭐ John Newton Mitchell, born in Detroit in 1913, served as U.S. Attorney General from 1969 to 1972, appointed by President Nixon. The two men had met when their law firms merged in 1967, and then Mitchell managed Nixon's presidential campaign. Mitchell was convicted of conspiracy, obstruction of justice, and perjury for his participation in the Watergate cover-up. He served 19 months in federal prison (1977-79) and died in 1988.

ALL THE PRESIDENT'S MEN

Other cabinet officers that hailed from Michigan:

Secretary of State
Lewis Cass under James Buchanan, 1857

Secretary of the Treasury
W. Michael Blumenthal under Jimmy Carter, 1977

Secretaries of Defense
Charles E. Wilson under Dwight D. Eisenhower, 1953
Robert S. McNamara under John F. Kennedy, 1961, and Lyndon B. Johnson, 1963

Secretaries of War
Lewis Cass under Andrew Jackson, 1831
Russell A. Alger under William McKinley, 1897

Secretaries of the Navy
Truman H. Newberry under Theodore Roosevelt, 1908
Edwin Denby under Warren Harding, 1921 and Calvin Coolidge, 1923

Attorney General
Frank Murphy under Franklin D. Roosevelt, 1939

Secretaries of the Interior
Robert McClelland under Franklin Pierce, 1853
Zachariah Chandler under Ulysses Grant, 1875

Secretaries of Commerce
Roy D. Chapin under Herbert Hoover, 1932
Frederick H. Mueller under Dwight D. Eisenhower, 1959

Secretary of Housing and Urban Development
George W. Romney under Richard Nixon, 1969

Secretary of Health, Education, and Welfare
Wilber J. Cohen under Lyndon B. Johnson, 1968

Secretary of Veterans Affairs
Jesse Brown under William Clinton, 1993

THEY CAME BY WATER

⭐ The first steamship to reach Michigan was the *Walk-in-the-Water* out of Buffalo in 1818. It was another seven years—1825, the year the Erie Canal was opened—before two more ships were added to the Great Lakes. But by the mid-1800s the Great Lakes belonged to the mariners. At the peak of the schooner era, more than 3,000 ships plied the waters around Michigan. The *Water Witch*, *Queen of the West*, *Forest Maid*, *Belle Sheridan*, *Twilight*, *Golden Fleece*, and *Silver Wake* all graced the Great Lakes.

In the early days, many seasoned sailors from the Atlantic were drawn to the Great Lakes due to the unique adventure that lake sailing offered along with high wages.

> *In the crew were sons of other lands*
> *Roundheads and Scots of a feather*
> *Who wandered the world for a drink and a bed*
> *In fair and stormy weather.*

Called chanteys, the hearty songs the sailors sang were loud and boisterous, and the cadence helped sailors work the heavy riggings in unison. Residents of nearby harbor towns were often greeted in the early morning by a crew loudly singing, their voices carrying far across the water. The chanteys also told of the tragedy and fear many dealt with as they sailed the Great Lakes. To this day stories of the "Gales of November" still strike fear in a sailor's heart.

The song (at right) tells of the story of the steamer *W.H. Gilcher*, lost with her crew in 1892 during the "Gales of November."

Yet another chantey tells the difficulty a Canadian vessel had trying to get lumber loaded on the Fourth of July:

> *On July Fourth in Cheboygan Port*
> *I tell you there was fun*
> *The sailors kicked and would not work*
> *Aboard the* Stewart H. Dunn
> *Did they work? No, they did not!*
> *They went out on a bum*
> *And all that day the timber lay*
> *'Longside the* Stewart H. Dunn!

⭐ In 1856, Chicago ship captain Albert E. Goodrich paid $16,000 for a used sidewheeler steamer, the *Huron*. He hauled freight and passengers up and down Lake Michigan and within three years had made enough to pay the $32,000 price tag for a new ship. By the end of the century, Goodrich's line of seven ships was the largest.

Today that $16,000 Goodrich laid out to buy a used steamer would cover its operating costs for only a 24-hour period! Maritime officials estimate it costs between $10,000 and $25,000 a day to operate a freighter with a crew of 30.

Maidens of the Great Lakes

Lost in Lake Michigan
They did not reach the shore,
The gallant ship and crew
Will sail the lakes no more!

The cost of doing business

Home one year after sinking

⭐ The *Ella Ellenwood* was loaded in her home port of White Lake. Her destination was Milwaukee, Wisconsin. She was eight miles north of the Milwaukee Harbor that October day in 1901 when disaster struck.

Run aground, she began to break up from strong winds and brutal waves. Some cargo was salvaged, but the *Ella Ellenwood* was abandoned and soon sank. One year later a surprise discovery was made at White Lake. A portion of the *Ella Ellenwood*'s wooden nameplate washed ashore. Somehow it had traveled all the way across Lake Michigan to her home port. The nameplate is on display in Montague City.

Madeline and the Edmund Fitzgerald

Although two Michigan ships were named *Madeline*, the original was a two-masted schooner built in 1845. Used for freight, she sailed between Mackinac Island and the North Shore. In the winter of 1850 the crew sailed the ship to Bowers Harbor, an inlet near Traverse City. They dropped anchor, allowing the ship to become locked in ice, a common practice then. The crew hired a schoolmaster and spent the winter learning how to read and write away from the distractions of port.

Three brothers who acquired education aboard ship were named Fitzgerald. All of them became shipping giants. John Fitzgerald was the great-grandfather of Edmund Fitzgerald, whose namesake, the *Edmund Fitzgerald*, sank in Lake Superior in 1975. The *Madeline* was later used to carry troops to Beaver Island to chase away "King" Strang, the controversial Mormon leader (see p. 131).

Graveyard of the Great Lakes

Whitefish Point marks the end of an 80-mile stretch sailors know as the "Graveyard of the Great Lakes." Raging northwest storms build up power over 200 miles of open water before reaching shore. These storms are known to have caused 300 recorded shipwrecks and hundreds of seamen lost. The first ship lost was the British schooner *Invincible*, in 1816. The most recent was the *Edmund Fitzgerald*.

The lakes won't give up their dead

⭐ The depth of the Great Lakes and the strength of the storms has made it nearly impossible for the dead to surface—but not always. On November 22, 1919, the steamer *Myron* sank in Lake Superior near Whitefish Bay. The crew attempted to use lifeboats while the captain stayed with his ship. Later the captain was found hanging onto a piece of wreckage. In 1920, the bodies of eight crewmen were washed ashore at Salt Point encased in ice. They were buried at Bay Mills.

Salty superstitions

⭐ If it were known that a vessel had any mishaps while being built or stuck while being launched, sailors often kept clear of her. A hatch cover found upside down aboard a vessel or a shattered compass glass meant misfortune. Some sailors wouldn't work aboard a vessel with a female cook, a cross-eyed sailor, or a cat named in honor of a person who had died.

Once a ship had a reputation for being unlucky, sailors were reluctant to work on her. The Detroit schooner *Walter H. Oads* suffered a series of mishaps. Finally it collided with another ship and sank in Lake Erie. The schooner *Augusta* collided and caused the passenger steamer *Lady Elgin* to sink in Lake Michigan, with 287 lives lost. Due to her jinxed reputation, the *Augusta* was sold and sent out to the Atlantic.

A slight list to the port of a loaded vessel was also a bad sign. Whistling aboard the ship was sure to bring headwinds, and many officers would not permit it! However, it was allowed during calms, because it might bring a wind!

⭐ The lakes' version of Davy Jones Locker is "Fiddlers' Green." And with it come many tales of sunken treasure on the lake. Gold, copper, whiskey, and more still lie in the bellies of great ships lost. (See p. 28 for a map of the underwater shipwrecks.)

Sunken treasure

The *Clairion* lies near the Detroit River in Lake Erie with her cargo of locomotives.

The *Lexington*, lost in 1846, sank with a cargo of kegged whiskey.

The *New Brunswick*, lost in 1859, also in Erie, carried a costly load of walnut and oak timbers.

The *Fay* sank in Saginaw Bay with steel bars worth $200,000.

The *City of Detroit* was filled with copper when she sank.

The *Westmoreland*, somewhere in the Straits of Mackinac, carried $100,000 in her safe, plus valuable cargo.

And somewhere near Escanaba, they say, lies an unnamed vessel which carried almost $5 million in gold bullion in her safe when she was lost.

Sailors give thanks to the Mackinaw

Cheboygan is home to the *Mackinaw*, a very special Coast Guard ship. She is credited with extending the shipping season at least six weeks into the winter, due to her special construction which allows her to break up ice floes that would otherwise block the shipping lanes.

Lighthouse guides sailors to safety

The first lighthouse in the state was built between 1818 and 1822. The oldest surviving lighthouse is located on Lake Huron at Fort Gratiot. It was constructed in 1825. Today there are 104 lighthouses dotting Michigan's coastline. The last lighthouse was automated by the Coast Guard in 1983.

St. Joseph Lighthouse

POLITICS AND PUBLIC FIGURES

Winning the Nobel

★ The career path selected by Detroit-born Ralph Bunche eventually affected the entire world. A graduate of UCLA in government, he earned a master's degree from Harvard University and did postdoctoral work at Northwestern University. He also studied in London and South Africa. In the early '40s, he played a major role in a monumental study of race relations in the United States.

Having helped lay the groundwork for the United Nations in 1944, Bunche served as UN undersecretary from 1955 to 1971. In 1950, he earned the Nobel Peace Prize—the first African-American to ever receive the award. He was honored for obtaining a cease-fire during the red-hot Arab-Israeli War after months of delicate negotiations. The NAACP honored Bunche with the Spingarn Medal in 1949, and in 1963, President Kennedy gave him the Presidential Medal of Freedom.

Priest collared for airtime outbursts

★ The Rev. Charles E. Coughlin was a Roman Catholic priest in Detroit who later became better known as the "Radio Priest" or the "Fighting Priest" because of his strong political views. Coughlin's 1928 radio show was intended to be a children's Sunday School program. Over the course of fourteen years the show became very political with Coughlin criticizing President Roosevelt and the New Deal. He also used the radio to preach against Communism, Jews, and Wall Street. During the 1936 presidential election, Coughlin delivered a tirade about "Roosevelt and Ruin" and called the president a liar and a scab. When the Roman Catholic Church pulled the plug on Coughlin's broadcasts in 1942, he had 40 million weekly listeners.

The name is Mudd

★ Retired Saginaw physician Dr. Richard D. Mudd continues the fight to have his grandfather, Dr. Samuel Mudd, cleared of conspiracy. Old Doc Mudd was found guilty of assisting John Wilkes Booth in the assassination of President Lincoln in 1865.

Dr. Mudd says his grandfather unknowingly set Booth's broken leg after the assassin showed up at his grandfather's farmhouse in Maryland, the morning after Lincoln was shot. Given the time frame, he says his grandfather couldn't have known about the assassination. He was committed to prison at Fort Jefferson in Florida's Dry Tortugas.

Despite Dr. Mudd's evidence, in 1992 the Army commission decided the original conviction would stand. Mudd's alleged involvement in the assassination gave birth to the phrase "Your name is mud!"

Malcolm X, Lansing, and the Nation of Islam

Malcolm Little, born in Nebraska, came to Lansing as a small child with his family. During his youth he saw his house burned down by the Ku Klux Klan and his father murdered. Becoming a small-time hustler and drug user by the age of 20, he served six years for burglary in Massachusetts. While in prison he learned about Black Muslims and the Nation of Islam.

Upon his release in 1952, he gave up his "slave" surname and began to use "X," which Elijah Muhammad, founder of the Nation of Islam, gave his members to represent the African name they could never know. Malcolm X split from the Nation of Islam and in 1964 made a pilgrimage to Mecca in Saudi Arabia where he saw blacks and whites praying together.

Upon his return to New York, he changed his name to El-Haji Malik El-Shabazz. He formed the Organization for Afro-American Unity and discussed the possibility of an interracial coalition. While speaking at the Audubon Ballroom in Harlem, Malcolm X was assassinated. Three members of the Nation of Islam were later convicted of his murder.

Malcolm X was one of the most influential African-Americans of his time. His influence continues to be felt today, as is reflected in songs by the rap group Public Enemy and speeches by Supreme Court Justice Clarence Thomas. In 1992, film-maker Spike Lee released a movie depicting the life of Malcolm X, entitled *X*.

The mayor who cared

The Panic of 1894 left thousands unemployed. Detroit Mayor Hazen S. Pingree announced all vacant city lots would be used for gardens. He supplied citizens with seeds which he paid for by selling his favorite saddle horse!

Popular mayor leads Detroit

⭐ In 1990, Coleman Young began his fifth term as mayor of Detroit. Young's climb to the city's highest office started when his family joined the great northern migration from Alabama to Detroit in 1923. Young grew up within blocks of the mayor's office.

In 1942 he became the first black bombardier in the Army Air Corps and was a member of the famed Tuskegee Airmen, the nation's first African-American aviation unit. His political career began in 1948 when he was elected director of the Wayne County Congress of Industrial Organizations. As he moved upward in the state senate, he became the first black member of the Democratic National Committee. In 1973, Young was elected the first black mayor of the city of Detroit. He received the Jefferson Award in 1979 and the NAACP presented him with the coveted Spingarn Medal for Distinguished Service.

Other Spingarn Medalists

Two other people Michiganders have been honored by the National Association for the Advancement of Colored People with its Spingarn Medal. **Damon Keith**, a jurist born in Detroit, received the medal in 1974. Actor **Richard Berry Harrison**, who was born in Canada but raised in Detroit, received the 1931 Spingarn Medal for his role in the Broadway production of Marc Connelly's *Green Pastures*.

A HAVEN FOR SLAVES

Slaves seek refuge

⭐ Michigan became a free state in 1837, the same year the Detroit Anti-Slavery Society was formed. The first known runaway slave was brought through the Underground Railroad into Cass County in 1836, by a Quaker minister. By the 1840s hundreds of slaves migrated to Michigan seeking protection.

The man with the branded hand

⭐ Prior to the Civil War, Captain Jonathan Walker was arrested off the coast of Florida for transporting seven slaves to their freedom in 1844. He was tried and convicted in federal court. The letters "SS" for "slave stealer" were branded on his right hand. He spent one year in prison and later settled on a farm outside Muskegon.

Kentucky Raid at Calvin Center

⭐ Calvin Center became a haven for runaway slaves after the Quakers established an Underground Railroad. Word of this place reached angry slave owners in Kentucky and led to the Kentucky Raid. In 1847, thirteen slave owners came to Michigan in covered wagons. They told the curious that they were salesmen for a new washing-machine firm.

Members of the Underground Railroad did not believe their story and told the slave owners to leave. They left, only to return and capture what they believed was their property. Three hundred Quakers came to the slaves' rescue. Later the slave owners filed suits against the Quakers. The cases dragged on unresolved. In 1859, they ended with a congressional decision in favor of the slave owners.

A single shot helps start a war

Adam Crosswhite and his four children were Kentucky slaves who fled to Marshall through the Underground Railroad (see map). Crosswhite settled on a farm, only to live in fear that his former owner would someday track him down. As a precaution, he told his neighbors he would fire a signal shot if trouble came to his doorstep. On a winter morning in 1846, two years after his escape, that shot was fired. Crosswhite's neighbors quickly came to the rescue and sent the entire family to Canada, out of harm's way.

The owner, enraged at the loss of his "property," called public meetings to condemn the residents of Marshall. He sued Michigan abolitionists and won. He even threatened the breakup of the Union if action to save other escaped slaves continued. The debate was picked up by other slave owners and their case was presented in Congress.

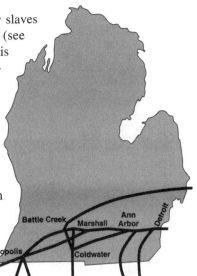

The Crosswhite/Marshall incident was instrumental in the creation of the Fugitive Slave Act of 1850. The first Republican legislature of Michigan passed a law that prevented recovery of fugitive slaves from Michigan, making it against the law for officials to cooperate with those trying to recover slaves.

MICHIGAN AND THE MILITARY

⭐ John Clem was smaller than most soldiers in Michigan's 22nd and for good reason—John Clem was only 12 years old when he participated in a battle at Chickamauga in 1863. During this conflict, three bullets pierced his hat. A rebel colonel took one look at his small frame and allegedly yelled, "Stop, you little Yankee devil!" Clem shot the officer dead on the spot. Later, General Rosencrans made Clem a sergeant and assigned him to special duty at headquarters.

Spunky 12-year-old

Custer: A Monroe museum remembers

Ohio-born George Armstrong Custer grew up in Monroe, Michigan. Raised by a half sister, he lived with her until he entered a military academy. Even after he had become a brigadier general, Custer continued to visit the little town on Lake Erie where he married his childhood sweetheart, Elizabeth Bacon.

The County Historical Museum has the country's largest collection of Custer's personal effects. Items include a buffalo hide he wore during a winter campaign in 1868 and his buckskin suit decorated with impressive beadwork and porcupine quills. His favorite Remington buffalo rifle is also on display in Monroe.

World War I

1st Lt. Harold Furlong (Detroit)

World War II

Col. Demas T. Craw (Traverse City)
Ens. Francis C. Flaherty
    (Charlotte)*
Owen F.P. Hammerberg (Daggett)*
Pfc. Oscar G. Johnson (Foster City)
S. Sgt. John C. Sjogren (Rockford)
Sgt. Maynard H. Smith (Detroit)
Pfc. William H. Thomas
    (Ypsilanti)*
Pfc. Dirk J. Vlug (Grand Rapids)
Pfc. Walter C. Wetzel (Roseville)*
2d Lt. Thomas W. Wigle (Detroit)*
2d Lt. Raymond Zussman (Detroit)*

Medal of Honor

The Medal of Honor is the highest award in the United States military, presented for exceptional bravery in combat. The medal originated in the Civil War. President Truman once said, "I'd rather have this medal than be president." The criteria for receiving the Medal of Honor is clear risk of life, voluntary act beyond duty, and two eyewitnesses. Those Michigan soldiers marked with an asterisk (*) were killed in action.

Korea

Hospital Corpsman C William R.
    Charette (Ludington)
Cpl. Duane E. Dewey (Muskegon)
Cpl. John Essebagger, Jr. (Holland)*
Sfc. Donald R. Moyer (Oakland)*
Pfc. Robert E. Simanek (Detroit)
2d Lt. Sherrod Skinner, Jr.
    (East Lansing)

Vietnam

S/Sgt. James L. Bondsteel (Jackson)
Spec 4 Dwight H. Johnson (Detroit)
Sgt. Paul Ronald Lambers
    (Holland)
Sgt. Peter C. Lemon (East Tawas)
1st Lt. Robert Leslie Poxon
    (Detroit)*
Pfc. Dewayne T. Williams
    (St. Clair)*

Is he or isn't she?

Genesee County officials had quite a problem on their hands. It seems that one of their very own enlistees, Franklin Thompson, was somewhat of a Civil War hero. Joining the Union Grays Company F, Second Infantry, in the 1860s, Thompson fought in the bloody battles of Bull Run and Antietam, as well as behind enemy lines.

The problem was Franklin Thompson's real identity. The soldier was really Sarah Emma Edmonds. County officials didn't argue that the hero deserved to be honored, it was just *how*. What pronoun should they use—he or she? The action was tabled until the county board could compromise. After leaving the service, she did receive a pension of $12 per month from the federal government. Edmonds was the only woman admitted to the Grand Army of the Republic.

An Unknown Soldier

⭐ The 102d U.S. Colored Troops is also known as the First Michigan Colored Infantry. Mustered into service in 1864, 1,387 African-Americans served. In 1986, the body of an unknown soldier who was a member of the 102d was removed from an isolated grave in Grand Rapids and reinterred at the Fort Custer Cemetery. It was the first grave of an unknown African-American soldier from that war.

Executed for desertion

⭐ During World War II, over 40,000 American soldiers in the European Theater deserted. Though many had been caught and convicted, their sentences were always commuted. Looking for a way to prevent more desertions, the army decided to execute one soldier as an example. A soldier had not been executed for desertion since 1864.

Twenty-four-year-old Michigan Private Eddie Slovik deserted but returned the next day. Court-martialed and found guilty, he was executed on January 31, 1945, in France. Strangely, the army kept the execution a secret, so his death did nothing to deter other deserters. Slovik's wife did not know he had been executed until 1953, when documents were declassified. Slovik's remains were exhumed from a war criminal's grave in France and reburied in Detroit. The story was told in the highly rated TV movie *The Execution of Eddie Slovik*.

WOMEN MADE A DIFFERENCE

⭐ Isabella, the slave of a wealthy Dutch landowner in New York, was raised speaking Dutch. By age 30, Isabella had given birth to five children. The four who survived were sold away from her. In 1827, she escaped to the home of Isaac and Maria Van Wagener, whose name she took. While with the Van Wageners, she was able to find some of her children and bring them home.

Slave turns abolitionist

Experiencing mystical voices and events over several years, Isabella developed an alliance with evangelist Elijah Pierson. A scandalous turn of events including the mysterious death of Pierson put the innocent Isabella into the midst of rumor and innuendo. She sued those who encouraged the rumors through newpapers and a pamphlet. The case was won, but Isabella had changed. After living quietly for several years in 1843, she changed her name to Sojourner Truth and began traveling throughout the East speaking the word of God and abolition. Audiences were drawn to Sojourner Truth by her striking gaunt figure, powerful speaking ability, and dynamic personality.

Moving westward as she preached, sheltering wherever space was offered, she reached Battle Creek in the mid-1850s. Harriet Beecher Stowe wrote of Sojourner Truth in the *Atlantic Monthly* in 1863, calling her the Libyan Sibyl. Other writers were not so impressed. Reporters even questioned her sex, claiming she was a man. Sojourner proved them wrong by baring her breast at an Indiana women's rights convention. After meeting Abraham Lincoln in 1864, she became involved in the movement to set aside land in the West for refugee blacks. During the Civil War she collected food and clothing for the African-American troops. Her travels as a speaker ended in 1875 when she returned home to Battle Creek. Her funeral in 1883 was considered one of the largest the city had ever seen.

⭐ Laura Smith Haviland and her husband arrived in Michigan in 1829 and began farming in Rasin Township. Soon after, with other Quakers, they formed the first anti-slavery society in the territory. They later opened their farm to orphans, founding the Rasin River Institute.

First anti-slavery society

Chief of staff denied membership

⭐ Although she was a dedicated and talented surgeon with skills beyond those of most men, Dr. Bertha Van Hoosen was still refused admittance into the medical societies. Van Hoosen, born in Stony Creek and raised in Pontiac, studied at the University of Michigan. She always had to finance her studies by teaching because her parents objected. She opened her obstetrical practice in Chicago in 1892. Within ten years she was teaching gynecology and obstetrics at Illinois University and Loyola University medical schools. She became chief of the gynecological staff at Cook County Hospital in 1913. Rejected by the regular medical associations, Van Hoosen established the American Medical Women's Association in 1915. Her autobiography, *Petticoat Surgeon*, was published in 1949.

Founder of the Seventh-Day Adventists

Born and raised in Maine, young Ellen Harmon and her family became converts from Methodism to the new Adventist group led by William Miller, who believed that the Second Coming of Christ was about to occur. Soon after Miller's date passed and nothing happened, Ellen, who suffered ill health all her life, began to have visions. As she preached around New England, her visions gave her the guidance to turn Miller's followers into a group called Seventh-Day Adventists.

Harmon married another Adventist preacher, James White. In 1855, they moved their family to Battle Creek, which became the center of the Seventh-Day Adventist Church. Among the 2,000 visions that she had during her life was the instruction that people should not eat meat, consume alcohol, coffee, or tobacco, and should live on nuts, grains, and vegetables. Her concerns with health led to the founding of a sanitarium that became the Battle Creek Sanitarium (see p.96).

Hall of Fame honors women

In 1983 the Michigan Women's Hall of Fame held its first annual awards dinner. It had been organized by the Michigan Woman's Studies Association to honor distinguished women. Some of those honored included:

• Pearl Kendrick (1890-1980) of Grand Rapids, an internationally known bacteriologist whose research resulted in the first successful vaccine against whooping cough;

• Caroline Bartlett Crane (1858-1935), an ordained Unitarian minister and reformer responsible for Kalamazoo's legislation requiring meat inspection, street-cleaning services, and a central charity referral agency. She was called America's public housekeeper;

• Martha Longstreet, a physician who gave 45 years of service to the Saginaw community. She founded a community center, a preschool children's clinic, and a home for the aged and for girls.

WOLVERINE WHISTLE-STOPS

From Indian villages to trading posts to railroad junctions, Michigan's villages and cities have been born from some awesome circumstances. Some started quietly, later earning comical or dubious reputations as time marched on. Still others earned their reputations based on man-made or natural creations.

Take Gay, for instance. On any given Sunday morning you could mistake it for a ghost town. But Gay's alive and kicking. It's just that most of the residents do their kicking—and on Sunday, their praying—somewhere else. There's no church in Gay, no school. Not much of anything, except the Gay Bar. It's open most mornings ready for business and the occasional prank phone call. A bartender admits they do get calls asking if it really is the Gay Bar. He takes it in stride and tells 'em, "Sure!"

Actually the community received its name from Josephine E. Gay, the director of the mining company. By 1915 the population swelled to a congested 800. Those boom days are gone, however, and today only 25 hearty residents and their sense of humor remain!

CITIES THAT COUNT

Among America's largest cities

🏠 Michigan includes only one city that is among the nation's top 50 in population—Detroit's 1990 population of 1,027974 makes it the seventh largest in the United States. Others with populations over 100,000 (though not for long at the rate some of them are shrinking) are:

- 83rd - Grand Rapids - 189,000 (down from 198,000 in 1970)
- 118th - Warren - 145,000 (down from 179,000 in 1970)
- 125th - Flint - 141,000 (down from 193,000 in 1970)
- 142nd - Lansing - 127,000 (down from 131,000 in 1970)
- 152nd - Sterling Heights - 118,000 (up from 61,000 in 1970)
- 170th - Ann Arbor - 110,000 (up from 100,000 in 1970)
- 193rd - Livonia - 101,000 (down from 110,000 in 1970)

THE NEXT TWENTY LARGEST MICHIGAN CITIES

Dearborn - 89,286
Westland - 84,724
Kalamazoo - 80,277
Southfield - 75,728
Farmington Hills - 74,652
Troy - 72,884
Pontiac - 71,166
Taylor - 70,811

Saginaw - 69,512
St. Clair Shores - 68,107
Waterford - 66,692
Royal Oak - 65,410
Wyoming - 63,891
Rochester Hills - 61,766

Dearborn Heights - 60,838
St. Joseph - 58,913
Redford - 54,387
Battle Creek - 53,540
Roseville - 51,412
East Lansing - 50,677

THE GOOD, THE BAD, & THE UGLY

A different kind of British invasion

🏠 The general manager of the Baltimore and Ohio Railroad gave the towns of Rudyard and Kipling their unique names in 1896. Fred Underwood was apparently a lover of words and poetry. As the railroad cut through the forests, creating a few small villages, it was Underwood's job to name them.

Rudyard was in the middle of a mosquito-infested forest. Some summer nights, settlers were unable to sleep due to the pesty insects and would travel to Soo, where they would swap 100 pounds of butter or eggs for a plow, calico, or candy. So remote was the village that mail carriers used snowshoes or dog sleds in the winter. The schoolteacher boarded week by week with the parents of students and sold Japanese oil and medicines to earn extra money.

Located in the Upper Peninsula, Kipling enjoyed brief prosperity during the logging years. For a time, its charcoal iron furnace, stone beehive-shaped kilns, and village docks were in great demand.

Many other Michigan villages were named with obvious English influence. This is due to railroad promoters selling securities to English investors in the British Isles. Either way, Rudyard Kipling was touched by the honor and wrote the Rudyard and Kipling poem at the right.

Carry Nation saves the day

The arrival of the Detroit-Milwaukee Railroad gave Holly the distinction of being the very first railroad junction in the state. With 25 trains passing through daily, the town drew a wide cross-section of personalities. Many congregated on Martha Street, which was soon lined with saloons. Fights and general rowdiness increased as the population grew.

In 1880 there was quite an uproar between local toughs and a traveling circus. The resulting bloody fisticuffs left so many bruised and beaten that locals started calling Martha Street "Battle Alley"! Local temperance leaders weren't about to allow such carrying-on to continue and called in the supreme hatchet wielder, Carry Nation. The Kansas saloon smasher and her followers arrived in Holly on August 28, 1908. The next day, umbrella in hand, she and her temperance-minded supporters invaded saloons, smashing whiskey bottles, clubbing patrons, and preaching about the evils of Demon Rum. Supposedly Carry Nation also attacked a nude painting hanging over the bar in the dispensing room at the Holly Hotel.

Today things are a little calmer in Holly, but residents still celebrate that day in August with the Carry Nation Festival. The twelve saloons that once lined Martha Street are now specialty shops. And by golly, you can still get a sip of that Demon Rum if that's your desire!

Rudyard and Kipling

Wise is the child who knows his sire
The ancient proverb ran
But wiser far the man who knows
How, where and when his offspring grows
For who the mischief would suppose
I've sons in Michigan?

Yet I am saved from midnight ills
That warp the soul of man
They do not make me walk the floor
Nor hammer at the doctor's door
They deal in wheat and iron ore
My sons in Michigan.

O, tourist in the Pullman car
(By Cook's or Raymond's plan)
Forgive a parent's partial view
But maybe you have children, too
So let me introduce to you,
My sons in Michigan!

Adam "Pump" Arnold was a successful businessman who created the first pump and water line manufacturing company. Despite his success, or perhaps because of it, he was considered a man of questionable character. He also had an on-going feud with Battle Creek Mayor William C. Gage. Once Arnold commissioned an iron statue of the mayor depicted as a bum and placed the statue in the mayor's front yard. Needless to say, it went over like an iron balloon. The statue has since had many different resting places.

The mayor as a bum!

Notorious   Although its reputation could have been started as a hoax, Seney's colorful residents more than lived up to the image. It all started when rumors of corruption in Seney were passed to a team of reporters, among them one of the few female newspaper reporters of the day, who promptly traveled to Seney.

Yes, the rumors from Seney were true, she wrote to readers back East. The place was a hell camp of slavery! Strangers were being shanghaied on the frontier, shunted into camp, held in chains, and tracked by fierce dogs when they attempted to escape. Forced to work in the forests by day, they were marched into camp at nightfall and held in the Ram's Pasture, a stockade unfit even for dumb animals. The place was so overcrowded that chained men were forced to sleep in shifts!

The story made headlines nationwide and a congressional committee went to investigate. Local politicians swore the whole thing was a hoax. The fierce dogs were mastiffs raised by a local saloonkeeper for sale to the general public. And Ram's Pasture was actually the main floor of a crowded hotel where the manager permitted men to sleep in eight-hour shifts with advance payment. The armed guards stood by to ensure prompt removal of the sleeping men at the end of their shift. Officials believed this version, but the reading public was never quite sure.

One Seney resident made national headlines. In 1901, Leon Czolgosz assassinated the twenty-fifth president of the United States, William McKinley, in New York.

And you thought your neighbors were bad!

We'll never know the truth about Seney, but we do know the tiny town was filled with an incredible collection of hellraisers. Most did whatever they wanted, whenever they wanted. Many of them enjoyed local celebrity.

Noted citizens include P.J. Small. Known as "Snap Jaw," he would earn drink and food by snapping off the head of a live snake or frog. Once he went too far and bit the head off a lumberjack's pet owl! Stuttering Jim Gallagher took the loss of his pet hard. Jim regularly laid out those who laughed at his stutter with a heavy handle or rough hobnail shoes. We don't know what happened to Snap Jaw.

Stub-Foot O'Donnell and Pumphandle Joe liked to meet incoming trains. They would stand strangers on their heads and shake out all the loose change. And Old Light Heart slept in two sugar barrels turned end to end and eventually lost his toes to frostbite. Whenever he got drunk after that, Pumphandle Joe and his buddy, Frying Pan Mag, would entertain themselves by nailing Old Light Heart's shoes to the floor!

Seney's fiercest battle is said to have been fought between Wild Hughie and Killer Shea. They bit off ears and gouged out eyes. The fight was finally stopped out of pure exhaustion and no man was declared the winner.

Say, mister, can you spare a dime?

Bogus Corners was the headquarters in the 1830s for a blacksmith whose gang of counterfeiters worked out of his shop. Apparently they filled a box with bogus silver coins, then approached a wealthy farmer. The counterfeiters explained they had to travel East immediately, adding the silver dollars were too heavy to carry. They asked the farmer to lend them a fraction of the coins' face value in paper money, promising to leave the silver as security.

The travelers said if they did not return within the week the farmer was welcome to spend the money. Several people were taken in by the story, but finally the blacksmith was imprisoned, and his gang driven out of the area.

Little Jake Seligman was a man who knew the meaning of promotion. His incredible merchandising adventures made him a legend. He was a banker and a real estate agent, and also operated a local horse-drawn street railroad in Saginaw.

Little Jake has last laugh in Saginaw

During the city's lumber boom, hundreds of loggers roamed the village, their pockets full of money. Seligman threw vests into the street, promising free coats and trousers to those who were able to hang on to them in the free-for-all that usually followed. Seligman kept his word and replaced the pants and coats. However, the vests were usually torn in half and could be replaced for $10 to $12!

His most visible sign of self-promotion was in 1890 when he commissioned a statue of himself and erected it on top of the Tower Building. The life-sized copper figure was only four feet, four inches tall, and was dressed in a long coat and top hat. When it was unveiled, many residents thought it was some Civil War general, which infuriated Seligman and he began to wear garments similar to those on the statue.

Seligman moved to Detroit and offered to sell the statue and clock tower to the city for $1,200. The council thought a more civic-minded resident would donate such items. However, when the dealing was done, the city paid Little Jake's sister-in-law $600 for the statue and clock and appropriated $150 a year to keep the clock in running order!

Ruling makes town butt of jokes

The village of Coldwater was incorporated in 1837, and the first criminal case ever tried by local authorities made the village the butt of jokes throughout the territory.

It seems a local man was found guilty of stealing a cow bell. He was sentenced to bend over a huge log and each person present was to give him a severe blow upon "the rotundity of the body with a piece of board four feet long and six inches wide." Apparently the whole town turned out and almost boarded the poor man to death. Several of those gleeful participants soon found themselves defendants in civil court when the victim brought suit against them. The litigation was moved from court to court through the Northwest and was known as the Cow Bell Suit. The case eventually disappeared from the records.

DYNAMIC DETROIT

Beauty is in the eye of the beholder

🏠 The Detroit Institute of Arts, established in 1885, is considered one of the nation's finest art museums. It houses treasures and history artifacts spanning 5,000 years in its 101 galleries. There are over 40,000 works in the permanent collection alone. The institute is home to the second-largest Dutch-Flemish collection, including several Rembrandts' and it also has the third largest collection of Italian Renaissance works outside of Europe. Diego Rivera, Mexican muralist, decorated the walls of the institute with a pictorial history of Detroit industry (see p. 137).

A fashionable library

Who created the miniskirt? Who developed polyester? Why do hemlines go up and down, and ties go wide and narrow? You can find out everything you ever wanted to know about fashion trends and designs at The Fashion Group International-Detroit Tavy Stone Fashion Library. It's located in the Detroit Historical Museum and is the only one of its kind in the Midwest. The museum is named in memory of fashion editor Tavy Stone, who wrote fashion columns for the *Detroit News* until her death in 1985.

Coneys, in Detroit?

In Detroit, the folks eat hot dogs they call "coneys," which are described as "the real heartburn kind, slathered with mustard, chili, and onions." Two master coney makers are located right next to each other on Lafayette Street. There's some friendly but spirited competition between the two, so don't be surprised if someone comes out and tries hard to persuade you to enter his establishment.

The Detroiter

Detroit is definitely a river city that heartily enjoys its location. Not only are there parks and islands to enjoy, but you can also take a cruise on the *Detroiter*, a paddle wheeler. During the summer, try and talk the captain into docking at the Baja Beach Club. There you'll find different theme bars anchored in the Detroit River, behind Cobo Hall.

It's not raining, it's pouring!

According to the *Guinness Book of World Records* in 1992, the world's tallest indoor waterfall is located in the lobby of Greektown's International Center Building in Detroit. The waterfall is 114 feet high and made of 2,525 square feet of marble!

Did "ja" know?
- Detroit has the most bowlers registered in the nation.
- They can't stop eating them—Detroit is a leader in potato chip consumption.
- In 1954, Detroit opened the nation's first shopping mall, the Northland.
- The city's People Mover (an elevated, computerized rail transit system) not only gets you to your destination but offers a lesson in art. In 1987, $2 million of artwork was commissioned to decorate its 13 stations.

WHAT'S IN A TOWN?

The Hastings House in Hastings was once famous for its dance floor. Not just your typical dance floor, it was constructed to absorb the heavy shock of dancing feet by swinging to and fro. Apparently so slight was the sensation that no dancers complained and the building's foundation was saved. The Hastings House also played host to a variety of important people of its day, including Zachary Taylor and General Lewis Cass.

The place was really jumping!

You can walk its beaches and listen to the sand sing or you can sit in the park and watch a musical performance by a massive water fountain. No, this isn't Disneyland, it's Grand Haven.

Singing sand bars have no cover charge

Geologists say it's one of the few places in the world where singing sand can be found. When walked upon, the tiny sand particles make a musical whistle!

When you get tired of tiptoeing through the sand bars, you can take in the entertainment at Dewey Hill. You'd better sit down for this. The musical water fountain has a repertoire of 1,875,352,500,000,000 possible musical/visual variations. It would require 4 billion miles of tape to record them all. And it takes over 20,000 feet of electrical wiring alone to make the thing work!

The largest fountain of its kind, it plays music with synchronized water and colored lights. Water is sprayed up to 125 feet, achieved by pumping 40,000 gallons of water through 18,000 feet of pipe in nozzles varying in size from $3/16$ to 1 inch. The sound system uses 12,000 watts, compared with 50 watts for a home stereo! During the holiday season it presents a 40-foot nativity scene.

Once a booming community, Fayette was founded in 1866 by Jackson Iron Company manager Fayette Brown. The company selected the site because of its deep, natural harbor and abundance of hardwoods and limestone. Numerous smelting furnaces were constructed and up to 1,000 people lived there at its peak. When the timber was depleted in the late 1880s, the company abandoned the site. Today, Fayette is a preserved ghost town open to visitors.

A ghost of its former self

Ship-to-shore gawkers

About 15 miles from Port Huron is the small town of St. Clair. Once a major shipbuilder of the 1900s, its claim to fame is the world's longest boardwalk facing fresh water. The 1,500-foot riverwalk runs exceptionally close to the river, giving board-walk browsers a chance to see those huge Great Lakes freighters and crews up close. The second favorite pastime on the boardwalk is walleye fishin'!

First to light up

Though Port Huron began in 1686 as Fort St. Joseph, the first permanent colony did not develop until 1790. Thomas Edison spent his youth here, which may explain why the city seems greatly interested in pioneering electrically. Edison developed the first electrical battery here in 1861. The first electric utility was formed in 1844.

The first underwater rail tunnel between the United States and a foreign country opened September 19, 1891. The 6,025-foot-long tunnel linked Port Huron and Sarnia, Ontario, Canada. In 1908, it was equipped with electricity. Still in use, its original cost was $2,700,000.

Hope it never gets a flat

You can see the World's Largest Tire if you take the Oakwood Boulevard exit off I-94 in Dearborn. Not just any tire, it's a white wall located right outside the Uniroyal Factory. Akron, Ohio, claims they're the rubber capital of the world, but where's their tire?

Working with one's friends

Most museums are built after a famous person is gone, but Henry Ford created his own. His friend Thomas Edison laid the cornerstone for the Henry Ford Museum in Dearborn on September 27, 1928. Today the museum and adjoining Greenfield Village span 254 acres, and cover 350 years of technology and inventions, with the majority reflecting Ford's personal tastes. Collections cover communications, transportation, industry, agriculture, and, of course, the automobile.

Many of the original exhibits are devoted to Ford's personal friends, such as Thomas Edison. The workshop where Edison invented the light bulb is included. Henry Ford even had the junkyard around Edison's New Jersey workshops excavated to find additional treasures.

The museum was dedicated October 21, 1929, on the 50th anniversary of Edison's invention of the incandescent bulb. Ford had his old friend re-enact the discovery while a roomful of dignitaries sat in candlelight. As Edison's carbonized fiber began to glow, switches were thrown, filling the room with light. Among those attending the ceremony were President Hoover, Madame Curie, Orville Wright, and Will Rogers. Albert Einstein made his contribution to the festivities by communicating from Germany over the radio.

Petoskey statue and stones

Petoskey is home to a unique tourist attraction. Located in Little Traverse Bay, it's 68 feet under the water. A life-size statue of Christ serves as an aquatic church for underwater worshipers. Those who like to do their sightseeing above the water can join the rockhounds looking for Petoskey stones. Petoskey stones are actually extinct coral which inhabited the shallow seas 350 million years ago. They may be extinct, but they're not forgotten: the Petoskey stones have been designated Michigan's official State Stones!

The Indians called it *Michilimackinac* or the "Great Turtle," but today it's known as Mackinac Island (pronounced Mackinaw). The island served as a frontier outpost for 115 years and in the mid-1800s was the center of fur trade when John Astor's fur company was based there.

The Great Turtle

Today the island remains a unique outpost from modern civilization. The only access to the island is via the massive Mackinac Bridge or by boat. Once there, travel is by horse power, foot power, or bicycle—no motorized vehicles are allowed.

This makes SR 85 possibly the only state highway in the nation on which a vehicle accident has never occurred. Mackinac Island is a treasure to be enjoyed. The island is three miles long and two miles wide. All original buildings in Fort Mackinac have been restored to their 18th-century splendor.

The Grand Hotel, built in 1887, is a resort of monumental stature and its white pillared porch is believed to the longest porch in the world. Also on the island is the Bark Chapel built by an early missionary in the 1600s, the Stuart House Museum of the Astor Fur Post, the Biddle House, the Mission Church built in 1829, and even an Indian Dormitory which houses Indian artifacts. Oh yes, some of the world's best fudge makers can be found on the island, too.

The "Big Mac" bridge

Land of wooden shoes, tulips

🏠 Holland was settled by Dutch immigrants seeking religious freedom in 1848. Today the descendants of those original settlers continue to practice many old traditions, right down to the wooden shoes.

Each spring thousands of tulips bloom, almost on cue, to celebrate "Tulip Time." In May, Holland plays host to a spectacular festival which includes street scrubbing by wooden-shoed participants. The De Klomp Wooden Shoe and Delftware Factory welcomes visitors to watch as wooden shoes are carved. The Dutch Village, just one mile from Holland, is lined with shops, carving exhibits, klompen dances, and more. The Netherlands Museum is another important attraction filled with folklore, pottery, and furnishings. Flower lovers had better not pass by the Veldheer Tulip Gardens. Over 100 different varieties of tulips and daffodils are on display during the flower season.

What goes around, comes around

What's been around since 1780, works as good as new, and is still earning its keep? If you guessed the DeZwaan located in Holland's 36-acre Windmill Island, you're correct. The 12-story windmill was brought from the Netherlands to Michigan's Holland. It still produces a fine graham flour which is sold on site.

Hidden treasure

Imagine the surprise of the coroner. Performing a routine autopsy, he discovers a missing gem valued at $35,000 inside a man's body. It all started when gangster Peter the Greek was shown a collection of gems in a New York hotel. Store clerks immediately realized the gem was missing, but a thorough search of Peter and the room turned up nothing. The Greek was eventually jailed in Michigan for perjury on a different matter and when he died one year later his treasure was discovered.

Cemetery filled with Who's Who

🏠 Oak Hill Cemetery in Battle Creek is the final resting place of many residents who made some impact on a local or national level. Among the more noteworthy are David Merrill, C.W. Post, and another cereal giant—W.K. Kellogg.

Sojourner Truth, a former slave turned temperance leader and abolitionist, found her resting place in Battle Creek. She worked on the Underground Railroad and was invited to the White House by President

Lincoln. Abolitionist Erastus Hussy also rests in the famed cemetery. As station manager for the Underground Railroad, he supplied food, clothing, and blankets to the slaves who sought freedom. He was also founder and editor of the *Michigan Liberty Press*, an abolitionist newspaper.

A not-so-well-known resident of Oak Hill Cemetery is Frank Kellog (no relation to the cereal guys). Cartoonist and sign painter, he owned a mail-order medicine business and sold anti-fat pills. One of Napoleon Bonaparte's personal guards during his banishment on St. Helena, English soldier Williams Palmer, also rests in peace there.

The wonderful world of Ziggy

If you happen to live in Chicago, you know that to be a Grabowski is the same as being called the ultimate Bears fan. However, if you live in Fenton and there's a Grabowski in your yard, it's probably a painting that's two stories tall! Ziggy Grabowski is a local artist who paints barns, but not in red. He actually recreates historic paintings. On Cronell Dexter's farm, down on US 23, he painted a black-and-white two-story reproduction of John Singletown Copley's *Paul Revere*. At Robert Wakeman's farm, Grabowski reproduced (see photo) a study of Raphael's *Baldassare Castiglione*.

MICHIGAN MONIKERS

🏠 Menominee, the southernmost city in the UP, translates from Indian as "rice men." The name was given to those who harvested the grain-bearing grass that grew wild on the banks of the river. A trading post was established there in 1796 by fur trapper Louis Chappee. By the 1890s the docks were jammed with lumber—making Menominee the largest shipper of pine lumber in the world.

The river itself was a rare find. Early history books claimed fish were so plentiful that dip nets were used to simply scoop out the bounty swimming below the surface. More than 500 barrels of fish were scooped, salted, and packed each season. In 1934, two fishermen working alone netted 4,200 pounds of smelt, in less than five hours! (But you should have seen the ones that got away!)

Fish 'n chips

🏠 Irish Hills is a portion of Michigan with gentle slopes, emerald green forests, and sparkling lakes. It was so much like his Irish home that founding father Reverend Lyster honored the area with Ireland's name. St. Joseph's Roman Catholic Church, which still stands today, was originally built as a small stone chapel in 1854 by Irish settlers.

Irish son finds home away from home

**It's mine! No, it's mine!
I was here first.
No, I was . . .**

🏠 Louis Campau and Lucius Lyon both thought the site on the west bank of the Grand River would be a good place to start a town. Campau established a fur-trading center in 1827 and three years later purchased a large tract of riverfront property.

Not to be outdone, Lucius Lyon purchased the land to the north of Campau's claim. Campau, called "The Fox" by the Indians—with good reason—immediately plotted his tract in such a way that Lyon's streets dead-ended into his cross-streets, which blocked Lyon's path to the river. Lyon retaliated by running his streets at odd angles. When Campau requested that the settlement be called Grand Rapids, Lyon used political pull to change the name to Kent.

The area remained Kent until 1842, when it was changed back to Grand Rapids. Evidence of this rivalry still exists today. Campau Square is an odd piece of land left undeveloped because of the way Lyon and Campau laid out their streets.

**You say Benton, we
say Bungtown**

🏠 Real estate was a bit too expensive in the St. Joseph area in the 1830s, so many hard-working settlers moved to the east bank of St. Joe's River. They called their new settlement Benton Harbor, but their snobbish neighbors referred to it as Bungtown Harbor. More folks could afford to live in Benton Harbor than in St. Joseph. Soon Benton Harbor was boasting a larger population than its neighbor.

As the town expanded, boundary disputes arose. St. Joseph had been incorporated as a village in 1836, Benton Harbor in 1869. But due to the conflicts, the state legislature decided to issue one city charter, incorporating the two cities. The cities were unable to agree on a name and in 1891 they were chartered separately. The rivalry went on for a long time before common interests prevailed. Today, the old rift has been set aside and the two communities promote togetherness by calling themselves Michigan's Twin Cities.

House of David

In 1903, a religious community was established in Benton Harbor. Benjamin Purcell developed the House of David and became the town's benefactor. He gave Benton Harbor a miniature railroad and amusement park which brought an influx in tourists. A more unusual contribution was his long-haired baseball team.

A touch of the grape

🏠 How to stay friends with your neighbors and still name a town after your wife. Together Elisha Rumsey and John Allen founded a town in 1855. Luckily for them, both their wives were named Ann. Since the women enjoyed visiting while sitting under a grape arbor, Rumsey and Allen decided to name the town "Ann Arbor." And everyone lived happily ever after.

🏠 That's what *Frankenmuth* means. In 1845, fifteen Franconians from Bavaria left their native land seeking religious freedom. They arrived in the Saginaw Valley and founded Frankenmuth. Many Germans followed. Until the early 1900s, German was the major language there.

"Courage of the Franconians"

Today, the traditions and heritage of those people lives on in the spirit, food, and architecture of this unique village. The former St. Lorenze Lutheran School is now the School Haus Square and features 25 specialty stores. The 35-bell carillon in the Bavarian Inn's Glockenspiel Tower plays three melodies, followed by the presentation of carved wooden figures telling the tale of the Pied Piper of Hamelin.

Frankenmuth Waterworks

🏠 In the 1970s a Scottish rock 'n' roll band was seeking an American name to help Americanize their product. Leaving it up to fate, they stuck a pin at random into a map. It landed on Bay City, Michigan. They went on to become the Bay City Rollers, but the good residents of Bay City have more than some longhairs to brag about.

It's not just for rock and rollers

Although originally a center for the lumbering industry, today the city serves as a distribution point for industrial and agricultural products as both foreign and domestic freighters grace its busy port. Also known as "Mural City USA," downtown Bay City has 50 different murals painted on the outside walls of many businesses. What started as a job for the local Pontiac dealer—painting murals—has spread like wildfire all over town!

🏠 Michigan towns received their names in a variety of ways and for many different reasons.

A collection of towns

• Descendants of the Pilgrims from Plymouth Rock settled in the Michigan Territory in 1825 and gave their new home an old, familiar name—Plymouth! (And you thought it was named after that car, didn't you?)

• Old Salt Saline was settled in 1824 and was named for the natural salt springs in the area. The Indians considered this a prized location and later Henry Ford did too! Ford purchased the Saline Gristmill, built in 1849, and used the soybean oil extracted in the finish of his autos!

• Grand Blanc, located near the Thread River, was named for a huge fur trader named Fisher who came to help divert the fur trade away from the British. Fisher's large stature caused the Indians to name him *Le Grand Blanc*, French for "The Big White." The Indian nickname was eventually used to name the trading post and, later, the settlement itself.

Then Came Bronson

🏠 The Indians called it *Kee-Kalamazoo*, which means "Where the water boils in the pot." That's what the Indians saw in the Kalamazoo River where hundreds of bubbling springs cause it to roll and boil. A trading post established on the site was given the same name in 1823. Then Titus Bronson, a man who, according to legend, loved his liquor, arrived in 1829 and the settlement's name was changed to Bronson. However, the good citizens did not approve of the town's new name—or the man it was named after. In 1836, the settlement became known as Kalamazoo.

Moscow on the Kalamazoo

Moscow enjoyed its brief claim to fame when stagecoach drivers used it as a stopping point on the journey between Detroit and Chicago. The road through Moscow became known as the Old Chicago Turnpike at the Kalamazoo River. So well known was the spot that once a letter, mailed in 1829, arrived there with only the above description, stampless!

A picture is worth a thousand words

🏠 When government surveyors traveled to southeastern Michigan, a broken ax was found at one site. Hence, the village of Bad Axe was born. Until the U.S. Post Office banned picture addresses, letters from distant writers addressed with only a sketch of a broken ax were routinely delivered to Bad Axe residents.

Telling it by the nickname

Every town wants some reason to stand out from the crowd, and Michigan has a mighty large number of nicknames that give its towns distinction. Here are some:

Battle Creek – Best Known City in the World, Best Known City of its Size in the World, Breakfast Food City, Cereal Food Center of the World, Health Food City
Beaverton – City Growing with Plastics
Bellaire – America's Bit O' Ireland in County O' Antrim
Belleville – Happy Town
Bronson – City the Depression Passed Up
Cadillac – Friendliest Area in the Northern Lower Michigan
Colon – Magic City (home of Harry Blackstone)
Detroit – Has 23 different nicknames, including – Dynamic Detroit, Ford's Greatest City, City of Destiny, Fordtown, Beautiful City by the Straits, Overgrown Small Town, Motown
Elk Rapids – City for the Vacation of a Lifetime
Frankfort – Gliding and Soaring Capital of the World
Grand Rapids – City in the Heart of 250 Sparkling Lakes and Streams, City of Happy Homes, Furniture Capital of the World, Hub of Western Michigan
Kalamazoo – Celery City
Mackinac Island – Fudge Capital of the World, Bermuda of the North
Mount Clemens – America's Bath City
Muskegon – Lumber Queen, Red Light Queen, Sawdust Queen
Sault Ste. Marie – Soo
Tawas City – Perchville USA
Wayland – Cow Town
White Cloud – City Where the North Begins and the Pure Waters Flow

TAKING CENTER STAGE

The state's first coup in the entertainment industry came on August 20, 1920. Detroit's WWJ, owned by the *Detroit News*, went on the air to become the nation's first commercial radio station. Several years later, George Trendle, looking for a way to promote patriotism, compassion, and fairness, created "The Lone Ranger," which made its debut on Detroit's WXYZ January 30, 1933, and became one of the longest-running radio serials ever. Trendle had just two rules for the Lone Ranger: he could not touch women or kill anything!

Then came William John Clifton Haley of Highland Park. Considered the father of rock and roll, Bill Haley and his Comets paved the way for the Beatles and Elvis. His song "Rock Around the Clock" was the first song to top the charts in 1955.

And if you're talking music, you can't ignore the little recording studio called Hitsville USA. It grew up to be Motown, and its artists and their music exploded on the music scene. In one week in 1966, three of the top five records were spinning Motown labels.

- Motown Magic
- Motown Moments
- Chart Busters
- Stage and Screen
- Awards and Applause
- The Silver Screen
- Laughter is the Best Medicine

MOTOWN MAGIC

It started in Studio A

Berry Gordy was a would-be professional boxer in the late 1940s, making a modest $150 per week. After a stint in the army, he returned to Detroit and opened a record store that soon failed. He eventually landed a job at Ford making $79.88 a week.

Gordy cut a demo record with an old friend, a singer named Jackie Wilson. The song, "Reet Petite," became a midsized hit. He also wrote "Lonely Teardrops" for Wilson. Gordy grew unhappy about the production quality of his records and was further soured when a publisher denied him $1,000 in royalties. Gordy borrowed $800 from his family and set up a small recording studio (Studio A) in a house on Grand Boulevard in Detroit and turned it into Motown.

The man who gave the push

Smokey Robinson is one of Detroit's greatest resources. Born in 1940, his musical genius surfaced early. He formed a group called the Miracles while still in high school and, in 1957, convinced Berry Gordy, Jr., to form his own record label.

As a singer/composer, Robinson's first hit, "Shop Around," surfaced in 1961. He shared his tremendous writing talent with other Motown artists. In 1971, he became a Motown vice president. In appreciation, he named his son "Berry William Borope" honoring both Gordy and his singing group, the Miracles: Bobby, Ronnie, and Pete. Ten years later, he returned to recording with the hit single, "Being With You."

Smokey Robinson and the Miracles

Climbing to the top

In 1961, Berry Gordy produced his first million-seller on his own label, the Miracles' "Shop Around." At its peak in 1966, 75 percent of the company's releases made the charts, at a time when the industry average was 10 percent. By 1970, Gordy's company had produced 22 number-one rock hits, and 48 number-one rhythm and blues hits.

First lady of Motown

Mary Wells was born into a poor Detroit neighborhood. As a baby she suffered from spinal meningitis and tuberculosis. Perhaps that is what made her a scrapper. At age 15, she marched down to the Motown recording studio to sell a song she had written for Jackie Wilson called "Bye, Bye, Baby." Gordy had her sing it instead and it became Motown's first number-one hit. She dominated Motown with her popularity and at 21 informed Gordy she would not sign another contract. Her absence opened the doors for other female singers. "My Guy," which went number one in 1964, was her most famous song. She died of lung cancer in 1992 at age 49.

MOTOWN MOMENTS:

- Detroit's music community was untapped in the 1960s. There were few managers, and performers worked without contracts. Gordy recruited the Temptations and Martha and the Vandellas and found Tammi Terrell, David Ruffin, Eddie Kendricks, and Paul Williams performing in Detroit clubs. The Marvelettes were discovered at a high school talent show.
- Anna-Tri-Phi Records was another Motown label. It was named after Berry's sister, Anna, who was married to Marvin Gaye. When they divorced, his album "Here, My Dear" contained songs about their married life. She received $600,000 in royalties due to its contents.
- Before approving a record for release, Gordy would listen to the song on a tinny-sounding radio. Since most people would hear the song in their car first, he could judge its commercial value this way.
- Berry Gordy was a tough boss. He rejected Smokey Robinson's first 100 songs. At one production meeting, 68 already produced songs were presented and only one (the Supremes' "Love Child") was released.
- Gordy encouraged up to four in-house producers to produce the same song, then he would select just one for release.
- Motown's recording studio had an ancient eight-track tape machine that would slow during recording sessions. To keep the reels turning at the right speed, someone had to turn them by hand!
- In the early Motown years, the volatile '60s, black singers' photos did not appear on record covers. Gordy tried to make Motown music more commercially acceptable to white audiences and used alternative artwork on album covers. For instance, the Marvelettes' "Please, Mr. Postman" had a line drawing of a mailbox with cobwebs, and the Isley Brothers' "This Old Heart of Mine" showed a white couple gazing into each other's eyes.
- The Motown Motor Revue served as a way for young talent to become seasoned and also gain market exposure. Up to 45 performers traveled in one bus and five cars. It was a tour on a shoestring. Costumes were hand-me-downs that often ripped at embarrassing moments.
- Prior to the civil rights movement, black performers had trouble finding hotels and restaurants that would admit them. Once a Motown employee got a room at the Hyde Park Hotel in Chicago and Smokey Robinson stopped to visit him. Later the hotel manager told the Motown exec he would have to leave since guests were not allowed to have black visitors.
- Berry Gordy earned $367 million in 16 years. In 1972, Motown moved its operations to Los Angeles. Today, Studio A is a popular museum.

From the projects to the penthouse

On March 26, 1944, a clerical error by a Detroit hospital staff member resulted in officially naming the Ross baby Diana instead of the chosen Diane. It was a name she would select after becoming a Supreme. At 14, her family moved into the Brewster-Douglas Projects, a government housing complex. That same year, when she failed to win a singing role in a school musical, Ross and two friends, Mary Wilson and Florence Ballard, decided to form their own musical group, the Primettes.

In 1960, their senior year, the three were hired by Motown to sing background for various artists and to play record hops with Marvin Gaye and Mary Wells. With their name changed to the Supremes, they toured with the Motown Revue. Their initial lack of success changed with "Let Me Go the Right Way." It was followed by "Where Did Our Love Go?" which hit number one. Over 10 years the Supremes had 15 consecutive smash-hit singles, and at one point had five consecutive records in the number-one position on the charts.

In 1969, Ross and Gordy became a couple, and he began grooming her for a solo career. The group's name was changed to Diana Ross and the Supremes. She broke from the group and moved into movies, which included *Lady Sings the Blues* (1972) and *Mahogany* (1974). She won a Tony for the Broadway musical of *The Wiz* (1984).

It's a wonder

Steveland Judkins Morris Hardaway, a.k.a.: Stevie Wonder, was born blind in Saginaw in 1951. He and his family later moved to Detroit. Discovering music early, he had mastered, by 10 years old, every instrument he played. Fate stepped in when a friend's brother, a member of the Miracles, heard Stevie. He introduced him to Motown and by the age of 12 he had recorded his first album, *Stevie Wonder: The Twelve-Year-Old Genius*, and also *Fingertips.*

By the age of 20, Stevie was recording his own albums. Averaging one per year, he produced such Top 40 hits as "I Was Made To Love Her," "My Cherie Amour," and "Uptight." Wonder earned Grammys for the Best Album in 1973, 1974, and 1976.

The deadly singers

Singer **Marvin Gaye**, the son of a minister in Washington, D.C., sang all his life. In the 1960s, he was signed to Motown as a sessions drummer playing on all the early hits by Smokey Robinson and the Miracles. And, he married Berry Gordy's sister. In 1962, Gaye recorded his first hit, "Stubborn Kind of Fellow," and over the next 10 years produced 20 hits. During a 1967 concert in Cleveland, his Motown partner,

Tammi Terrell, collapsed in Gaye's arms. First thought to be exhaustion, her illness was later diagnosed as a brain tumor. Eight operations couldn't save her, and in 1970 Tammi Terrell died at the age of 24. Shattered, Gaye did not tour again for four years. In 1971, he released "What's Going On?" which was followed by "Let's Get It On." In 1982, he divorced and signed with Columbia Records where he sang the Grammy-winning single, "Sexual Healing." On April 1, 1984, Marvin Gaye was shot to death by his father.

⭐ Martha (Reeves) & the Vandellas started out as the Dell-fi's with Martha, Rosalind Ashford, Annette Sterling, and then lead singer Gloria Williams. Their first label credit came when they sang backup on J.J. Barner's "Won't You Let Me Know" in 1960. But when their own recordings languished in record-store bins, Detroit-born Martha decided to go solo under her real name, Martha Lavaille.

The right place at the right time

Auditioning for Motown, she took a job as a secretary at $35 per week. In 1962, Mary Wells failed to show for a recording session and Martha recommended her old group be used as a replacement. The Dell-fi's changed their names to the Vells and recorded "There He Is (at My Door)," which flopped.

Renamed Martha & the Vandellas, a name Martha took from Detroit's Van Dyke Avenue and singer Della Reese, they sang backup for Mickey Stevenson. When Wells missed another session, Martha & the Vandellas recorded "I'll Have To Let Him Go." Their big break came with "Heat Wave" in 1963, followed by "Dancing in the Street" in 1964 and "Nowhere to Run" in 1965.

⭐ One of the most talented musical families of our time was discovered by Bobby Taylor and the Vancouvers—not Diana Ross, whose name was lent to the discovery for marquee value. During a 1968 performance at Chicago's Regal Theater, the Jackson 5 from Gary, Indiana, was spotted as an emerging talent. (One of the Vancouvers was Tommy Chong, later of Cheech and Chong fame!)

The family that sings together . . .

The five young brothers sang and danced, with the youngest, Michael, often singing lead. Taken to Detroit to record, the Jacksons' first hit with Motown was "I Want You Back," released in 1968. More hits followed, as well as a cartoon series and TV specials. Young Michael went solo, and recorded his first album, *Got To Be There*. In 1975, the group broke from Motown and moved on to Epic Records.

⭐ Gladys Knight and the Pips was based in Atlanta. The undisputed lead singer was Gladys, who sang at churches at age 5, and at 7 won the Ted Mack Amateur Hour. The Pips came together in 1952 after an impromptu performance at a birthday party. They included Gladys's oldest brother, Merald, William Guest, and Edward Patten. They toured with Jackie Wilson and Sam Cooke, all before Gladys was 13! After achieving one hit, "Every Beat of My Heart," they signed as a guest act on the Motown Touring Revue. They left Motown in 1973. Later hits include "Midnight Train to Georgia" and "Best Thing That Ever Happened To Me."

Must be in the genes

More Motown groupies

The Marvelettes were just five schoolgirls from Inkster who recorded a number-one hit, 1961's "Please, Mr. Postman." The great singing and dancing group called **the Temptations** began as the Distants in 1958. They had 21 Top 20 hits between 1964 and 1971. A mutual friend happened to introduce four Detroit boys to each other in 1954. They cut one record on a small Detroit label as the Four Aims, then changed their names to **the Four Tops** in 1956. Joining Motown, their recording of "Baby, I Need Your Loving" went to number one.

CHART BUSTERS

Making do

Born Thomas Gregory Jackson, singer Tommy James moved to Niles when he was 11 and put together a band, the Shondells, from his seventh-grade band buddies. Weekdays after school he worked at a record store and met a distributor with a recording studio. At 12, his band recorded their first record, "Long Pony Tail," which sold a whopping 500 copies. His second single, "Hanky Panky," did somewhat better, becoming a local hit in Indiana, Illinois, and Michigan. Two years later, a Pittsburgh disk jockey began playing the song on the air. The original Shondells had broken up, so James quickly found another group in a Pittsburgh nightclub, the Raconteurs, and they became his new Shondells. For two weeks in 1966, "Hanky Panky" enjoyed the number-one berth on the charts.

We got you, babe!

Detroit-born Salvatore "Sonny" Bono moved with his family to California when he was a teenager in 1954. He dreamed of being a star from an early age—his first song was inspired by a package of cookies with a catchy name! Recording under the names Sonny Christie and Ronny Sommers got him nowhere. Then he met Cherilyn Sarkisian LaPierre at a Hollywood coffee shop and his luck changed. Borrowing $135 to pay for Cher's recording session at RCA studios, he found her so nervous that at the last minute he recorded "Baby Don't Go" with her.

In 1965, their number-one hit, "I Got You, Babe," established them as an international recording duo. Now a restaurateur and divorced from Cher, Sonny became the controversial mayor of Palm Springs, California, in 1988, and lost a bid for the U.S. Senate in 1992.

⭐ Son of a Detroit preacher, Vincent Damon Furnier never considered following his father's profession. Nor did his folks ever think he would take on a girl's first name and become an international rock star known for his on-stage antics with a boa constrictor and black eye makeup. Alice Cooper's theatrical concerts put him in the forefront of "shockrock." He produced a hit album in 1975, *Welcome to My Nightmare.*

Alice doesn't live here any more

⭐ Casey Kasem's voice is among the most recognizable in the world. A radio personality for 18 years, he was the youngest person inducted into the Radio Hall of Fame. Born Kemal Amin Kasem in Detroit in 1933, he dreamed of becoming a baseball player but ended up announcing sports in high school. Majoring in speech and English at Wayne State University, he coordinated radio drama on the Armed Forces Network while stationed in Korea. Kasem has done voice-overs on 2,000 episodes of cartoons, including "Scooby-Do," "Super Friends," "Mister Magoo," and "Transformers." His most popular show is "American Top 40s" on the radio.

What a voice!

A star for all reasons
Singer/actress/TV personality Della Reese was born Deloreese Patricia Early in 1932 in Detroit. Reese began her career as a gospel singer. In 1957, the singer turned to pop. Her numerous gold records include the mega-hit from 1959, "Don't You Know?" She broke ground with her 1969 TV show, "Della," on which she was the first female to host a TV variety show. She has appeared in several hit television series, including "Sanford and Son," "The Love Boat," and "Chico and the Man." Reunited with actor Redd Foxx (who had played Fred Sanford) on the 1991 TV series "Royal Family," she tried to keep it going after his unexpected death.

Among her silver screen performances were *Let's Rock* and *Psychic Killer.*

They were a Detroit band first

Brainchild of former Detroit DJ Terry Knight, Grand Funk Railroad broke all the rules. Made up of four music-loving Michigan boys—Mark Farner, Craig Frost, Mel Schacher, and Don Brewer—the late '60s rock-and-roll group sold over 20 million records during its lifetime. A July 1971 New York concert grossed $5,000 a minute! They're remembered for their 1973 mega-hit album, *We're an American Band*.

Soaring with the eagles

Singer/guitarist Glenn Frey started his career in Detroit's punk rock scene, then started a country band and moved on to form the Eagles, a famous American rock band of the 1970s. The Eagles sold over 50 million records worldwide, won four Grammys, and had four top hits, "Best of My Love," "One of These Nights," "New Kid in Town," and "Hotel California," before the group disbanded in 1980. Frey now records alone.

Took his name from a car

When Coopersville-native Charles Westover's first record, "Runaway," rose to number one in 1961, he was working at a carpet store in Battle Creek during the day and appearing nightly at the Hi Lo Club. He changed his name to Del Shannon. The "Del" was a shortened form of the boss's car, the Cadillac Coupe de Ville, and "Shannon" was a local wrestler he once met. He followed his first hit with "Hats Off to Larry," "Hey! Little Girl," "Little Town Flirt," and "Sea of Love," to name a few.

Still battling depression, but sober, Shannon admitted that he spent much of his thirties and forties drunk. In 1979, the tides turned as a remake of "Sea of Love," produced by Tom Petty, made a strong showing on the charts for four weeks. With new lyrics, "Runaway" was used for the TV show "Crime Stories." It was rumored that Shannon was in line to take Roy Orbinson's spot in the Traveling Wilburys. On February 8, 1990, in California, Del Shannon committed suicide with a rifle.

Mad City Mad Man

The "Mad City Mad Man," rocker Ted Nugent, summed up his philosophy of life during an appearance on Dr. Ruth's cable TV show by saying, ". . . life is one big female safari and Dr. Ruth is my guide." Nugent began playing guitar at age nine and never turned back. Very popular in his hometown of Detroit, his first group, the Amboy Dukes, recorded the 1968 classic, "Journey to the Center of the Mind." In the '70s, his high vocals with Styx became a rock standard for many imitators. The Dukes split in 1975, with Nugent going solo.

The controversial star shocked the public in January of 1978 by signing an autograph on a fan's arm with a Bowie knife. He has been an avid hunter and environmentalist for years and publishes a monthly hunting magazine, *Ted Nugent's World Bowhunters*. Nugent had a chance to show off his hunting skills on the band's 1991 tour. An eight-foot wooden Saddam Hussein popped up on stage each night. Standing sixty feet away, Nugent aimed his bow and arrow and hit the plywood Hussein in a very sensitive area as crowds cheered "USA!"

In 1989, Nugent formed a new rock-and-roll band called "Damn Yankees," a group with a "chainsaw" spin. Their debut album sold two million copies.

When she's bad, she's very good

Madonna (a.k.a.: Louise Veronica Ciccone) likes to portray herself as a Catholic girl gone bad, and she does it well. Born in Bay City in 1959 into a family of eight children, she lost her mother at age six and was raised by a very strict stepmother. When a junior high school teacher told her she had a beautiful "Roman face," she decided to devote her life to ballet. Following a year at the University of Michigan, she moved to New York to pursue her dance career with the Alvin Ailey Dance Troupe. After a trip to Paris, she returned to New York where she promoted her first song, "Everybody," by dancing in front of a DJ's booth at a local nightspot. The crowd loved it, the DJ remixed some of her demo tapes, and Sire Records signed her in 1983.

By 1985, Madonna, at age 25, was the hottest recording star in the nation with two hit LPs, "Madonna" and "Like A Virgin." *Desperately Seeking Susan*, a 1986 hit movie, opened the way for her film career. Married briefly to actor Sean Penn, she also co-starred in the big screen production of *Dick Tracy*, with then current love interest Warren Beatty.

Creating controversy as often as she changes her hair color, Madonna's 1992 book, *Sex*, caused the expected gasps. Madonna said the explicit photos were meant to be therapeutic, but one critic wasn't convinced. "Six months from now it will be the first aluminum-covered soft-porn book ever to grace the remainder bin."

Johnny Desmond started out as Giovanni Alfredo de Simone in Detroit. His singing career began in 1941 with a Detroit-based band, the Downbeats, performing on local radio. While serving in the Air Force, he was discovered by the great Glenn Miller. He sang in Miller's Air Force Band billed as the "GI Sinatra." He appeared regularly on "Don McNeill's Breakfast Club." Although he was never a big fan of rock and roll, he sang on "Your Hit Parade" in 1959.

The GI Sinatra

Sex, soccer, and Rod Stewart

How can a concert lead to divorce? Well, when Patricia Boughton attended a Rod Stewart concert at Clarkston's Pine Knob Music Theatre in 1989, she didn't expect to get hit with a soccer ball. Rod Stewart, a former soccer player, traditionally kicks balls off the stage at the end of his concerts. When the middle finger of her left hand was struck by one, Boughton claimed it was disfigured so badly that her sex life suffered. She sued Stewart and two theater owners, winning $17,000 in judgments in 1992. Her husband testified that the painful injury contributed to the end of their 14-year marriage.

Old-time rock and roller

Still a Michigan resident, rock and roller Bob Seger is goin' strong after almost thirty years in the business. Perseverence and a distaste for "marketing" and "image" characterized his slow ten-year rise to fame. Born in Detroit in 1945, Seger always loved rhythm and blues and the Chuck Berry style. As early as 1964, Seger was a local hit at teen clubs and lounges with the Omens. Del Shannon stepped in and paid for some of Seger's early demos.

His first solo recording, "East Side Story," was released in May of 1966 and sold 50,000 copies in Detroit. In 1968, he made a deal with Capitol Records, even though Motown offered more money. His Silver Bullet Band, composed of local unknowns, came together in the early 1970s, and "Night Moves" (1976) cemented Seger's fame and his long association with the Silver Bullet Band.

Queen of soul

Named one of Michigan's natural resources in 1985, although she was born in Tennessee, singer Aretha Franklin grew up in the same neighborhood that produced such greats as Smokey Robinson, Diana Ross, and the Four Tops. She learned to play piano from records, but her four-octave voice was coached by various family friends including gospel great Mahalia Jackson. Daughter of a famous gospel preacher, Aretha often sang at his revivals.

In 1952, she dropped out of high school and devoted herself to singing full-time. She enjoyed some success on the gospel circuit and was encouraged by friends to change her style. In 1966, she signed with Atlantic Records, a label specializing in rhythm and blues. A string of hits in the late '60s and '70s, including "Respect," "Natural Woman," and "Chain of Fools," followed. Today the "Queen of Soul" has 21 gold records and 15 Grammy awards—the latest for "One Lord, One Faith, One Baptism," which was recorded in the same church where she started. Inducted into the Rock and Roll Hall of Fame in 1987, Aretha was the first female rock star to be so honored.

Biggest in North America

Over 750,000 jazz fans crowd downtown Detroit for the largest free jazz festival in North America. Held every September, the Montreux-Detroit Jazz Festival started in 1980 and today includes more than a hundred open-air concerts staged in outdoor theaters.

Songwriter Harry Von Tilzer published 2,000 songs during his prolific career. Born in Detroit in 1872, Harry, like his brother Albert (who wrote "Take Me Out to the Ball Game"), changed his surname from Gumm to Von Tilzer, his mother's maiden name.

By gumm, it's a Tilzer!

Harry joined the circus as a teenager, and finally moved on to songwriting. His hits recall memories for the senior generation: "A Bird in a Gilded Cage," "I Want a Girl Just Like the Girl that Married Dear Old Dad," "In the Sweet Bye-and-Bye," and "Wait Till the Sun Shines, Nellie."

Contemporary gospel duo Benjamin "Bebe" and Priscilla "CeCe" Winans are just part of the family business based in Detroit. All ten Winan children are involved in gospel music, probably because their father is a minister. Several of the brothers sing as a group called the Winans, three of the sisters perform as the Sisters (BeBe produces them), and Daniel, another brother, won a Grammy singing alone. When BeBe and CeCe first appeared together in 1982 as PTL singers, they had no idea they'd have four Grammys by 1990. Sometimes called controversial in gospel circles, they describe themselves as ". . . just two young people trying to bring a smile to people's faces."

All in the family

STAGE AND SCREEN

Certain he'd immediately be a Broadway success, Detroit-born actor George Peppard had his phone number unlisted after his stint at the Lee Strasberg acting school. But the phone never rang and he had to accept bit roles. In 1957, the actor finally made his screen debut in *The Strange One*. Other films he appeared in were *Pork Chop Hill, Home From the Hill, How the West Was Won, The Carpetbaggers, The Blue Max*, and *Breakfast at Tiffany's*.

Saved by the A-Team

In the 1980s Peppard's luck almost ran out. About two weeks before the series "Dynasty" went into production, he was replaced by John Forsythe for the lead role of Blake Carrington. Facing tough financial times, Peppard was worried he might even lose his house but was saved in 1983 by a casting call for the TV series "The A-Team."

That's my boy!

Jason Robards, Sr., was a popular leading man between 1921 and 1961 and appeared in over 100 films. The Hillsdale-born actor is also the father of Jason Robards, Jr. His namesake established himself as a great actor in his own right and won an Oscar for *All the President's Men*. He was also once married to Lauren Bacall, but they don't give out awards for that.

Betty Hutton in The Perils of Pauline

Pistol-Packin' Betty

Her real name is Elizabeth June Thornberg and she was born in Battle Creek in 1921. But to millions of movie buffs, she's Betty Hutton, the skinny blonde with the distinctive voice. According to Hutton, she "shoved and clawed" her way through vaudeville, night-clubs, and contests to get into the movies. In 1941, she got her first movie part in *The Fleet's In.* By 1947, she got the lead in *The Perils of Pauline.* Her big break, just like in the movies, came when Judy Garland turned down the role of the singin', gun-totin' Annie Oakley in the 1950 production of *Annie Get Your Gun.* In 1953 she had to learn to fly through the air for Cecil B. DeMille's circus extravaganza, *The Greatest Show on Earth.*

Bond's favorite bad guy

☆ Actor Richard Kiel, at 7 feet, 2 inches tall, made the perfect bad guy to face off against James Bond in *The Spy Who Loved Me.* The Redford-born actor also appeared in *Moonraker.* Other films include *The Longest Yard,* and *Force 10 From Navarone.* On TV, Kiel has appeared in the "The Riflemen," "I Spy," "Barbary Coast," and "Klondike."

Three hits on the little screen

☆ Robert John "R.J." Wagner, Jr., was born in 1930, the son of a wealthy Detroit metals manufacturer. Kicked out of several prestigious prep schools, he moved to California and landed a job at Warner Brothers Studio. He appeared in over 40 films as a bit player before finally making an impression with his one-minute portrayal of an injured soldier in *With a Song in My Heart.* In *All the Fine Young Cannibals,* he appeared with his future wife, former child star Natalie Wood. Although he acted in more than 30 movies, Wagner, often called the "Cary Grant of the small screen," achieved real stardom through his three hit TV series: "It Takes A Thief," "Switch," and "Hart to Hart."

His personal life has been a constant source of copy for the industry rags, beginning with his Hollywood-style wedding to Natalie Wood in 1957. They divorced four years later and, after Wagner's brief marriage to Marion Donen, they remarried in 1972 and had three daughters. Tragically, Wood drowned in 1981.

He started out as Harry Bratsburg when he was born in Detroit and later changed his name to Harry Morgan. Though he started acting in movies, he's been a fixture on television since an early sit-com called "December Bride." He enjoyed great success as Officer Bill Gannon, Detective Friday's sidekick, on the second (or was it third?) go-around of TV's "Dragnet" in the '60s. To millions of "M*A*S*H" fans around the world, he will always be lovable Colonel Sherman T. Potter, a role he played from 1975 to 1983.

Colonel Sherman T. Potter

Entertainer and humanitarian Danny Thomas was born Amos Muzyad Jacobs in Deerfield on January 6, 1914, the son of Lebanese immigrants. He called August 12, 1940, his second birthday because that's the day he performed publicly at the 5100 Club in Chicago. During those years, Thomas didn't know if he should pursue a show business career. He prayed to St. Jude for guidance and that day was offered a job in showbiz. He later built a shrine to honor St. Jude.

A promise kept

A high school dropout, Thomas was a successful radio performer on the "Baby Snooks Show" in 1945 and went on to star on the big screen in *Call Me Mister* and *The Jazz Singer*. It was TV's "Make Room for Daddy," which ran for eleven years (1953-1964), that assured his fame. A nightclub headliner, he also produced numerous hit TV series, including "That Girl," which starred his daughter, Marlo. In 1981, he was nominated for a Nobel Prize and in 1987 he received the Presidential Medal of Honor.

A multimillionaire many times over, he never forgot the guidance he received. Today St. Jude Children's Research Hospital in Memphis, Tennessee, is a world-famous medical center. Until his death in 1991, Thomas was intimately involved with fund-raising for the organization.

The big picture

It's a movie usher's worst nightmare. How to keep a theater filled with 5,041 people quiet? That's how many customers the ushers at Detroit's Fox Theater handle at one time. Opened in 1928, it's the largest movie theater still in existence, though it was eventually turned into a theater for live entertainment.

H-e-e-e-r-e's Ed!

He's the best known second banana in the world. Born in Detroit in 1923, Ed McMahon is best known as Johnny's sidekick. They got together in 1954 when Carson hosted a daytime quiz show called "Who Do You Trust?" In 1984, Ed began hosting TV's "Star Search" and also co-hosts "TV Bloopers and Practical Jokes." One of TV's top pitchmen, he has hawked everything from beer and dog food, to magazine sweepstakes.

Play it again, Sam, er, Richard

Actor Richard B. Harrison is best known for one role, a role he performed 1,656 times! His characterization of "De Lawd" in "Green Pastures" earned him national acclaim and the 1931 Spingarn Medal from the NAACP. Born in Canada in 1864, he moved to Detroit as a young boy and later studied drama.

Girls just want to have fun!

Hostess Perle Mesta didn't aspire to intellectual pursuits, she just wanted to have fun. Born in Sturgis about 1891, Mesta was sent east by her father to meet all the "right people," and she did. Known as "the hostess with the mostest," she got her start during the Truman Administration, entertaining at her Washington mansion, "Les Ormes." Perle's parties were attended by the biggest names in town—Eisenhower even sang at one. Apparently partying wasn't enough and in 1949 Perle was appointed ambassador to Luxembourg. They loved her over there! Her wealthy husband, George, died in 1925, and she remained the widow "who always had a good time" until her death in 1975. The Broadway musical *Call Me Madam* is based on Perle Mesta's career.

Daddy's little girl

Mary Margaret Truman, daughter of the 33rd president, was 23 when she made her professional singing debut with the Detroit Symphony Orchestra, in 1947. Columnist Paul Hume wrote a scathing criticism of the performance and Margaret's papa responded with an angry letter. Hume's paper, the *Washington Post*, refused to publish it. An angry father doesn't give up so easily so Truman sent the letter to the *Washington Daily News*, which did!

AWARDS AND APPLAUSE

No ordinary award

Detroit-born author Judith Ann Guest wrote *Ordinary People* in 1976. In 1980 it was made into an Oscar-winning movie directed by Robert Redford. The movie focuses on a family who is trying to deal with—by ignoring—the boating-accident death of one of their two sons and the suicide attempt of the surviving son. Mary Tyler Moore, Donald Sutherland, and Timothy Hutton starred. Residents of Lake Forest, Illinois, where the story takes place, were amazed at the clear picture the nonresident author had of the town.

A desired actress

Detroit-born actress Kim Hunter is best known for her role in the stage and film version of *A Streetcar Named Desire*. The 1951 film version earned her an Oscar for Best Supporting Actress. Hunter was "discovered" in 1922 by David O. Selznick of *Gone With The Wind* fame while performing in *Arsenic and Old Lace* at the Pasadena Playhouse.

Selznick gave her a contract and she co-starred in the 1943 movie *The Seventh Victim*. She went on to make *A Stairway to Heaven* with David Niven and, in 1947, *A Canterbury Tale*.

Not afraid to take a chance

Winner of five Oscars, Francis Ford Coppola was born into a family that valued "art" more than money. Coppola once said, "So what if my telephone is turned off again at home? . . . Or my credit cards canceled? If you don't bet, you don't have a chance to win." The Detroit-born director and writer was raised in Queens, overcoming polio and paralysis at a young age. His movie breakthrough came in 1963 when he directed a low-budget horror flick, *Dementia 13*. He went on to phenomenal success with big-budget movies, winning Oscars for co-writing *Patton* (1970), for the screenplay of *The Godfather* (1972), for the screenplay, direction, and best film for *The Godfather Part II* (1974). *Apocalypse Now* (1979) was honored at the Cannes Film Festival with two awards.

Out of Michigan

Screenwriter Kurt Mamre Luedtke was born in Grand Rapids, but it was another country which brought him recognition. In 1985 he won an Oscar for *Out of Africa*, starring Robert Redford and Meryl Streep.

From Detroit dropout to film fame

Detroit-born actress Ellen Burstyn wrote her first Oscar acceptance speech when she was seven. She was over 40 before she got a chance to read it. Edna Rae Gillooly quit school in 1950, married director Paul Roberts, and moved to New York where she became Keri Flynn, Erica Dean, and Edna Rae, depending on which job— model, cook, or fashion coordinator—she was doing while waiting for her big acting break.

Making her Broadway debut in *Fair Game* in 1957, she was hired for her smile, not for her acting abilities. But that changed. She left for Hollywood as Ellen McRae and got her break in *Tropic of Cancer* (1969) as Ellen Burstyn, taking her third husband's surname. Appearances in *The Last Picture Show* (1973), *The Exorcist* (1973), and *Harry and Tonto* (1974), led up to her 1974 Oscar-winning performance in *Alice Doesn't Live Here Anymore* (1974). She also won a Tony in the same year for her Broadway performance in *Same Time Next Year*. She is now the director of Actors' Studio in New York City.

A chip off the old block

Marlo Thomas, daughter of legendary showman Danny Thomas, starred in the TV hit show "That Girl!" The Detroit-born actress won Emmys for 1974's "Marlo Thomas and Friends," then in 1977 for "Free to be. . .You and Me," and in 1986 for "Nobody's Child." She is married to talk-show host Phil Donahue, whom she met while appearing as a guest on his show. Above, she is visiting children at her dad's St. Jude Children's Research Hospital.

Bet on a winner

She wasn't very popular and so found solace in acting, but Julie Harris went on to become one of the most acclaimed actresses of our time, earning 20 major acting awards including two Emmys and five Tonys. Born in Gross Pointe Park, Harris first made a name in the 1950 film *A Member of the Wedding*. Among her other films are *East of Eden* and *The Belle of Amherst*, which was based on her one-woman Broadway show. She won Tony awards for best actress in a drama for *I am a Camera* (1952); *The Lark* (1956); *Forty Carats* (1969); *The Last of Mrs. Lincoln* (1973); and *The Belle of Amherst* (1977). She also appeared on the long-running TV series "Knots Landing" from 1979 on.

THE SILVER SCREEN

Big Bay murder

Big Bay was catapulted into the spotlight after a sensational murder trial was turned into a best-selling novel by the judge who presided over

the actual trail. *Anatomy of a Murder* was made into an Academy Award-winning movie by director Otto Preminger. Starring Lee Remick, Eve Arden, and Jimmy Stewart, it was filmed on location, with many Big Bay residents as extras.

It all started on July 31, 1952. At 12:30 A.M., Korean War veteran Lt. Coleman A. Peterson walked into the Lumberjack Tavern and pumped six shots from a 9-mm Luger into proprietor Mike Chenoweth. Prior to the incident, Peterson's wife had told him that Chenoweth had raped her after she accepted a ride home from him to the nearby trailer camp where they both lived. After the shooting, Peterson, a former state policeman, still holding the gun, returned home and turned himself in.

On September 15, 1952, the Marquette County jury found Peterson not guilty by reason of temporary insanity. Judge John Voelker presided over the murder trial. He was a State Supreme Court judge when his novel, *Anatomy of a Murder*, was published under his pen name, Robert Traver. Although the book was fiction, its story line ran parallel to the murder trial. Voelker would never admit the story was based on the murder.

Two movies set in Michigan

The Big Chill (1983) – Friends from the University of Michigan gather for the funeral of a friend and rekindle a college friendship. It starred Glenn Close, Tom Berenger, Kevin Kline, William Hurt, and Meg Tilly.

Robocop (1987) – A series of brutal cop killings in Detroit brings the first "robocop" to the city. It starred Peter Weller.

Features filmed in Michigan

Part or all of many movies have been filmed in Michigan. This list starts back in 1946 with *This Time for Keeps.* Look for Michigan city or country in the following:

Action Jackson	Collision Course	Lunatics	Singing Birds
American Beauty	Detroit 9000	Midnight Run	Somewhere in Time
American Cops	Die Hard II	Moontrap	Tiger Town
American Cops II	Forever My Dog	One Step Closer	Tom Edison
Aspen Extreme	Full Circle	Only the Lonely	Tough Enough
Assignment Berlin	Hemingway	Prancer	True Romance
The Betsy	Hoffa	Presumed Innocent	Truth or Dare
Beverly Hills Cop	House Sitting	Roger and Me	Word of Honor
Beverly Hills Cop II	Jimmy B. & Andre	Rosary Murders	XYZ Murders
Blue Collar	The Land	Secret Honor	Young at Heart
Chameleon Street	Let's Kill All the	Singapore Harbor	Zebrahead
Checkpoint	Lawyers		

LAUGHTER IS THE BEST MEDICINE

★ Comedian Dick Martin of Battle Creek was part of the comedy team of Rowan and Martin. Together they co-hosted the TV comedy hit show "Rowan and Martin's Laugh-In," from 1967 to 1973. It changed the kind of humor that appeared on TV. The two comedians were responsible for adding such phrases as "Sock it to me," "Ring my chimes," and "You bet your bippy" to everyday American slang.

Laughter plus one

★ Detroit-born comedienne Lily (Mary Jean) Tomlin introduced her special brand of humor to TV audiences in 1969 by being part of the ensemble that created "Laugh-In." Viewers enjoyed the weekly adventures of "Ernestine" the incompetent telephone operator. Her 1971 comedy album won a Grammy award. Tomlin has appeared in both television and big screen productions, including "The Music Scene." She won an Emmy for 1974's "Lily: The Lily Tomlin Show" and an Emmy in 1981 for "Lily—Sold Out." Her motion pictures include *The Incredible Shrinking Woman, Nashville, Moment to Moment*, and *Nine to Five*. She also created and appeared in one-woman Broadway shows: *Appearing Nitely* and *The Search for Signs of Intelligent Life in the Universe* in 1986, which got a Tony award.

That's the way it is . . . pshgubhgn!

★ Sandra Bernhard's career really blossomed in 1988 when she appeared in a critically acclaimed one-woman off-Broadway show, *Without You I'm Nothing*. Bernhard and former gal-pal Madonna were inseparable for a time, tantalizing talk-show audiences about the real nature of their sexual relationship. After their falling out in 1992, Bernhard went on to enjoy more notoriety without her famous partner. Appearing in the TV comedy "Roseanne," she broke ground by playing a lesbian divorcee.

Has the last laugh

Gilda was one of a kind

 Comedian Gilda Radner was named after a nightclub singer that actress Rita Hayworth portrayed in the 1940s. The daughter of a Detroit real-estate investor, she loved to perform as a child. The first stop after drama school at the University of Michigan was a job as a ticket taker in an Ontario theater, but then her work in several stage productions earned her a job on Second City TV with John Belushi, John Candy, and Dan Aykroyd. Spotted by "Saturday Night Live" producers in 1975, she became one of the original Prime Time Players. Radner and her characters, Lisa, Roseanne, Baba, and Emily, were extremely popular. She answered Belushi's fan mail when he wouldn't. She married comedian Gene Wilder in 1984, and on May 20, 1989, she died of ovarian cancer.

More Power!

He's the guy that wears a tool belt like a coat of armor and grunts in delight when the conversation swings to horsepower. Comedian Tim Allen is the star of "Tool Time," which is, of course, the fictional TV show featured on the real TV sitcom hit "Home Improvement."

The 39-year-old comic had been doing stand-up for about 12 years before getting the show. But his life wasn't always funny. At the age of 11, his father was killed by a drunk driver. His mother remarried and moved her family to Birmingham, where Allen showed a flair for comedy. After graduating from Western Michigan in 1976, he was charged with possession of narcotics and sentenced to eight years in prison, but was released after 28 months. Fourteen years later, he came forward with the story of his past when Disney proposed "Home Improvement." His honesty paid off—he got the part. The TV show has been in the top five since the start, and today men across America are proud to lust after a power saw.

Taking a chance on comedy

 Family and basketball were the biggest parts of young David "Sinbad" Adkins life. One of six children in a minister's family, he wanted to be Benton Harbor's own "Wilt Chamberlain." At 6 feet, 5 inches, he might have made it, except his knees gave out while playing ball at the University of Denver. Instead, he joined the Air Force and discovered his new career during the Air Force Talent Show.

Winning in the MC category whetted his appetite for stand-up comedy. He tried his luck at comedy before making it to the finals of Ed McMahon's "Star Search." Hearing that the pilot for a new show, "A Different World," was in the works, he got booked as warm-up comic for an episode of the "The Cosby Show," hoping to use it as a springboard to the new show.

After Sinbad's act, Cosby came out of the audience, grabbed the mike, to Sinbad's surprise, and said, "This guy oughta be on TV every week." Three weeks later he had a guest spot on Cosby's show, and later became a regular on "A Different World." He's never forgotten his roots or his family. In 1992 he returned to Benton Harbor to donate renovated basketball courts.

TAKING CARE OF BUSINESS

Michigan is so closely connected to the automobile industry that it's easy to forget the state's success in other areas. Michigan is a sprawling state of 58,527 square miles, filled with rich mines, lush forests, productive farmland, and orchards. There are 63,000 farmers, and 11.4 million acres of farmland under cultivation. Twenty-six crops produced in the state are ranked fifth or higher in national production. The value of timber taken from Michigan's forests in the last century exceeded the value of gold mined in California!

Many Michigan residents, through dedicated experimenting or by accident, invented something that changed the way we live. Cornflakes started out as a kitchen mishap. The first carpet sweeper was invented to ease the discomfort of an allergy to dust. Even commercial baby food was created by a dad wanting to save time. The state is home to 21 Fortune 500 companies.

- Home-grown Michigan
- The Mighty Timbers
- The Good Earth
- Dreams Become Reality
- The Men Behind the Machines
- Power of the People
- The Printed Word
- Making Life Easier
- It's Their Business

HOME-GROWN MICHIGAN

Silk thread was an important industry

$ In Ionia County, a man named Hirman Belding settled near Patterson Mills in the 1860s. A practitioner of animal husbandry, he soon had six silk mills in operation. By 1925 over 2,000 people worked in the Belding silk mills. The company produced 95 percent of the silk thread in the nation. The discovery of rayon and other man-made fibers ended demand for the special thread.

Floriculture is a bloomin' success

$ Ah, the sweet smell of success! There are 470 commercial flower growers in Michigan and their production puts the state fifth in the nation in floriculture. In one year Michigan produced 40 million gladioli spikes, 1.1 million Easter lilies, and 275,000 bedding geranium flats. There was 26.1 million square feet of greenhouse space alone!

A little dab will do ya!

Did you know it takes just one pound of spearmint oil to flavor 135,000 sticks of gum? On average, Michigan farmers get about 36 pounds per acre. The oil is extracted from mint through a steam distillation process and most spearmint goes into gum, medicine, soap, and toothpaste. Fresh mint leaves are used by restaurants for garnishes.

First ag college

$ In 1857 the Michigan State College of Agriculture in East Lansing opened and was the first college of its kind. Later it became part of Michigan State University.

Celery as a miracle cure?

Celery as a cure for nervousness? As a cough syrup? An aphrodisiac? In 1866 a Dutch immigrant in Kalamazoo cross-bred celery with a newer, paler variety. The end result was christened "ivory pascal" and by 1887, over 5,000 acres of celery was planted.

Kalamazoo celery, considered a delicacy, started turning up in everything from soup to stew. People fried it, creamed it, and even served celery sauce over boiled fowl. In medicinal form, celery was claimed to be a cure for nervousness, headaches, sleeplessness, and general depression! Some even used it as a diuretic and an agent in cough drops! (Celery drops?) Believe it or not, celery tonic bitters was promoted as an aphrodisiac!

THE MIGHTY TIMBERS

In the beginning

$ Before 1820, forests covered all but one-eighth of Michigan's 37,000,000 acres! So dense were the forests it was said a squirrel could travel completely across the northern Lower Peninsula by running across the treetops, never having touched ground!

$ Because the great forests seemed inexhaustible, no thought was given to conservation. By 1849, there were 558 sawmills statewide, employing 2,730 people. It was only the beginning. During the peak of the lumber drive, a 20-year period from 1870 to 1890, more than 10,000 lumberjacks were cutting and sawing away the state's timberland. And the timber fell at a rate of 33,000 acres each year! In their wake, loggers left acre after acre of barren land scarred with stumps.

And then there were none

$ The huge virgin forests that had flourished in what is now Michigan long before Columbus discovered America are gone forever. Thankfully, recovery is well underway as second- and third-generation forests fill the land once again. Today both pine and hardwood trees cover over 20 million acres in the northern half of the Lower Peninsula and most of the UP.

Awesome recovery

About 12 million acres are owned by private logging companies. Today, logging companies plant more trees than they cut. Someday soon, a squirrel may once again dance on treetops across the Lower Peninsula.

Logging at Hermansville

$ The little fur-trading post of Grand Rapids exploded with the onset of the lumber boom. Enormous quantities of logs were floated downstream to sawmills. Along the Grand River, small mill owners watched with envy as valuable lumber floated past them. Soon many began stealing some for themselves, turning the bootleg logs into lumber.

Log thefts produce new breed of logger

Known as "hoggin'," the practice caused brawls to erupt up and down the river. In response, lumber companies began using daredevil river drivers. Riding the wet, rolling logs downriver, these adventuresome men helped protect their companies' product.

Check your boots at the door, please

⑤ The lumberjacks brought their own form of general rowdiness and some unique problems as well. It seems the heavy caulked boots of the river drivers caused the boardwalks in Grand Rapids to break into matchsticks. To save his floors, the proprietor of the Eagle Hotel had a rack of carpet slippers positioned at the door and required river drivers to change their shoes before entering!

World's largest hardwood floor

Demand for lumber increased as settlers moved into the territory. When all was said and done, Michigan had produced more lumber than any other logging state. How much? Enough to build 10 million six-room houses—160 billion feet of pine. Or enough to cover the entire state of Michigan with enough left over to cover Rhode Island, too!

Branded logs

⑤ Loggers banked their logs until the spring thaw, then sent them downriver. To make sure the right logs were claimed at the end of the river run, loggers began branding both ends of the logs with a specific symbol or initial, much like the branding of cattle in the West. At the mill, loggers would reclaim their company's logs and pound a metal eye into one end. Eventually a rope would be fed through the eyes, creating a raft. The rest of their logs would be banked up behind the "raft" and held at the mill.

Logs on the rampage

⑤ Both ice and log jams were responsible for great damage to many riverfront logging towns, and Grand Rapids was no different. In 1838 the streets were jammed with huge ice cakes and the town was almost submerged. In 1852, after heavy rains, 150 million feet of logs broke away from the booms and crashed into three railroad trestles. The runaway logs left a trail of destruction throughout the city. In 1904, more than 1,500 houses were flooded due to a log jam and the city was without electricity for several nights.

A diamond in the rough

Despite all the tales of ruthless lumber barons and bareknuckle fighting, there were a few men who encouraged positive growth within their community. English-born mill owner Charles Hebard was such a man and his concern for Pequaming can be seen in the way he laid out the village in 1879. He routed boardwalks around shady oak trees and built houses with lawns filled with even more trees.

His business practices were unique. There were no time clocks and no complicated rehiring process. After a layoff, the plant whistle blew and the men simply returned to their jobs. Hebard provided rent, water, and light at no charge to the workers. Firewood was free for the taking. He built the Union Church Building and attended services alongside the hired help.

THE GOOD EARTH

⑧ Rich iron ore strikes were made near Negaunee and Ishpeming in 1844. Four years later iron was smelted for the first time in forges known as "bloomeries" in the Superior area. The first forge was built at Negaunee by the Jackson Iron Company. When the Sault Ste. Marie canal and locks opened in 1855, mining operations accelerated. In its first year 1,447 tons of iron ore passed through the locks and that total increased to 11,600 tons in just one year! By 1860, 120,000 tons of iron ore were passing through the locks. By 1886 there were 60 mines operating in the state, pulling out about 2,000,000 tons of iron ore per year. Michigan still produces almost 25 percent of the nation's iron ore.

Iron ore mining

The Soo Canal
August 26, 1852, marked the passing of a bill making it possible for the Soo Canal (the first ship canal within U.S. borders) to be built through the U.S. military reservation connecting Lake Superior and Lake Huron at Sault Ste. Marie. Michigan, with 750,000 acres of land granted by the U.S., began building the canal in 1853. It was 5,674 feet long and had two locks in tandem. Each were 350 feet long, 70 feet wide, and $11^1/_2$ feet deep, with a lift of 9 feet. The job was completed in two years at a cost of $999,802. Continual renovation and expansion of the Soo Canal system by the federal government has made it one of the busiest in the world.

Octonagon Boulder causes stir in the wilderness
As early as 1667, explorers heard rumors of a five-ton copper boulder sitting on the river bank of the Octonagon River. In 1843, Alexander Henry was taken to the boulder by Indians. He hacked off a 100-pound piece. Soon after that, Julius Eldred of Detroit paid Indians $150 for the rest of the boulder. Federal government officials allowed Eldred to mine in the area, but declared themselves owners of the boulder. They changed their minds and sold the boulder to Eldred for $1,365—the boulder's copper content value was $600.

Eldred decided to take the boulder to Detroit and charge admission to see it. Once he got the boulder to the mouth of the river, the War Department seized it. Again the officials changed their minds, letting him take it on to Detroit. Eldred displayed it, then the ever-fickle government officials changed their minds again. They paid Eldred $5,644.98 for his expenses and transported the boulder to the Smithsonian Institution.

DREAMS BECOME REALITY

Clegg brothers made state history

$ The first self-propelled vehicle driven in the state was a little steam-driven auto built in the winter of 1884-85 by the Clegg brothers, John and Thomas. The auto was built in Memphis, about 50 miles north of Detroit.

What if . . .

Henry Ford worked on his auto inventions at night and worked for the Edison Illumination Company by day. He was a good worker and was made a chief engineer at a salary of $125 per week. Alex Dow, president of the firm, offered Ford an additional $40 a week if he would quit experimenting on the newfangled carriage and concentrate on his day job. Ford quit his day job instead!

First paved road

$ Michigan had the first mile of concrete highway, which opened in 1909 in Wayne County. The first urban freeway was opened in 1942.

Charles King produced early gas auto

$ Engineer Charles C. King dabbled in auto design in his free time. He drove the first gasoline-powered horseless carriage in Detroit in 1896, a vehicle he had designed two years before. The auto featured a steering wheel instead of a lever on the left-hand side and a single cylinder engine.

Electric traffic lights

$ By the early 1900s Detroit was dealing with hundreds of horseless carriages and inexperienced drivers. Detroit police officer William L. Potts must have seen more than his share of flared tempers and near misses. He eventually came up with a simple idea that revolutionized the way people drive. Taking a tip from the railroads, he rigged up an electric light system using red, green, and yellow lights to control traffic. Installing the lights in a tower, Potts was able to control three intersections instead of one!

Horseless carriage puts new demands on city

$ Detroit was a tree-shaded port city until the automobile made its noisy appearance on her dignified streets. One by one the inventions of Ford, Olds, Durant, the Dodge Brothers, Chevrolet, Buick, and others caused a ruckus and the city changed almost overnight.

Tree-lined streets disappeared as roads were widened to accommodate increased traffic. Elegant Georgian mansions were turned into boarding houses. The city seemed to explode as workers migrated from around the world to Detroit, the land of plenty, where jobs, money, and opportunity were available for the taking. Between 1880 and 1900 Detroit's population more than doubled as auto suppliers moved into the area.

THE MEN BEHIND THE MACHINES

$ He was born July 30, 1863, in Wayne County, the son of Irish immigrants, and no one expected Henry Ford to revolutionize the nation with his inventions. But he did. Quitting school at 15, within one year Ford had built a steam-threshing machine—just to see if he could. At 17 he moved to Detroit, intent on becoming a machinist's apprentice. He also intended to develop a watch he could make cheaply and sell for $1. The young inventor became enthralled with the idea of a gasoline engine and the production of the horseless carriage. The rest is history. In 1982, he was named to the National Inventors' Hall of Fame for his patents on transmission mechanisms.

First goal was to sell a $1 watch

20,000,000 Fords

In 1931, the "Star Spangled Banner" was adopted as our national anthem, the Empire State Building opened, Wiley Post and Harold Gatty flew around the world in the *Winnie Mae*, and the Ford Motor Company produced its 20 millionth auto on April 14, 1931. Once it rolled off the lines, Henry Ford and his son, Edsel, drove the car to the Ford Museum in Dearborn and parked it right next to the very first car Henry built.

Henry Ford proudly displays his 1904 racing car

$ Despite his wealth and inventions, even Henry Ford could not stop the Rouge River from flooding. On April 7, 1947, the river flooded the great tunnels under his estate, knocking out the power, electricity, and phone. That night Henry Ford, the man who brought great technology to the world, died of a cerebral hemorrhage, by candlelight. His estimated worth at the time of his death was between $5 million and $7 million. Not bad for a boy who wanted to build a watch he could sell for a $1.

Ford dies by candlelight

$ The only child of Henry and Clara Ford, Edsel was born in 1891. At age eight he drove his own car to school! After school he would drive to the Ford factory, where he spent time shadowing his father. Edsel Ford was only 28 in 1918 when he took the helm of the family company. Despite his favored upbringing, Edsel Ford was a man who knew how to roll up his sleeves, and he worked under the hood with ease. Not so easy was having to deal with his father's interference in running the company. Edsel should be best remembered for establishing the Ford Foundation, which has pledged almost $5 billion to assist in education, research, arts, environment, communications, and causes around the world. However, he's probably best remembered as the source of the name of a new Ford in the 1950s which, for reasons that seem inexplicable now, became the laughingstock of the car industry.

Edsel, Henry's son before he became a car

The keys to the kingdom

⑤ Henry Ford II, the oldest son of Edsel and grandson of Henry, was just 28 years old in 1942 when he became vice president of Ford. Although he dropped out of Yale, he worked his way to the president's office by 1945, and became chairman of the board when Henry Ford I died two years later.

Ford received first license to drive

⑤ Henry Ford's first practical motor car had two cylinders and ran on 28-inch wheels. It ran so well that the Detroit Common Council was forced to pass the city's first motor traffic regulation and Ford became the nation's first licensed driver. In 1896 he sold the original model for $200 after driving it 1,000 miles. One year later he bought it back.

Chicago dentist bought first Ford

⑤ The first Ford ever sold by the Ford Motor Company went to a dentist from Chicago. In January 1904, Dr. E. Pfennig paid $750 for the car, plus an additional $100 for the tonneau seat. Ironically, for 75 years it was believed that Dr. Pfennig was a general practitioner. His purchase of the Ford was flaunted as proving physicians were the first professional group to use autos on their rounds.

Ford researchers contacted his granddaughter in 1978 and discovered Pfennig was a dentist. Most likely he purchased the auto for fun, not house calls! Either way, the historic first purchase was misspelled in Ford's ledger as "Phenning." The purchase did, however, save Ford from bankruptcy. Unlike his competitors, Ford had built the cars first, then worried about finding buyers. By the end of 1904, Ford had sold 658 automobiles.

Olds first to export autos

⑤ The first horseless carriage made by Ransom Olds in 1887 was so odd looking that he tested it at night to avoid drawing a crowd. It looked like a surrey with a fringed top. The rear wheels, which were smaller than the front, were hidden by a curtain to avoid scaring the horses. The auto did feature a revolutionary new engine that eliminated gearing and transmission.

In 1893, a medicine firm in London, England, contacted young Olds and requested that one of his autos be sent to their Bombay, India, branch. Olds set the price at an astronomical $400, thinking the price would be too steep. It wasn't. Olds, reluctant to sell, drove the car for several months before shipping it off. It was the first car ever exported from the United States.

Durant: Born to sell

William Crapo Durant, the "Godfather of the Automobile Industry," reigned as president of General Motors from 1916 to 1920, but it was a hard climb to the top. He purchased the struggling Buick Motor Company and gathered such car whizzes as Charles W. Nash, Walter P. Chrysler, and Louis Chevrolet to help market the Buick.

Within four years Durant turned Buick into a sales leader and by 1908 the Buick outsold the Ford. In 1908, he bought Cadillac, Oakland, and Oldsmobile, changing his organization's name to General Motors. He even tried to buy out Ford, but the banks wouldn't lend

William Crapo Durant

him the $8 million Henry Ford was asking, because they didn't think the company was worth it!

In 1910, sales hit a slump and Durant went broke. To save the company, he sold his shares of GM stock and left the company he had created. Never giving up, Durant joined forces with Louis Chevrolet. He became president of Chevrolet and in 1916 regained controlling stock of GM. The postwar economic glut sent Durant out the door once again. He established Durant Motors, Inc., in 1921, but that also failed.

⑤ French race-car driver Louis Chevrolet made a name for himself at 27 during a three-mile race in New York. Chevrolet beat out two favorites by driving a daring 90 mph in his Italian Fiat. That was 1905. In 1912 he founded the Chevrolet Motor Company and his first model, a six-cylinder car, sold for $2,150. The company sold 3,000 cars during the first year.

Chevrolet began as a race-car driver

Chevrolet was unhappy with the small car Durant gave his name to and sold his share of the company. Chevrolet had no legal recourse to reclaim his name. After he left the company, he designed cars for the Indianapolis 500. He was the only man to design two successive Indy winners, in 1920 and 1921. After retirement he made axles at the Chevy division of GM and died of a cerebral hemorrhage in 1941.

First American sports car: '63 Stingray

In 1953, GM unveiled the Chevrolet Corvette. The laminated fiberglass sports car listed for $3,250 and had a powerglide transmission as standard equipment. It was GM's answer to European sports cars. Even after a powerful V-8 engine replaced the original V-6 in 1956, consumers couldn't decide if the 'Vette was a true sports car or just a Chevy with a fancy exterior. Then along came the sporty and powerful 1963 Stingray and all debate was set aside. Popularity of the Corvette soared. Even today the car is a cult object among auto buffs and is very much in demand as a collectors' item.

Buick bathtubs? It almost happened!

David Dunbar Buick was first known for discovering the process of fusing porcelain onto cast iron! By 1882, he and partner William Sherwood began producing enameled bathtubs. In 1899, Buick sold his interest for $100,000 to Standard Sanitary Manufacturing.

He used the money to form Buick Auto-Vim and Power in Detroit to produce marine and stationary engines. It was there he created the powerful Buick Model F engine, which had an engine valve directly over the piston. However, his company began to founder, and in 1908 he sold it to William Durant.

DeLorean's designs were futuristic

$ John Zachary DeLorean, who had been an up-and-comer at General Motors, was lured away to Ford. Then, with the help of government financing, he established the DeLorean Motor Company in northern Ireland in 1975. With the company under great financial strain, DeLorean allegedly smuggled millions of dollars worth of cocaine into the U.S., apparently hoping to pour the drug money back into his company. The FBI arrested him but, despite videotaped evidence, he was acquitted. DeLorean also beat a government tax charge and other civil lawsuits. Although he was able to avoid the law, DeLorean succumbed to bankruptcy. DeLorean's automobiles are now collectors' items.

Dodge Brothers: from stove parts to autos

$ Horace and John Dodge began their careers by making stove parts and bicycles, but moved quickly into the new auto industry. They originally made engine parts for the Ford Motor Company and transmissions for the Olds Motor Works. On November 14, 1914, the first Dodge automobile was introduced with the industry's first all-steel body.

The Dodge Brothers, both in their 50s, died of natural causes in 1920, but the innovations continued. The 1925 model featured a sprayed-on lacquer finish, vacuum windshield wipers, a one-piece windshield, and an adjustable rear window. In 1928 Walter Chrysler purchased Dodge.

Chrysler: locomotives to luxury

$ As a young man Walter P. Chrysler went to work for the American Locomotive Company in Wamego, Kansas. He made $12,000 a year and was soon made plant manager. In 1908, he purchased a Locomobile for $5,000, just to take it apart.

Intrigued, he went to work for Buick in Detroit. By 1917 he was president of General Motor's Buick Division. After making it the strongest of the General Motors group, he resigned in 1920 and six months later became vice president of the Willys-Overland Company and president of the Maxwell Motor Company.

Chrysler pushed a luxury car, the first to carry his name, into production. It was the star of the New York Auto Show in 1924. The six-cylinder Chrysler "70" featured a high-compression engine and torsion bar suspension. The company's name was changed in 1925 to Chrysler Corporation. He later bought out the Dodge Brothers and introduced the Plymouth line to compete nose-to-nose with Ford and Chevrolet.

Did "ja" know?
Uriah Smith of Battle Creek tried to keep everybody happy by attaching a dummy horse to the front of his horseless carriage.

$ Lido "Lee"Anthony Iacocca decided at 16 that he wanted to work for Ford Motor Company, and his goal was to become president by the time he was 35. He was off by one year. At the age of 36, in 1970, he was named president.

Iacocca: A name to reckon with

Six years prior to landing the big office, Iacocca introduced the Ford Mustang, still one of the most popular cars made. Once the golden boy of Ford, he eventually had a bitter parting with the company and was named CEO of Chrysler in 1979. He inherited Chrysler's $1.7-billion debt load and was able to negotiate $1.5 billion in government loan guarantees. By 1984, the loans were repaid and Chrysler was on its feet again. Iaccoca retired in 1993, after introducing a new line of wide wheel-base cars.

Iacocca's 56 for 56 brainstorm

Lee Iacocca was a struggling Ford salesman in Chester, Pennsylvania, in 1956. Fords were not selling as they should, so Iacocca put pencil to paper and figured with 20 percent down, consumers could end up with 36 monthly payments of $56. It was a sum he believed most could afford.

Iacocca told his salesmen to drive around supermarket parking lots looking for well-kept used cars. Once found, he told them to look up their value in the price guide and write it on the "wujatak" ("what would you take" offer). When the shoppers returned to their cars, they found a dollar offer for the vehicle in exchange for a new Ford, plus a bag of chips with the message, "56 for 56! The chips are down. We're selling cars in '56 for $56 per month!" It was an instant success, and within a few weeks Iacocca's district was leading in sales.

The Chrysler Technology Center, a 3.3-million-square-foot building in Auburn Hills, cost about $1 billion. Nearly 7,000 employees work on design, engineering, and manufacturing at the facility.

Bicyclists get state to improve roads

Surprisingly, it was cyclists who first called for road improvements, beginning in 1879. The League of American Wheelmen pushed for new roads in Michigan for 26 years! In 1905, Governor Fred M. Warner finally signed an act creating the Michigan State Highway Department, and appropriated $20,000 for the first year's budget. Horatio S. Earle, a hard-core bicycle fan, was named commissioner. When the American Road Makers' Association met in Port Huron that year, they accused Earle of turning the state's dirt roads into speedways because Earle offered prizes for the best travel time made by convention delegates.

POWER OF THE PEOPLE

Labor union steps

⑤ The first labor organization in Michigan was the Detroit Mechanics' Society, formed in 1818 and incorporated in 1820. So widespread did labor organizations quickly become that even Ypsilanti, with a population of only 240, had one in 1830!

The carpenters' union was the only one to survive the depression of 1837. The printers' union, formed between 1835 and 1855, is the oldest union in Michigan to have continuous existence. In 1864, the iron miners of Marquette organized, and struck for an 11-hour day with a daily wage of $5.50.

Michigan workers begin to strike

⑤ Labor organizations were beginning to flex their muscles as early as 1837. That year, nine strikes occurred in the nation. On April 4, 1837, in Detroit, journeymen carpenters took to the the street demanding, "Ten hours a day, and two dollars for pay."

The strike had been precipitated by the unbelievable growth of Philadelphia. In 1837, over 200,000 people arrived by ship alone! Buildings went up at great speed. In 1819, wages in Detroit were as low as 12 cents per day, while unskilled workers were getting up to $2.25 per day in Detroit. The carpenters' walkout was the first organized protest against lower wages and increased hours.

Ten hours or no sawdust!

⑤ By July 1885, there were more than 5,500 lumbermen in the Saginaw Valley, many of them children. The loggers demanded that their workday be limited to 10 hours, with no reduction in pay. Strikers in Saginaw chartered a steamboat and headed upriver, stopping at every mill town along the way. When they finished the journey, all 78 mills in the valley were silent. Twenty companies of the state militia and 250 Chicago Pinkertons arrived and arrested strike leader Thomas Barry. After three months of silence, however, the strikers won.

⑤ The Crash of '29 took its toll on car production, which dropped one-fifth in the 1930s. By 1933, more than half of the state's industrial workers were without jobs. Unrest and violence grew throughout the nation. On March 7, 1932, 3,000 hunger marchers headed from Detroit into Dearborn. Detroit police ignored the fact that no march permit had been filed. Dearborn was a different story. The police were considered Ford's property since his company accounted for 62 percent of the city's tax base. The police waited for the marchers at the city limits. When the resulting skirmish was over, four men lay dead and many were wounded. Within three years Michigan workers and union leaders would organize the United Auto Workers (UAW).

Death on the line

⑤ UAW strikers backed by the CIO began a strike at General Motors in Flint on December 30, 1936. Workers reported to work but refused to do their jobs until officials met with them.

Sit-down strike new tactic

"If the boss won't talk, don't take a walk, sit down, sit down," the workers chanted. The National Guard was called in, prepared to take over the building, when GM management agreed to recognize the UAW and negotiate. By February 11, 1937, workers received a wage increase and Chrysler later approved a similar agreement.

⑤ Walter Reuther, the son of a trade-union activist from West Virginia, was 20 when he talked himself into a $1.05-an-hour job at Ford. Four years later he talked himself out of the job while trying to organize workers there. In 1936, he was elected president of the UAW Local 174. Successful in getting the workers a post-war raise, Reuther was elected president of the UAW Union in 1946. Two years later he survived a gunshot blast through his kitchen window by an unidentified gunman. Elected president of the Congress of Indus-

Reuther becomes union leader

trial Organizations (CIO) in 1951, he helped merge the union with the American Federation of Labor (AFL). In 1969 the UAW withdrew from AFL-CIO and joined the International Brotherhood of Teamsters, led by Jimmy Hoffa. In 1970, Reuther and his wife were killed when their chartered plane crashed near Pellston in foggy rain.

The mystery of Hoffa's disappearance

The disappearance of former Teamster boss Jimmy Hoffa continues to intrigue thousands. He became vice president of the International Brotherhood of Teamsters in 1952. Under constant scrutiny by the federal government, Hoffa was found guilty of jury tampering in 1967 and sentenced to 13 years in prison. In 1971 he was pardoned by President Nixon. Under a court order not to be involved with the union until 1980, Hoffa immediately attempted to gain control. On July 30, 1975, he dined at a Detroit restaurant and was never seen again.

The chief suspect is Anthony "Tony Pro" Provenzano, former boss of the Northern New Jersey Teamsters. He and Hoffa had some run-ins at Lewisburg penitentiary. Hoffa's body has never been found but rumors have it hidden in Pine Barrens Nature Preserve in the New Jersey wetlands or under the playing field of the Meadowlands Sports Complex in East Rutherford, New Jersey. He was declared legally dead July 30, 1982, in Oakland County, Michigan.

THE PRINTED WORD

First newspaper rolls off presses

⑤ On a printing press belonging to Father Gabriel Richard, James M. Miller printed the first newspaper in the state on August 31, 1809. The paper folded after one issue due to lack of sales. Population in the Michigan territory at this time was only 4,762. On July 25, 1817, John P. Sheldon and Ebenezer Reed issued the first copy of the *Detroit Gazette*, which was printed until 1830.

First newspaper printed on a train

⑤ The very first newspaper ever printed on a train was done by Thomas Alva Edison as he traveled between Port Huron and Detroit. The first issue of the *Weekly Herald* was dated Port Huron, February 3, 1862. The 21-year-old Edison printed the paper on both sides of one sheet, then distributed it at stops along the way! He had gotten the idea as a 12-year-old delivering papers from a railway train.

Editor sued by Teddy Roosevelt

⑤ On May 26, 1913, *Roosevelt vs. George Newitt* came to trial in Marquette. One year earlier the Ishpeming newspaper editor had written an article accusing Teddy Roosevelt of getting drunk frequently. Roosevelt, insisting his character had been defamed, sued. Newitt knew he couldn't beat Roosevelt, who came to town with hotshot lawyers and witnesses. When Newitt took the witness stand he stated he wasn't able to find any witnesses to corroborate his story. The judge awarded Roosevelt damages of six cents, the minimum allowed by state law.

⑤ In the 1830s, Bark Shanty Point was just a collection of crude bark shanties built for lumberjacks. Things were pretty easygoing and none too fancy. The town did have a newspaper of sorts, however. The circulation wasn't very high—just one copy per issue—but many publishers today would welcome the low overhead of the *Bark Shanty Times*. There was no editor, proofreader, printer, or paperboy. Sheets of newsprint and a supply of lead pencils were simply left on the counter of the local general store/post office. As residents, visitors, and traveling salesmen passed through, they were invited to scratch out their news on the sheet. After the paper was perused by everyone interested, it was filed away in a book!

Readers wrote their own news!

⑤ Since 1932, two newspapers, the *Detroit Free Press* and the *Detroit News* together have been honored with five Pulitzer Prizes. The first such award was presented in 1932 to the *Detroit Free Press* for reporting. In 1945, the paper earned the Meritorious Public Service award for investigating corruption in the state government, in 1956 for local reporting, and in 1968 for coverage of the riots. In 1982, the *Detroit News* received a Meritorious Public Service award for coverage of the death of a Navy seaman.

Pulitzer Prize winners

⑤ Debra Bonde of Livonia wants to get all kids hooked on books, even blind kids. She founded her company, Seedlings, in 1984. It's a nonprofit organization dedicated to providing reasonably priced books for 40,000 blind school children nationwide.

"Seedlings" plant dreams for children

Her company's name came from the Braille dots which Bonde said reminded her of seeds, and she says giving a child a book is like planting a seed. Children's books in Braille are expensive. For instance, *Charlotte's Web* can cost up to $43. Bonde wanted to offer books at lower prices, so she began her publishing venture with an eight-inch slate and stylus, after taking a community college class in Braille. Although the task is huge (*Superfudge* by Judy Blume, for example, weighs seven pounds in Braille), she is now producing books by computer, with the help of a Braille printer.

⑤ When window washer Stephen Holcomb presented a 100,000-German-mark note to National Bank and Trust in Traverse City, all appeared well. The bank gave Holcomb $39,000 in cash and Holcomb immediately went on a buying spree. He bought several guns, a delivery truck, and a cockatoo, and gave an elevator operator a $900 tip!

Con man bilks bank with bogus bucks

The bank finally realized that the German note, printed in 1923 at the height of German post-war inflation, was worth less than a penny. The police arrived in time to stop Holcomb's buying spree, but not before he had spent over $18,000.

MAKING LIFE EASIER

Early writing machine

$ The tiny burg of Washington was named for the first president of the United States. It is also the home of William A. Burt, who invented the first writing machine, a springboard to the modern typewriter. He received a patent for the invention in 1829 and went on to invent the solar compass in 1836 and the equatorial sextant in 1844.

Breakfast barons created by accident

$ It's hard to believe the man who invented an entire new industry was selling brooms for his father at the age of 14, but that's what Will Keith Kellogg did. His older brother, Dr. John Harvey Kellogg, as director of the Seventh Day Adventist Western Health Reform Institute, later to be known as the Battle Creek Sanitarium, hired his brother as a business manager.

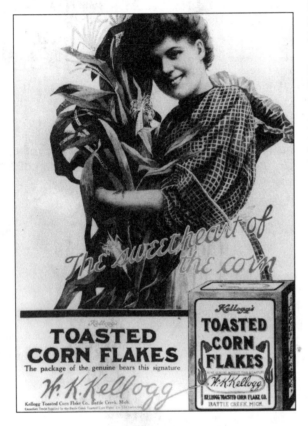

The sanitarium promoted treatment by eating healthy foods and banned the use of caffeine, alcohol, tobacco, and meat. The brothers created substitutes for the banned foods. In 1894, while W.K. Kellogg was experimenting with a new wheat bread recipe, a batch of boiled grain was forgotten. The next morning W.K. returned and when he rolled it out, it broke into small flakes. Intrigued, he baked the flakes and served them with milk.

The patients seemed to like it, and together the Kellogg Brothers developed an item called Granose, a flaked-wheat cereal. They formed the Sanitas Nut Food Company mainly as a mail-order firm to send the cereal to patients when they returned home. The cereal idea was quickly copied and by 1902, 40 different cereal companies sprang up in Battle Creek! W.K. formed the Battle Creek Toasted Corn Flake Company in 1906; it became the Kellogg Company in 1922.

Invention really cleans up!

$ An idea born during the Great Depression brought its creators fame and fortune. Elizabeth G. MacDonald of Saginaw and an aunt who was a chemist concocted a powdered cleaning agent they called "Spic and Span." Along the way they also created a new type of market. Until then, cleaning products were considered a hardware item and were not found in grocery stores. MacDonald sold local grocers in Saginaw the idea that area shoppers would buy cleaning products from them. In 1945 the MacDonalds' company was bought out by Procter and Gamble.

Mother's helper

Mothers everywhere can thank Fremont's Dan Gerber. His impatience with his wife preparing baby food by forcing vegetables through a strainer prompted him to create Gerber Products Company. Working in his father's successful cannery in 1927, he began making baby food. His own baby and others in Fremont were recruited to test the new concoctions. Using the first market survey to test consumer demand, Gerber ran an ad in *Good Housekeeping*. He offered readers a chance to purchase six cans of baby food for $1 if they would write the name of their grocery store on the order blank. With list in hand, Gerber was able to convince store owners there was enough demand to carry his new product. His baby food was priced at 15 cents per can and that first year Gerber sold 590,000 cans. Today, the original line of five products has grown to 180. Through the purchase of the largest baby food and juice company in Poland and Central Europe, Gerber is turning into a superbrand.

Gerber's baby

The baby's face that has adorned billions of Gerber Baby Food jars and boxes was created by artist Dorothy Hope Smith. Despite rumors which surfaced in the late 1920s that the adorable baby was a very young Humphrey Bogart, Smith's subject was a neighborhood baby, Ann Turner. She had sent the unfinished charcoal sketch to Gerber in response to a contest.

The artist indicated she could finish the sketch once she knew what age and size of baby the company wanted. Company officials and, later, consumers fell in love with the bright-eyed baby and in 1931 it was adopted as the official trademark. By the way, Ann Turner Cook raised four children, and taught English in Florida, where she served as chairman of the English Department until her retirement in 1990!

$ The Upton Machine Company was founded in St. Joseph in 1911 to produce electric motor-driven wringer washers. Considered a modern convenience every housewife needed, it was being advertised by Sears and Roebuck within five years. The Upton Machine Company merged with the Nineteen Hundred Washer Company of New York and, two years after World War II ended, the company's very first fully automatic washer was introduced. In 1948, a Whirlpool-brand washer was unveiled, and finally the Nineteen Hundred Corporation was renamed Whirlpool.

Whirlpool gets its start

A clean sweep!

$ The Bissells, Melville and Anna, operated a small crockery shop in Grand Rapids in the 1870s. All was well until Mel developed an allergy, a great problem since most of the inventory was shipped in straw. Out of desperation he created a lightweight sweeper which picked up the excess straw dust from the shop floor.

The sweeper worked so well that when customers saw it in action they wanted to buy it. In 1876, Mel and Anna formed the Bissell Carpet Sweeper Company. Soon Melville, who was always a bit of a ham, kept prospective customers enthralled as he dramatically scooped dirt from the street and poured it onto the shop floor. After a few quick passes with his sweeper the mess would be gone and Bissell had more than likely sold another sweeper.

Young doctor establishes Upjohn

$ A young doctor from Hastings, William E. Upjohn, received a patent in 1885 for the friable pill, one which dissolves easily. One year later, with his brothers, he established the Upjohn Pill and Granule Company in Kalamazoo. The company produced 186 different pill formulas. First-year sales totaled $50,000. By 1890 the company had opened its first sales branch office in New York City. Because the company was now producing liquid extracts, too, its name was changed to the Upjohn Company.

Reproduced courtesy of The Upjohn Company

IT'S THEIR BUSINESS

Pickled in Detroit

$ Joseph Vlasic was a master promoter who knew how to target specific audiences with the right product. He began his successful venture as a teenager, building a night-time milk run into the state's largest wholesale milk company. In 1937 a small pickle plant asked him to distribute a new home-style pickle. Vlasic agreed, but only if the labels would carry his name. He then set about targeting the large Polish community in Detroit, even printing the labels in Polish. The pickles were an instant hit. In 1978 Vlasic Pickles was bought by Campbell Soup. The stork is a registered trademark of Vlasic Foods, Inc.

Stroh's Beer still family owned

Bernard Stroh, having left Germany to escape political turmoil, arrived in Detroit in 1850. He used a nest egg of $150 to establish a small brewery. Early success permitted him to build a substantial brewhouse a short time later.

Stroh opted to produce a light lager beer in copper kettles at a time when most brewers were producing ales and dark porters. Eventually the brewery became the largest in Detroit and the seventh-largest brewery in the nation. In the 1970s the company passed the six-million-barrel sales mark.

In 1981, Stroh acquired New York's Schaefer Brewing Company and in 1982 purchased the Joseph Schlitz Brewing Company, the thirdlargest brewery in the nation. These purchases allowed Stroh's products to be distributed nationally rather than just regionally. The Stroh Brewery Company is still family operated. Peter Stroh, great-grandson of the founder, runs the business today.

From pizza . . . an enterprise grows

The next time you have pizza in Detroit, you might get an urge to watch a hockey game. But don't worry, there's a simple explanation. Mike Ilitch, the guy who owns the Detroit Red Wings, founded Little Caesar's Pizza back in 1959. Born and raised in Detroit, Ilitch spent four years in the Marines and three with the Detroit Tigers farm team. After some soul searching, he decided he'd really rather open a restaurant.

In 1959, he and his wife opened their first Little Caesar's restaurant in Garden City. Two years later they opened a second restaurant and by 1992 there were 4,100 Little Caesars in all 50 states and Canada. Along the way Ilitch made a few other acquisitions. In addition to the Detroit Red Wings, the Adirondack Red Wings (Detroit's affiliate in the American Hockey League), Olympia Stadium, the Fox Theatre, and Meadowbrook Music Festival, he purchased the Detroit Tigers in 1992 from Thomas S. Monaghan, who owns Domino's Pizza! Ilitch gives back, too. In 1985, Little Caesar's Love Kitchen was created. Its two mobile restaurants are used to feed the homeless. As of 1992, the man with a big bank account and a heart to match had fed 750,000 in the U.S. and Canada.

Domino's Pizza is another familiar face

Domino's Pizza is as familiar to fast-food fans as those arches. The company was founded by Thomas S. Monaghan and his brother, James, in 1960. They bought DomiNicks pizza store in Ypsilanti for just $900. Later James traded his half of the business to Tom for a Volkswagen Beetle! Tom opened his first franchise store in Ypsilanti in 1967. Today there are 5,500 pizza stores in the nation with 31 international markets.

Post creates own special cereal

⑤ Charles William "C.W." Post was a traveling salesman from Illinois. In Battle Creek, he sought treatment at the Kellogg Brothers' sanitarium, where he was given the opportunity to taste their cornflakes. Knowing a good thing when he saw it, he offered to go into partnership with them. The Kelloggs refused and Post went on to develop his own cereal.

On January 1, 1895, he created his first batch of Postums and began an intensive door-to-door marketing campaign. He introduced the first ready-to-eat cereal, Grape Nuts, and, in 1904, Post Toasties, originally called Elijah's Manna. During the next 18 years, the company added such brands as Jello and Maxwell House. The company's diversification called for a name change. In 1922 it became General Foods.

In his personal life, C.W. Post waged ferocious battles against the unions. In 1914, while recovering from an appendectomy, Post committed suicide.

Economist tells 'em to "Stuff It!"

Ruth Siems is the home economist who invented Stove Top Stuffing for General Foods. All she got for her effort was a $125 bonus and a plaque. To add insult to injury, she lost her job after 33 years when the company was taken over by Philip Morris. In 1984, when the one-billionth package of stuffing rolled off the assembly line, no one bothered to invite the woman who started it all to the ceremony marking the event. However, Siems had the last word. On the back of the commemorative T-shirt designed to celebrate the event, Siems had a special message printed. It simply said, "Stuff It!"

BOOMmmm!

⑤ Herbert Henry Dow, better known as "Crazy Dow," had more persistence than money or management skills. The son of a Cleveland mechanic, the teen-aged Dow invented the first egg incubator. But a customer stole his idea. He never made any money off it!

During his senior year of college, a science project called for natural gas. Dow knew natural gas could be obtained from brine (saltwater) and he soon discovered it was full of bromine, which was used in medicines and film developing. He tried to produce it cheaply and in mass quantities, but his first two companies were financial failures. After more experimenting, he decided to make chlorine. While in the process of making it, he blew up several plants.

In 1897, he founded the Dow Chemical Company in Midland. The plant was rocked by explosions from time to time, but Dow was finally successful. Ironically, he also discovered an ingredient used to make explosives during World War I. Dow, the man, was named to the National Inventors' Hall of Fame in 1983. Dow, the company, at one time supplied most of the world with aspirin. Today Dow is a world leader in chemicals.

Sew it was

⑤ In 1927, an advertising salesman named James Shapiro decided sewing patterns could be made and sold for as little as 15 cents at a time when most companies charged $1. He was right. Simplicity Patterns were an immediate success. To keep up with demand a factory was established in Niles in 1931. After testing a perforated pattern, officials decided a printed pattern was better. The factory began printing the patterns in 1935. Today, the patterns are printed in several languages and can be purchased in 60 countries around the world.

$ You gotta believe! That's what Rich De Vos and Jay Van Andel will tell you, and they've put their money where their mouths are. The dynamic duo turned a simple soap company into a $3-billion-plus industry that includes thousands of distributors around the world.

They're positive!

Originally selling vitamins, Vos and Andel decided they could do better on their own when the company began experiencing financial woes. They created a little company called Amway, whose first product was a multipurpose cleaner. The company was founded in 1959 in the basement of Van Andel's Ada home.

But it's not just soap anymore. Amway has branched off into total consumer product needs, and its massive headquarters in Ada has its own research laboratory. The company owns the Amway Grand Plaza Hotel in Grand Rapids and the Peter Island Resort, as well as the Mutual Broadcasting System, with 800 affiliate stations.

$ William Russell Kelly pioneered the temporary help concept in 1966 in Detroit. Today, the company has over 180,000 customers. Annually more than 500,000 Kelly employees (who can no longer be called "Kelly girls" because many are men) work as temporary helpers and are based in one of the 950 branch offices around the world.

Temps ready for action

The little train that could

Lionel Trains, Inc., in Chesterfield has probably got the best visitors' center of all. It started as a dream of Lionel employees who volunteered their time to make it happen. The center is built around trains and everything that goes with them. The 560-square-foot operating center features 1,000 feet of track and 7,775 feet of wire. There are 5,000 hand-cut and painted track ties. Ten Lionel trains run simultaneously through a network of villages and railroad stations, over mountains, and into factories. Thirteen transformers power the trains, gates, and other accessories. And best of all, visitors get to push the buttons that make it all happen!

Time marches on in Zeeland

$ Zeeland is just a small community, but it's home to the nation's largest clockmaker, Howard Miller Clocks. First opened in 1926, the company originally made mantel clocks and in 1948 expanded into grandfather clocks. It is still family owned and operated.

Last of the red-hot playboys

$ Hugh Hefner rose to fame and fortune in 1953 with a magazine he called *Playboy.* Riding on the crest of the sexual revolution, the magazine's popularity spun off a wild life-style and an international chain of private "key" clubs. As the sexual revolution began to crumble, the clubs closed, one by one. In 1988, Lansing's Playboy Club was the last in the nation to shut.

K mart calls Michigan home

$ Sebastian Spering Kresge's climb to fortune began when the owner of a Wilkes-Barre, Pennsylvania, tinware company offered him a job. He had heard that Kresge had bought up some rusted cast-iron stoves, refurbished them, and sold them at a profit. For five years Kresge worked as a traveling salesmen. When he made his biggest sale ever to Frank W. Woolworth, he got his first introduction to chain-store retailing and saw its potential.

Kresge saved $8,000 and opened a store in Detroit in 1899. He and his brother-in-law operated stores in Detroit and Port Huron, then Kresge bought out his brother-in-law and expanded his S.S. Kresge Stores in six major cities in the Midwest. In 1962, when dime stores had stopped being dime stores, the company took a big chance and started a chain of discount superstores, called K mart! The chain is headquartered in Troy. By the time Kresge died in 1966 at the age of 99, he had donated $63 million to the Kresge Foundation.

Goin' to that big doghouse in the sky

Gone are the days when pet owners simply disposed of their late, beloved pets by either flushing them (depending on their size, obviously), to burying them efficiently (cheaply) in the backyard. These days, thanks to companies like the Hoegh Pet Casket Company in Gladstone, you can purchase a pet casket and bury your beloved pet in style. At last count, the caskets came in seven different sizes and the smaller caskets were available in pink and blue.

For the cat who has everything

$ Pet pampering is big business and Heath Company of Benton Harbor wants to cash in on the craze with its electronic cat door opener. For about $150 the purchaser gets a cat door that gives off a radio signal which is stopped only by a "key" collar worn by the cat. The latch is released and in goes the pet—or out if you get the deluxe two-way-passage model!

Atlas and cosmetics

$ Floyd Bostwick Odlum was born in Union City but was living in New York when he helped create the investment firm of Atlas. He emerged untouched by the Great Crash of 1929 and took advantage of the situation by buying up weakened businesses such as Greyhound Bus Lines, Bonwit Teller, and RKO Movies. In 1936, Odlum married aviation pioneer and cosmetics queen Jacqueline Cochran.

THE SPORTS ARENA

The sporting arena has dealt with some very tough Michiganders. Joe Louis and Sugar Ray Robinson boxed their way out of the Detroit neighborhoods to become world champions. Earvin Johnson brought (you guessed it) magic to the basketball court. The state's universities, University of Michigan Wolverines and Michigan State University Spartans, have always been deemed tough teams to reckon with.

Let us not forget the professionals. Detroit is the home of four professional teams—the Lions, Tigers, Pistons, and Red Wings. The Detroit Tigers have had the unique distinction of having been owned by two pizza giants. Thomas Monaghan, founder and owner of Domino's Pizza, and Mike Ilitch of Little Caesar's Pizza fame (see p.99). Must be lots of dough in sports.

Then there are those obscure sports like cherry spitting. The next few pages will give you a smattering of the famous and not-so-famous participants in the Michigan sports arena.

- Tigers at Play
- The Boys of Summers Past
- Women in Sports
- The Lions' Roar
- Legends of Gridiron
- Collegiate Football
- Bad Boys of the NBA
- College Roundball
- Taking It on the Chin
- Sticks and Ice
- Sports for All Seasons

TIGERS AT PLAY

What's in a name?

◄ In the old days, the Tigers were called Detroit, the Detroits, or the Wolverines. In 1894, they were called the Creams. Baseball historians credit Philip J. Reid, city editor of the *Detroit Evening News*, with calling the Detroit baseball team the "Tigers" for the first time in 1896. But team manager George Stallings claimed credit for the name when he put his players in black-and-brown striped stockings which he said reminded fans of tiger stripes.

However both were wrong. One year earlier on April 16, 1895, the *Free Press* printed a headline . . . "Stouther's Tigers Showed Up Very Nicely." On the same page a list of baseball notes was headed "Notes of the Detroit Tigers of 1895."

From then on the *Free Press* regularly used the moniker and in May 1895, *Sporting Life* began using it in its dispatches. Many believe the unknown *Free Press* headline writer created the Tigers' name.

Tiger nicknames tickle fans' fancy

Detroit Tigers players have had their share of unusual nicknames. Take, for instance, Schoolboy Rowe, Pepper Poploski, Soldier Boy Murphy, and Sailor Stroud. Then there was Piano Legs Hickman, Baby Doll Jacobson, and the Wilson trio, Mutt, Icehouse, and Squanto. Others included Mark "The Bird" Fidrych, Hooks (Dauss), Snooks (Dowd), Razor (Ledbetter), Rip (Radcliffe), Hack (Simmons), Rocky (Colavito), Muddy (Ruel), Stubby (Overmire), Tubby (Spencer), Baldy (Louden), and Slim (Love). It must have been fun for fans to shout at John Francis Gammon and call him Phenomenal Smith!

Nothin' like a home game

◄ One of the oldest ballparks in the country, Tiger Stadium, was constructed in 1900 one year before Detroit became a charter member in the American League. It was originally called Bennett Park, then Navin Park in 1912, Briggs Stadium in 1938, and finally Tiger Stadium in 1961. A major renovation began in 1977 after it was sold to the city of Detroit for $1 and leased back to the Tigers for 30 years with a 30-year renewal option. Tiger Stadium covers $8^1/_2$ acres and has a seating capacity of 52,416 with 11,732 box seats.

THE BOYS OF SUMMERS PAST

Who's on first? Who's on second? Who's on third?

Grand Haven native Neal Ball has the distinction of executing the very first unassisted triple play in the National League. On July 19, 1909, the right-hander was playing shortstop for Cleveland against Boston. He made a leaping catch on a line drive with runners on first and second. Next, Ball stepped on second to double off one runner and tagged out the other runner between first and second!

Baseball's most feared hero

Ty Cobb is considered one of the greatest baseball players ever. He was an unbelievable competitor on the field. But he was also so hostile that he had few friends and even roomed alone when other baseball players bunked together. Said one of his teammates, "He had such a rotten disposition it was darned hard to be his friend."

However, no one would dispute that the "Georgia peach" could play ball. He played 22 years with the Detroit Tigers and managed the team for six years. He had a lifetime batting average of .367, with 4,191 hits, 12 batting titles—achieving his first at age 20—and he had three .400 seasons. He was named to the Baseball Hall of Fame in 1936.

Cobb had a knack for making news. In 1912, his actions brought about the first genuine baseball strike in history. It was over principle rather than pay. On May 15 of that year an abusive spectator and reporter, Claude Leuker, kept taunting Cobb. The taunting from the stands came to a climax when Cobb cleared the fence and battled it out with Leuker. Reporters sided with Leuker, the umpire ejected Cobb, and the American League president, Ban Johnson, suspended Cobb indefinitely. Although he wasn't his teammates' best friend, they rallied around Cobb, claiming the president's action was unjustified and threatening a walkout. Cobb's suspension remained and the team left the field. Unlike modern strikes, the next game with the Philadelphia A's was not canceled. Replacements were brought in from nearby St. Joseph's College. The game was a sorry one for the Tigers with a 24-2 loss. Future games were canceled until the strike ended. Johnson fined every Tiger $100. The principle of it had gone too far for Cobb and he told his teammates to go back to work. Cobb settled for a $50 fine and 10-day suspension.

◀ Larry MacPhail was one of the greatest baseball promoters of all time, outshone, perhaps, only by Bill Veeck. Born in Cass City, MacPhail served as general manager of the Cincinnati Reds. During this time MacPhail introduced night baseball in 1935, red uniforms for the players, and cigarette girls and usherettes in satin pants. In 1937, when MacPhail moved to Brooklyn, fans were greeted by a merry-go-round in the middle of the field.

He is credited with opening the doors to make radio broadcasts of the game profitable for the teams. He sold the broadcast rights to Dodger games for $70,000. By 1950 the Dodgers averaged $210,000 from broadcast rights. He was inducted to the Hall of Fame in 1978.

Putting baseball on the air waves

Tigers in the Baseball Hall of Fame

The Detroit Tigers have produced a number of Baseball Hall of Famers. In addition to such greats as Ty Cobb, they include:

First baseman **Henry "Hank" Greenberg** was the first Jewish player ever inducted into the Baseball Hall of Fame. He played for the Detroit Tigers from 1933 to 1941, and later, from 1945 to 1946. He was elected in 1956, receiving 164 out of 193 ballots.

Tiger outfielder **Al Kaline** was named to 18 All-Star teams! In 1971, Tiger management wanted to reward him for his outstanding performances by making him their first $100,000 player. Kaline refused, saying he hadn't earned it because his last season wasn't that great. Kaline told them to give it to him when he deserved it! He was named to the Hall of Fame in 1980 and, as of 1992, has spent 17 seasons analyzing Tiger baseball on WDIV-TV.

Michiganders in the Baseball Hall of Fame

Second baseman **Charlie Gehringer** (Detroit Tiger), born Fowlerville 1903, elected 1949

Boston Red Sox owner **Tom Yawkey**, born Detroit 1903, elected 1980

Right fielder **Kiki (Hazen S.) Cuyler** (Pittsburgh Pirate), born Harrisville 1899, elected 1968

- First baseman **Dan Brouthers,** 1945
- Infielder **Charlie Gehringer,** 1949
- Catcher/manager **Mickey Cochrane,** 1957
- Outfielder **Sam Crawford,** 1957
- Outfielder **Goose Goslin,** 1968
- Outfielder **Earl Averill,** 1975
- First base/manager **Bucky Harris,** 1975
- Manager **Edward G. Barrow,** 1953
- General manager **Billy Evan,** 1973
- General manager/scout **Rick Ferrell,** 1984

Detroit's Prince Hal

◄ Harold Newhouser was known as "Hal" or "Prince Hal" to Detroit Tiger fans. The left-handed pitcher born in Detroit was a standout for the old American Legion Post 286 team. Following high school graduation, the 17-year-old Newhouser received from the Tigers an offer of a $400 bonus and $150 per month to play with the home team. After signing with Detroit, Newhouser was offered $15,000 in cash and a new car to join the Cleveland Indians. Cleveland didn't get their hands on Newhouser until he was 33. The pitcher won consecutive American League MVP awards in 1944 and 1945.

Scandal rocks 1919 series

◄ Edward "Eddie" V. Cicotte, right-handed pitcher born in Detroit, went on to play for Detroit, Boston, and Chicago. His 14-year career was filled with impressive stats including 35 shutouts and playing in two world series.

It was the 1919 series that ended his career. Cicotte gave the Reds five runs in the fourth inning of the opener, for a 9-1 loss. He made two additional errors in the fifth inning of the fourth game, allowing both of the runs in the 2-0 loss. Despite the fact he pitched to a 4-1 victory in the seventh game, Cincinnati beat Chicago five games to three.

Based on the errors that occurred during eight of nine games, rumors of bribes and payoffs surfaced. Eight players were indicted: Cicotte, Claud Williams, Oscar Felsch, Charles Gandil, "Shoeless" Joe

Jackson, Fred McMullin, Charles Risberg, and George Weaver. Only one player, Shoeless Joe, admitted to taking a bribe. The grand jury cleared all the other players. Cicotte's career ended with the shadow of the Black Sox scandal hanging over his head.

WOMEN IN SPORTS

◄ The All American Girls Professional Baseball league (AAGPBL), which was recently portrayed in Penny Marshall's big screen hit, *A League of their Own,* was once an important part of the state's sports menu. The league was created in 1942 by Philip K. Wrigley to fill the void left by male players who were fighting in World War II.

Replacing the Boys of Summer

Sophie Kurys of Flint set five all-time league records in 1946. She had the most walks, 93! She had one of the best fielding averages for a second baseman at .973 and stole 201 bases plus scored five runs in one game. She played for the Rockford Peaches and was named the AAGPBL MVP in 1946.

Johnny Rawlings and Max Carey both managed the Grand Rapids Chicks and Dottie Hunter and Doris Tetzlaff were chaperones for the team. Other AAGPBL teams from Michigan included:

Grand Rapids Chicks - 1945-1954
Muskegon Lassies - 1946-1950-53
Muskegon Belles - 1953-1954
Kalamazoo Lassies - 1950-1954
Battle Creek Belles - 1951-1952

◄ In 1975, a women's fast-pitch league, the International Women's Professional Softball Association (WPS), was founded by Billie Jean King and other female pro athletes. Bud Hucul founded the Michigan Travelers, a team which had six owners, four of whom were women. Detroit area teacher Sally Johnson was president. The league was divided into two divisions and teams played 80 games within their division and 40 with the other divisions.

Women get a crack at organized play

The Travelers' first draft pick was Linda Mueller, a left-handed second basemen. She signed for the standard $100-a-week pay, plus the $8 meal money on the road. Mueller was a physical education teacher and coach at Royal Oak Shrine High School. The Travelers opened against the Connecticut Falcones and lost. Opening day drew 5,800 fans and tickets ranged from $1.25 to $2.75. They finished in the Eastern division basement with a 42-77 record. The league's last year was 1977.

◄ Grand Rapids-born Marion Ladewig is often called the greatest woman bowler of all time. She won the All Star Tournament eight times consecutively and the WPBA National Championship in 1960. She has been voted Bowler of the Year a record nine times. Ladewig was named to the Women's Sports Hall of Fame in 1984.

Pinned

Women's BB standout

◄ The lack of organized women's sports slowed Denise Sharps down, but it sure didn't stop her. The 5-foot 10-inch Muskegon basketball player gained experience while playing in the Heights City League. She attended school before enforcement of the Title IX legislation, so she was limited in her chance to compete in organized ball.

Her career resumed at Muskegon Community College. In 1974, Sharps's help led the Lady Jayhawks to a 7-4 season, while averaging 25.9 points per game. She returned to MCC in 1975 and continued in the spotlight, averaging 24.7 points and 16 rebounds per game. She accepted a scholarship from Indiana State University. Repositioned to point guard, she continued her rampage on the courts and set several scoring records, averaging 18.1 points per game.

Following graduation, she joined the Women's Pro Basketball League, playing with the Iowa Cornets. Sharps led the Cornets to the Midwest Division co-championship and later played for the Chicago Hustle and Minnesota Fillies before the league disbanded in 1981.

Helped found the PGA

◄ Sally Sessions was a founding member of the Professional Golf Association and in 1987 was named to the Muskegon Area Sports Hall of Fame. As a young woman, she left the U. of M. and a successful career on the tennis courts to concentrate on golf. Her amateur career highlights include low medal of honors in the Western Amateur in 1944, the Michigan Women's Title, and a 10th-place finish at the Tam O' Shanter Tournament in Chicago in 1946. Sessions also finished second at the Women's U.S. Open Championship in North Carolina. She turned pro in 1948 by competing in the Tampa Women's Golf tourney which offered a $3,000 first prize. Sessions, who paved the way for other women golfers, died in Detroit of leukemia in 1966.

Queen of Drag Racing

Her nickname is "Cha Cha," but Shirley Muldowney was definitely not a Calypso dancer when she strapped herself to a supercharged, nitro-burning dragster and hit a speed of 243.90 mph in 1976 at the National Hot Rod Association Spring Nationals. In 1975, Muldowney was the first woman driver in NHRA history. And in 1977, the Mt. Clemens native became the World Top Fuel Champion.

◀ When Merrily Dean Baker was hired as athletic director at MSU she became the first woman at a Big Ten university to hold the title. Baker oversees 25 sports programs in which 800 MSU students are involved. A coach since 1969, Baker began her career at St. Lawrence University as field hockey and later gymnastics coach. She became director of Marshall College's first women's athletic program in 1969, then moved on to Princeton in 1970 where she served in the Department of Athletics. Among other accomplishments, she also spent time as coach in Istanbul, Turkey, and swam five miles across the Bosporus Strait, which separates the continents of Europe and Asia!

MSU hires female athletic director

THE LIONS' ROAR

◀ Believe it or not, there was football before the Lions. Back in 1920, the Detroit Heralds were a charter member of the American Professional Football Association, the original NFL. They played just two years. Then in 1925, the Detroit Panthers made an appearance. They were also gone after two seasons. In 1928, the Detroit Wolverines played just one season and also disappeared.

Detroit pigskin pros

Since the Lions, there have been the World Football League Wheels, who played in 1974, and the Michigan Panthers, who were part of the U.S. Football League in the 1983-84 season.

◀ In 1930, the National Football League was 10 years old. A franchise from Portsmouth, Ohio, called the Spartans, was added. After four seasons the team was purchased for $15,000 by radio station owner George Richard who spent an additional $6,500 paying off team debts. He moved them to Detroit using his radio station to host a contest to name the team. Detroit Lions football was born that year and a contract was signed stipulating the team would play their games at the University of Detroit Stadium.

Lions for sale

Early owner Fred Mandel suffered through some bad seasons after he bought the team in 1940 and decided, eight years later, enough was enough. Mandel sold the Lions at a loss, for $1,850,000 to several Detroit sportsmen such as D. Lyle Fife and Edward J. Anderson. They hired Indiana coach Alvin "Bo" McMillian on a five-year contract. That year they contracted end Bob Mann, the Lions' first black player. He caught 33 passes for 560 yards. The Lions finished last for the third year in a row.

William Clay Ford, the son of Edsel and grandson of Henry, saw his first football game with his father in 1934 during the Lions' maiden season in Detroit. In 1956, he became a club director and in 1961 president of the Lions. Two years later he purchased the team for $4.5 million. His son and namesake, William Clay Ford, Jr., has been treasurer of the Lions since 1979.

Locked out, shut out!

◄ The newly formed Detroit Lions played their first game, against the New York Giants on September 23, 1934, winning 9-0. There were 12,000 fans in attendance for the home game, about half the capacity of the stadium.

The Lions went on to win their next nine games, executing six more consecutive shutouts. They managed a feat that hasn't been matched—in the first seven games of the season they didn't allow an opponent to score. The Pittsburgh Pirates finally managed to pass 62 yards for a touchdown. (But the Pirates still didn't win!) Only Green Bay and Chicago managed to beat them that first year.

Game gets air time

◄ To close that first season out, the Lions played two games against the Chicago Bears, the first of which was held on Thanksgiving Day. Lions owner George Richards decided to broadcast the game coast to coast with 94 stations picking up the transmission. The game sparked so much interest that all 26,000 tickets to the University of Detroit stadium were sold out. The Bears beat the Lions 16-19. Today, the Thanksgiving game is a Lions' tradition.

Starting quarterback: George Plimpton?

◄ Adventurous author George Plimpton had trained with the Detroit Lions in the early 1960s, then played quarterback during a scrimmage. The experience led to the bestseller *Paper Lion*. In 1971, ABC filmed a TV special on Plimpton and asked the Baltimore Colts to let him play in a real game.

It turned out to be against his old friends the Lions, and Plimpton went in after the first half at Ann Arbor on August 22. It was the real thing—it just didn't count in the game's scoring. Plimpton was quarterback for four plays, gaining 21 yards.

Detroit Lions "Fearsome Foursome" in 1964 to 1965 were (from left) Sam Williams, Roger Brown, Alex Karras, and Darris McCord

◄ The Pontiac Silverdome has been home to the Detroit Lions since 1975. It is considered one of the finest sports facilities in the world and has the second-largest seating capacity (80,494) of all NFL stadiums. The first game the Lions played there was against the Kansas City Chiefs in a pre-season game on August 23, 1975.

Home in the Dome

- It's the largest air-supported roof in the world, according to the 1992 *Guinness Book of World Records.*
- Measuring 522 feet wide and 722 feet long, the cable-restrained facility is the largest of its kind in the world and is the first successful example of a fiberglass fabric roof system.
- It takes 5 pounds of air pressure per square inch to keep the 10-acre translucent fiberglass roof from falling in. Built at a cost of $55.7 million, it was occupied just 23 months after ground was broken for the project.

LIONS HALL OF FAMERS

Detroit Lions who have been inducted into the Pro Football Hall of Fame are:

Defensive back **Jack Christiansen** (inducted 1970)
Quarterback **Earl "Dutch" Clark** (1963)
Halfback **Bill Dudley** (1966)
Fullback **John Henry Johnson** (1967)
Defensive back **Dick "Night Train" Lane** (1974)
Defensive back/punter **Yale Larry** (1979)
Quarterback **Bobby Layne** (1967)
Linebacker **Joe Schmidt** (1973)
Halfback **Doak Walker** (1966)
Center/linebacker **Alex Wojciechowicz** (1966)

LEGENDS OF THE GRIDIRON

◄ George Gipp, born in Lauriam in 1895, went on to become a famed halfback for Notre Dame. He died unexpectedly of pneumonia at the end of the 1920 season. From his deathbed, he instructed Notre Dame coach Knute Rockne, "When things are wrong and the breaks are beating the boys, tell them to go in there with all they've got and win one just for the Gipper!"

"Win one for the Gipper"

Rockne relayed the message during the halftime of the Army-Notre Dame game in 1928. The Irish were trailing by just one touchdown. The boys went out and scored two touchdowns, winning the game 12 to 6. Warner Brothers immortalized the story in *Knute Rockne—All American,* starring Pat O'Brien as Rockne and future President Ronald Reagan as the Gipper.

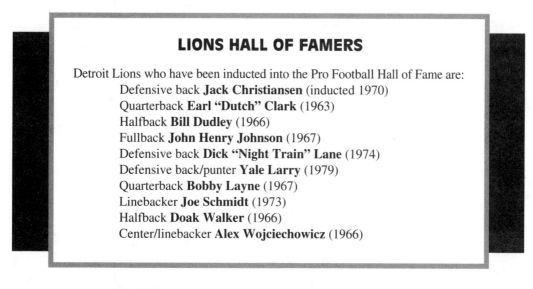

Another winner . . . and another . . . and another . . .

The best coaching record for the least amount of losses in professional football history belongs to George Allen of the Washington Redskins. The Detroit-born coach also coached the L.A. Rams and was the only NFL coach who never had a losing season.

Created the flying tackle

◀ Gustave Sonnenberg's talent first surfaced when he was a tackle with a Detroit team and later as guard with the Columbus Tigers in 1923. He stayed at guard and played for the Detroit Panthers and Providence Steamrollers. In 1930, he retired from football and his interests moved toward professional wrestling. There he introduced the flying tackle and won the heavyweight championship from Strangler Lewis in 1932. The Ewen resident died eight years later.

COLLEGIATE FOOTBALL

The president was an MVP

◀ Gerald Ford would become president of the United States in 1974, but in 1932 his main concern was earning varsity letters at the University of Michigan. (Between 1932 and 1934 he would earn three.) Wearing number 48, Ford played starting center in the All-Star game against the world champion Chicago Bears and was named MVP his senior year. He was later honored with the *Sports Illustrated* Silver Anniversary All-American Award honoring the football player who contributed the most to his fellow citizens.

One of the greats: Tom Harmon

His football coach described him as the greatest competitor he had ever known. University of Michigan's Tom Harmon was closely compared to the legendary Red Grange, breaking many of his football records. A running back, Harmon was awarded the Heisman in 1940.

At that time Michigan did not offer sports scholarships, instead it helped student athletes find summer work and part-time jobs. Tom Harmon said, "That's why I have no feeling for these guys who say they can't study and play football, too. That's a crock." Harmon graduated with a B average.

Harmon was one of few men to escape death twice in World War II. He was forced to bail out over dense jungles twice in seven months. Both times he was given up for dead only to resurface from the jungle six days after the first bailout and 32 days after the second. After the war, he signed a two-year pro contract with the Los Angeles Rams, where he played mostly defensive back. After his football career, he went into sports broadcasting full-time. He was the father of actor Mark Harmon (who is married to Michigan actress Pam Dawber) and singer Rick Nelson's widow, Chris.

◀ University of Michigan Wolverines had the second-longest winning streak in college football history: 56 games from 1901 to 1905. The University of Chicago broke their perfect record with a 0-2 score.

◀ It all began in 1903 when the University of Michigan Wolverines traveled to Minnesota for the game of games. Until then no one had beaten Coach Fielding H. Yost's Point-a-Minute team, or even tied them. The Golden Gophers were probably the only team at the time who could challenge the Wolverine machine. It promised to be all-out war!

The Battle for the Little Brown Jug

Water carts were not used yet, so when Minnesota sent over a supply of water, the Michigan team, not sure how "pure" the water was, sent student manager Tommy Roberts out to buy something to hold water. The jug was bought for 30 cents at a nearby variety store. (For the record, it was a five-gallon jug colored putty—not brown—and at five gallons, it wasn't little.) The Golden Gophers tied the game at 6-6 and the frenzied Minnesota crowd surged onto the field. The Wolverines left the field quickly, leaving the little jug behind.

The next day Minnesota's equipment manager, Oscar Munson, found the jug. A message was sent to Coach Yost. It read, "We have your Little Brown Jug. Come and win it!" The challenge had been issued. The next game, in 1904, was so brutal both schools severed all athletic competition until 1909. The challenge was still fresh in the minds of players and fans. Michigan won the jug back with a 15-6 victory. Since then, Minnesota and Michigan have fought to reclaim the Little Brown Jug each year.

Paul Bunyon, a spittoon and a megaphone

The Michigan State University Spartans battle for three different trophies each year. The Paul Bunyan Governor of Michigan Trophy goes to the winner of the Michigan State-Michigan game. It has been presented each year since 1953 when Govenor Mennen Williams made the first presentation to the victorious Spartans.

The Old Brass Spittoon goes to the winner of the Michigan-Indiana game, and it was initiated in 1950 by juniors and seniors at Michigan. The spittoon was selected because it was believed to be more than 100 years old and existed when both schools were founded.

The Megaphone Trophy (at right) is a prize that Michigan and Notre Dame vie for each fall. Started in 1949 by the Michigan/Notre Dame Alumni Club of Detroit, it was first presented in 1949.

National College Football Hall of Fame

PLAYERS

University of Detroit

Vincent Banonis inducted 1941

University of Michigan

Neil Worthington Snow inducted 1901

William M. Heston - 1904

Adolf Schulz - 1908

Albert Benbrook - 1910

John F. Maulbetsch - 1914

Henry Vick - 1921

Harry C. Kipke - 1923

Benjamin Friedman - 1926

Harry L. Newman - 1932

Francis Wistert - 1933

Thomas Harmon - 1940

Robert Westfall - 1941

Albert Wistert - 1942

Elroy Hirsch (also played with Wisconsin) - 1943

Merv Pregulman - 1943

Robert Chappuis - 1947

Chalmers Eliott (also played with Purdue) - 1947

Alvin Wister - 1949

Ronald J. Kramer - 1959

Ron Johnson - 1992

Michigan State

John Spencer Pingel - 1938

Don E. Coleman - 1951

Charles A. Smith - 1966

George D. Webster - 1966

COACHES

University of Michigan

Herbert Crisler - 1954

George Little - 1955

E.E. Wieman - 1956

Michigan State

Clarence Munn - 1959

Charlie Bachman - 1978

Hugh Duffy Daugherty - 1984

Headed for Tokyo Dome

The MSU Spartans head to Japan for the 18th annual Coca-Cola Bowl in 1993. MSU will face the Wisconsin Badgers in a Big Ten contest on December 5. Michigan and Wisconsin will be the first two Big Ten teams to ever appear there. It also is the first time the Spartans will play an intercollegiate football game in a foreign country. The Coca-Cola Bowl has been played since 1976; since 1988 the game has been held in the Tokyo Dome.

Spartan Stadium one of the biggest

Michigan State University's Spartan Stadium is the 13th-largest college-owned structure of its kind designed solely for football. It is the fifth largest in the Big Ten, with a seating capacity of 76,000. Rival Michigan's stadium is the biggest, with seating for 102,000 fans.

Since the original structure opened in 1923, the Spartans had, through 1992, played 359 games on the field with 245 wins, 101 losses, and 13 ties. The Spartans racked up 19 consecutive home stadium wins from the third home game of 1950 through the last home game of 1953.

Has four Super Bowl rings

Michigan State University's head coach George Perles has had amazing success since he took over the helm in 1982. He's had seven winning regular seasons, competed in six bowl games, and saw the Spartans win the 1988 Rose Bowl Championship. His team captured Big Ten titles in 1987 and 1990. MSU ended in the top 20 in three of the last five years, based on national wire polls.

The Detroit native was defensive coach with the Pittsburgh Steelers for 10 years, three as assistant head coach. He is among an elite group of coaches who has four Super Bowl rings—all with the Steelers. Perles was offered $2.25 million to become head coach for the Green Bay Packers in 1988, and turned it down. He later turned down an offer by the New York Jets.

BAD BOYS OF THE NBA

Piston facts

The Detroit Pistons were actually established in Fort Wayne, Indiana, in 1941, and played in the National Basketball League through the 1947-48 season there. In 1948, the Pistons joined the Basketball Association of America for one season and in 1949-50 became a member of the National Basketball Association.

The team moved from Fort Wayne to Detroit in time for the 1957-58 season. Up through the 1991-92 season, 220 players had worn a

Piston's uniform. Head coach Ron Rothstein is the 18th Pistons coach. Today the team is owned by Bill Davidson and 10 business partners.

Isiah: Player, author

◀ What can you say about a guy who plays basketball like Isiah Thomas? Beginning the 1992-93 season, Isiah was the all-time high Pistons scorer with 16,575 points to his credit. He was named the NBA Most Valuable Player during the 1990 NBA Finals when he averaged 27.6 points, 7.0 assists, and 5.2 rebounds while leading Detroit over Portland.

During his 10th appearance in the NBA All Star game he finished with 15 points, 5 assists, and 3 steals. In 1992, he hit a season high against Utah when he scored 44 points, the second highest of his career. He was named to the NBA All-Star team on each of his first 11 years in the NBA. He is a two-time All-Star Game MVP Player—in 1984 and 1985.

In his personal life, Thomas is considered one of the NBA's leading spokesmen against drugs. Married, he earned a degree in criminal justice in 1987. He has also co-authored a book, *Bad Boys: An Inside Look at the Detroit Pistons 1988-89 Championship Season*, written with Pistons public relations director Matt Dobek.

Leads in rebounds

◀ Bill Lambeer is the Pistons' all-time leader in rebounds, and is expected to reach his career 10,000 during the 1992-93 season. He began the year with 9,925 to his credit. As of the 1991-92 season, he started at center in all but one game, 765 out of 766 with Detroit. In 12 years of pro ball, he has logged 2,000 minutes of play for the 11th time. He surpassed Vinnie Johnson for the all-time Pistons' record in games played (847) through the end of the 1991-92 regular session. During the 1988-89 season he went over the 10,000 career point total.

Lambeer came to Detroit from Cleveland with Kenny Carr in a 1982 trade and has been on the NBA All-Star team four times. He won the NBA rebound title in 1985-86 when he averaged a career best—13.1 rebounds per game.

BASKETBALL HALL OF FAME

Coach and administrator
William A. Reid
born Detroit, elected 1963

Referee **James E. Enright**
born Sodus, elected 1978

Defensive forward **David A. DeBusschere**
born Detroit, elected 1982

COLLEGE BASKETBALL

A touch of magic

◀ They called him "June Bug" because he was a chubby kid. He grew up one of seven children living in a small three-bedroom home in Lansing. Basketball was as natural to Earvin Johnson as breathing. In high school he helped lead Everette High School through several big winning seasons. In his senior year, a

sportswriter for the Lansing *State Journal* came into the locker room and told Johnson he needed a nickname and proceeded to give him one, "Magic." It stuck.

As a member of the 1978-79 squad, he helped bring magic to Michigan State's winning the NCAA tournament. Magic led the team with 25 points and 17 rebounds against unbeaten Indiana State University and a future nemesis—Larry Bird (number 33—facing Magic in photo at left).

Magic went on to play with the Los Angeles Lakers in 1979. He was the NBA's all-time leader in assists in regular season, playoff and All-Star Game competition, led the Lakers to five NBA titles during the 1980s, and was two-time All-Star Game MVP.

In 1991, he married his college sweetheart, Earleatha "Cookie" Kelly of Detroit. His biggest battle started that same year. Magic Johnson shocked the sporting world on November 7 by announcing that he was HIV Positive, meaning he had a probability of developing AIDS, and was retiring. He served on the President's National Commission on AIDS, but resigned in the fall of 1992, complaining that the administration ignored the panel's work.

Although retired, Magic played in the All-Star Game and became the most popular player on the 1992 Olympic Dream Team. Acting on doctor's approval, Magic announced on September 29, 1992, that he was returning to basketball and was given a $14.6-million contract with the Lakers, payable whether he played or not. It was also the largest, single-season deal in history for a professional athlete. Magic would retire number 32 permanently later that same year.

First fieldhouse is built

◀ University of Michigan and Coach Fielding Yost can be credited with constructing the first fieldhouse in the nation. Yost wanted a large house that could cover a sports field and be used for multiple sports year round. The Yost Fieldhouse was constructed in 1923 and such basketball greats as Bennie Oosterbaan and Cazzie Russell regularly filled the fieldhouse to its 8,500 capacity. The fieldhouse was used until 1967, when the University Events Building (now named the Crisler Arena) was built.

TAKING IT ON THE CHIN

A sweet punch leads to title

◄ Sugar Ray Robinson is often labeled the greatest fighter pound-for-pound in the history of boxing. Born Walker Smith in Detroit, he took the name Robinson from the certificate of an amateur boxer whose identity enabled him to meet the age requirement for getting a match in Michigan. The "Sugar" came from his having been dubbed "the sweetest fighter" by sportswriters and fans.

As a 10-year-old boy, Robinson had watched Detroit neighbor Joe Louis train for an amateur boxing career. Growing up in Detroit and later New York, Robinson learned the ropes at Salem-Crescent Gym. He turned professional in 1940 and boxed until 1965. During his career he set a record of 175 wins with 110 knockouts. He suffered only 19 losses and one knockout.

Sugar Ray won the welterweight championship in 1946, taking the title away from Tommy Bell. He won the middle-weight championship by beating famed boxer Jake LaMotta in 1951. He lost and regained the crown several times during his career. After Robinson turned pro, his financial savvy astounded many. For instance, he negotiated 45 percent of the gate and a $225,000 TV guarantee by holding steadfast in the face of promoters during his 1958 fight with Carmen Basilio.

Sugar Ray Robinson suffered from Alzheimer's disease and diabetes in his later years. Before his death in 1989, he founded the Sugar Ray Robinson Youth Foundation for Underprivileged Children.

The Brown Bomber, still a legend

Perhaps it was the harsh life as a sharecropper's son in Alabama that made him tough. Whatever it was, it took Joe Louis all the way to the heavyweight championship.

He moved to Detroit as a young boy and took up amateur boxing. He won 50 out of 59 before turning pro in 1934. Louis quickly gained a reputation in the Midwest and in 1935 went east to meet Primo Carnera, a former champion who was then staging a comeback.

Louis knocked out Carnera in six rounds and earned his nickname, "The Brown Bomber." He went on to hold the heavyweight championship longer than anyone else (11 years, 8 months, 7 days) and defended it more often than any other heavyweight champion. His 25 title fights were more than the combined total of the eight champions who preceded him. He died in 1981 at the age of 67. In his memory, a four-ton, 24-foot-long bronze statue of the arm and fist of the great world heavyweight champion is located in Detroit.

STICKS AND ICE

The Detroit story

◀ The Detroit Cougars played their first NHL game as a team on November 18, 1926. They lost 2-0, but finished the season 12-28-4 on a 44-game schedule.

The 1928-29 season was the beginning of a new attitude for the young hockey team from Detroit. Jack Adams rode into town and when he left 35 years later, he was headed for the Hall of Fame. It happened like this. The team finished third that year, making its first of 41 play-off appearances in 66 seasons. They changed their name to the Falcons, mostly due to the urging of local media, who hoped a name change would bring the team good luck, but Detroit again sat out the play-offs.

In 1932, industrialist James Norris bought the franchise and renamed them the Red Wings. He had played for a Canadian team called the Winged Wheelers. He took their insignia, a winged wheel, and changed it to look like an auto tire with a flying wing attached. It is still used today with minor changes.

Today, the Red Wings are owned by the founder of Little Caesar's Pizza—Mike Ilitch. He purchased the team from Bruce Norris in 1982. Ilitch was raised in Detroit by immigrant parents. A sports lover since he was a child (he spent three years with the Tiger's farm team, a team which he now owns!), Ilitch's donations make it possible for over 50,000 children to participate in sports each year.

Hall of Famers

The United States Hockey Hall of Fame has inducted the following Michigan players:

Frank W. "Nick" Kahler, born in Dollar Bay (inducted 1980)

Victor Des Jardins, born Saulte Ste. Marie (1974)

Clarence J. "Taffy" Abell, born Sault Ste. Marie (1973)

Joseph C. Linder, born Hancock (1975)

Edward F. Olson, born Hancock (1977)

Could he play hockey? And Howe!

For 32 seasons, Canadian-born Gordie Howe played hockey, and 25 of those were with the Detroit Red Wings. A rival player said that Howe was "everything you'd expect an ideal hockey player to be. He's soft-spoken and thoughtful. He's also the most vicious, cruel, and mean man I've ever met in the hockey game."

Howe was nicknamed "Blinkie" after a near-fatal accident left him with an uncontrollable eye twitch. He was the league's top scorer four times and won the Hart Trophy, which goes to the league's most outstanding player, five times between 1952 and 1960. His wrist shot traveled at 114 mph. Howe was so strong he needed a special hockey stick, because as the Red Wings trainer explained, "Give Gordie a stick with an ordinary handle and he'll break it like a toothpick. He is so strong that when he shoots, that handle bends like a banana."

Howe retired in 1971 from the Red Wings. He came back to join the Houston Aeros of the World Hockey Association and in 1977, he joined the Hartford Whalers of the National Hockey League. He retired permanently at the age of 52 in 1980. His son, Mark, is now a player for the Red Wings.

SPORTS FOR ALL SEASONS

Sticks and chalk

The first billiard game to ever draw international attention occurred April 12, 1859, in Detroit. Challengers Michael Phelan of New York City and John Seereiter of Detroit met for the championship title and played on a 6-foot by 12-foot four-pocket table with four balls. A purse of $15,000 was offered. Phelan, "father of billiards," won with a score of 2,000 against Seereiter's 1,904.

Their game is the pits!

Pit spitters from around the world compete for a chance to be listed in the *Guinness Book of World Records* at the Cherry Spitting Championship at the Tree-Mendus Farms in Eau Claire. You get three tries and no funny business. To date, the longest spit on record belongs to the 1988 champ, Rick Krause. He came all the way from Sanders, Arizona (he is a former Eau Claire resident), to spit 72 feet $7^{1}/_{2}$ inches. Krause has won eight times total.

◄ Located in the Wayne County Building in Detroit is the International Afro-American Sports Hall of Fame and Gallery. It is the only Sports Hall of Fame of its kind, honoring outstanding black athletes. Elmer Anderson founded the hall in 1977. Since then many great black athletes have been honored.

Afro-American Sports Hall of Fame

Hall of Famers as of 1992 include: track star Wilma Rudolph; boxer Muhammad Ali; basketball player Samuel Lee Washington; baseball coach Ronald Teasley; bowling pioneer Lafayette Allen, Jr.; the Brewster Old Timers; Richard "Night Train" Lane; William J. "Will" Robinson; "The Brown Bomber" Joe Louis; track coach Leroy Dues; golfer Thelma Cowans; football player-basketball player "Jumpin' " John Kline; Sugar Ray Robinson; baseball player Norman "Turkey" Stearnes; baseball player Jackie Robinson; tennis player Althea Gibson; baseball player Marshall Williams; golfer E. Ben Davis; and softball player Samuel Gee.

◄ Norwegian Carl Tellefsen introduced skiing to America. Tellefsen came to Ishpeming and helped create the Norden Ski Club, possibly the first ski club in the nation. The group held its first jumping contest in 1888. Three years later they hosted jumpers from three states. In 1905, Tellefsen became the first president of the National Ski Association. (Today it's called the United States Ski Association.) Ishpeming is considered the birthplace of organized skiing in the U.S. and is home to the National Ski Hall of Fame. The museum houses Olympic memorabilia and a replica of the arctic type skis and poles used 4,000 years ago by Stone Age skiers. Probably the most important artifact is Oscar Gunderson's "yoompin' " sticks, which he used in 1909 when he made a record 138-foot jump.

They're yoomping in Ishpeming

What's in a name?

What do the Tunas, Gryphons, Speedboys, and Dreadnaughts all have in common? They're names of high school sports mascots in Michigan. The Gryphon is the mascot for the Greenhills School in Ann Arbor. The Gryphon has the body of a lion and the head of an eagle and was created in 1970 when students decided their new gym needed a new mascot. Then there's the Dexter High School Dreadnaughts (at left), and the Our Lady of the Sea Tunas.

The Bessemer High School team named their teams the Speedgirls and Speedboys, using a winged, sandaled foot as their mascot. The name was created in 1933 when the school had small but speedy backs on the football team. Newspapers made notes of this and the school changed their name from the Golden Hurricanes to the Speedboys!

The Olympics and Michigan

The Olympics brought glory to many athletes from Michigan. Grand Rapids-born **Russell Vis**, called the "greatest wrestling champ of the century," began wrestling as a teenager in Portland, Oregon. He won a gold Medal in lightweight freestyle wrestling in the 1924 Olympics. That same year, Buchanan resident and track star **Jackson Volney Scholz** finished second during the Olympic competition. He used the experience as the topic for his book, *Chariots of Fire*, which became a hit movie in 1981.

Birmingham resident **Sheila Young** won an Olympic gold medal and world championships in speed skating. And in bicycling she had to beat 28 rivals during the National Bicycle Track Championship in 1976 prior to competing against national and world champion Sue Novara to win the best two of the three series in the 1,000-meter course. Young won the 1975 World Sprint Championship in speed skating and set the women's world record of 37 seconds for skating 500 meters. She is the only athlete to ever become world champion in two sports.

Sports Hall of Oblivion

Ever hear of the Macon Whoopees or the Toledo Swamp Angels? What about the Michigan Stags or the Akron Firestone Nonskids? If it weren't for Chuck Hershberger of Pleasant Ridge, those teams and thousands of others like them would be forgotten forever. He has immortalized them in the Sports Hall of Oblivion located in Where, Michigan.

The social studies teacher got interested in defunct teams while growing up in Detroit when he tried to get into the Tigers games. Tickets were easiest to purchase when a losing team was in town. One by one the old teams faded away or were swallowed up by other franchises, but Hershberger didn't forget them.

He has 5,000 pieces of sports trivia concerning entire leagues and teams in his Sports Hall of Oblivion. Hershberger has identified 3,500 extinct professional teams. He continues to gather information including material on phantom teams that never set foot on playing fields, like the Miami Screaming Eagles of the World Hockey Association. Ironically, Hershberger recently learned that his birthplace—Detroit's Grace Hospital—was constructed on the site of Recreation Park, which served as the home of the Detroits, the city's first professional baseball team—a team that no longer exists, of course!

MICHIGAN MISCELLANEA

What kind of people live in Michigan? What have they accomplished and how does that affect you? You'd be surprised! Michigan is not only home to the automobile, carpet sweeper, baby food, and cereal, it has produced famous astronauts, leaders in politics, religion, and science, not to mention entertainment. Then there's the everyday people who may not have discovered the cure for cancer (yet) but, nonetheless, their awesome ability to laugh at themselves has somehow made us all richer.

- The Animal Kingdom
- Taking Wing
- Unique Feats
- Michigan: The State of Education
- Who was First?
- Spiritual Living
- Pioneers of the Final Frontier
- Scientific Michigan

THE ANIMAL KINGDOM

Big Benny breaks record

Benedictine Jr. Schwarzwald Hof is a St. Bernard who gets a lot of attention. Most of it has to do with his size. At last count, Benny weighed in at 310 pounds, the heaviest St. Bernard on record, and stood 39 inches high at the shoulders. He is owned by Thomas and Anne Irwin of Grand Rapids—or he owns them.

What's a ton or two among friends?

◆ Sometimes, stories have a way of snowballing and this is one of those, although the significance of the feat is none the less impressive. It was reported on February 26, 1893, that two Shires with a combined weight of 3,500 pounds pulled an astounding 144-ton load of logs on a sled for a distance of 1, 320 feet on a frozen road.

However, eyewitnesses to the event, which was held at the Nester Estate in Ewen, said the tonnage was greatly exaggerated. The load was actually comprised of 50 white pine logs measuring 36,055 board feet, weighing in at a mere 47 tons!

Land of the giants

Some horses are big and some are small. Then there was Tritonis, a Canadian thoroughbred gelding who was a giant. The show jumper stood 19.2 hands ($6^{1}/_{2}$ feet) and weighed 2,100 pounds. Tritonis set a record for being the tallest non-draft horse. He was owned by Christopher Ewing of Southfield. The gentle giant died in 1990 at the age of seven.

TAKING WING

The Lone Eagle

◆ Following the Lone Eagle's first solo nonstop flight between New York and Paris in 1927, the whole world wanted to claim him as their own. However, Detroit has the honor of being the birthplace of Charles Augustus Lindbergh, Jr. One of the world's greatest pilots, he was born there on February 4, 1902.

The Lindberghs moved to Little Falls, Minnesota, when Charles was a child. Finishing two years of college at the University of Wisconsin, he took off on his motorcycle to Nebraska where he had his first flying lesson. He became a barnstormer, an Air Reserve cadet, and a test pilot. He also delivered air mail and was famous for practical jokes. In fact, he played so many jokes, it is said that one Midwest airfield manager used to announce his arrival by saying, "Bellies to the ground! Here comes Slim!"

Hearing of a $25,000 prize offered for the pilot who could complete the first solo flight between the United States and Europe, Lindbergh spent many months developing plans and obtaining financial backing for an attempt at the prize. With spare fuel tanks weighing down *Spirit of St. Louis*, he took off from New York on a foggy morning—May 20, 1927. Thirty-four exhausting hours later, he arrived at Le Bourget Field in Paris, stunned to find himself an international celebrity. When all was said and done, Lindbergh received some 15,000 awards and medals. He had movie offers, and George M. Cohan even wrote a song about him.

Lindbergh married Anne Morrow, the daughter of the U.S. ambassador to Mexico. In 1932, their infant son was kidnapped from the second-floor nursery of their New Jersey home. After an intense search and international coverage, the baby was found dead. Eventually, Bruno Hauptmann was found guilty of the deed and was executed.

Lindbergh moved his family to England and later to a remote French Island. He spoke out against U.S. involvement in the beginning of World War II, causing many people to wonder if he were a secret Nazi. However, when war broke out he became a brigadier general flying combat missions. He was awarded a special Medal of Honor by the U.S. Congress.

❖ The story of the first African-American pilots to fly during World War II is told at the National Museum of the Tuskegee Airmen in Detroit. Airmen trained at an isolated air base near Tuskegee, Alabama, and studied at Tuskegee Institute. The graduates formed the 99th Fighter Squadron under the command of Colonel Benjamin O. Davis, Jr., who later became the first black lieutenant general in the Air Force.

The "Black Birdmen" are honored

The 99th was later joined by three other black fighter squadrons and was redesignated the 332nd Fighter Group. The 99th completed 1,578 combat missions in North Africa, Sicily, and Europe with the 12th Tactical U.S. Army Air Force. They were called the "Black Birdmen" by the Germans and were feared and respected. The 99th is credited with being a major force in causing the eventual disappearance of segregation in the military. Among the members of this prestigious group was Detroit Mayor Coleman Young.

Invented the word "aircraft"

◆ Detroit eccentric Alfred William Lawson's birth was declared by some to be the "most momentous occurrence" in recorded history. Lawson was truly a Michigan Renaissance man, labeling himself a physicist, nutritionist, educator, economist, novelist, aviator, and baseball player.

Lawson founded the first magazine devoted entirely to airplanes, *Fly*. He is credited with inventing the word "aircraft," as well as the double-decker passenger plane. In 1919, he established his own airline, Lawson Aircraft Corporation.

Lawson's idea for "direct credit," to end the gold standard and replace it with "valueless money with no purchase power" was extreme-

ly popular during the Great Depression. His philosophical three-volume work, *Law-sonomy*, detailed his thoughts on subjects ranging from suction and pressure to how the brain works. These works and others provided the complete instructional materials for his university, Des Moines University of Lawsonomy.

Teachers were called "Knowledgians." Lawson was, of course, the "Supreme Head and First Knowledgian." It took 10 years to complete the course work, but there was no tuition. Tobacco and alcohol were forbidden because Lawson promoted good health habits. His regimen included never breathing by mouth, eating raw fruits and vegetables including skin, pits, and seeds, and always sleeping in the nude. Disease-causing kissing was to be avoided at all costs.

Boeing founded United Airlines

◆ Detroit-born entrepreneur William E. Boeing was in the process of establishing a lumber business in Seattle when he learned to fly for fun. After cracking up his airplane, he became certain he could build a better one. He established Pacific Aero Products Company near Seattle in 1916, and his products were quickly purchased by fans of this new form of sport. Fortunately, the Boeing Airplane Company was fully functioning when World War I began and the U.S. government decided that airplanes were needed. Boeing and his partner made training aircraft and flying boats.

Following the war, Boeing turned to making furniture but kept on building airplanes and selling them when he could. Then in 1927, Boeing bid on a government contract to fly airmail. Awarded the bid, he founded Boeing Air Transport. In 1928, his company merged with Pratt & Whitney Aircraft to become United Aircraft and Transport. The following year they started a friendly little company called United Airlines. The government forced United to split in 1934, and Boeing Aircraft Corporation had to separate from the airline. During World War II, Boeing designed the famous B-17 Flying Fortreess.

Fly Henry's skies

◆ Henry Ford, who was convinced he could do just about anything, entered the airline business in 1925 by starting scheduled commercial airline service from Chicago to Detroit.

◆ Helen Richey was the first woman to fly an airmail transport on a regular schedule. She arrived in Detroit on December 31, 1934, after making stops in Pittsburgh and Cleveland. Richey became a copilot for Central Airlines and flew a 12-passenger Ford Tri-Motor transport— decades before the hoopla about the "first" woman airline pilot.

Air-female arrives in Detroit

UNIQUE FEATS

And for my next act . . .

Some folks crave the spotlight and some folks just want to be left alone. Then there's Livonia's Jim Purol. Some folks say he doesn't know when to leave well enough alone! It all began in 1976 when Purol played the drums nonstop for 320 hours. The next year he played the drums underwater. Then in 1979, he crawled 25 miles on his hands and knees. Purol was no dummy. He strapped tire treads to his hands and knees. For an encore, he ate 12 slices of pizza during the journey. Then, he squeezed 12 (we assume, very good) friends onto a mattress.

During the Great American Smokeout Day, he stuffed dozens of lit cigarettes in his mouth. His record to date is 151 smoking cigarettes. He followed the event by briefly smoking 41 cigars and 40 pipes. Some folks say he's a little backward, and if Purol gets his way, he'll prove 'em right. Purol wants to drive a car from New York to Los Angeles backward! Once there, he wants to sit in each of the 104,464 seats in the Rose Bowl in Pasadena!

◆ Detroit secretary Jackie Wells was a student at Wayne State University in 1958 when she posed nude for Norman Rockwell, best known for his wholesome *Saturday Evening Post* covers. In 1990, the painting, Rockwell's only known nude, sold for $50,000 at a Detroit art auction. The painting was purchased by Tom Sullivan of Bloomfield. The painting is known as *Portrait of Miss Jackie Wells* and also *The Manapessa*. Apparently Rockwell gave Wells the finished product.

Rockwell's only known nude

◆ Michigan has a "Timid Motorist's Program" which helps gephyro- phobiacs—those afraid of crossing a bridge. In 1991, 830 drivers were helped across Michigan's famed Mackinac Bridge. The big bridge is 200 feet high and 5 miles long. Some drivers just needed to talk to someone while they drove across, but others needed to lie in the back seat and be driven. (Out of sight, out of mind?)

Trying to bridge the gap

◆ We may never know how it started, but when it was all said and done, John J. Makinen, Sr., had built a house out of 60,000 soft-drink bottles. He finished in 1941, and forty years later the house became a museum. Located in Kaleva, the House of Bottles is home to historical items from the lumbering industry, farming, homemaking, railroads, schools, and more. So if you're thinking about adding a wing to the old family homestead, maybe you should consider pop bottles as an alterna- tive building material!

All bottled up

Any which way but lost

❖ If you're lost and heading in the wrong direction, you can look for moss on the north side of the trees, search the skies for the North Star, or wait for the sun to set in the west. But if you're in Montague all you have to do is look at the weather vane. The world's largest weather vane, that is. Overlooking White Lake, it stands 48 feet high with a 26-foot wind arrow. It weighs 3,500 pounds, and is adorned with a 14-foot replica of a 19th-century Great Lakes schooner.

Clean finish

❖ In 1914, Allen S. Browne and some businessmen formed a club in Detroit called the Benevolent Order of Brothers.
The name was changed in 1915 to Kiwanis, which they said meant "we trade." The translation was later revised to include "we have a good time" or "we make noise." Browne was kicked out when members thought he was making too much money from initiation fees. In 1919, after the club paid him $17,500, Browne gave up his rights to the Kiwanis name. Today the service club has over 300,000 members nationwide.

MICHIGAN: THE STATE OF EDUCATION

Organized the 3 Rs

❖ John D. Pierce and Issac E. Crary are responsible for the organization of the public education system in Michigan. They met in Marshall in 1835 and Pierce was appointed the nation's first superintendent of public instruction. Supposedly the great oak tree under which these plans were laid was located on the lawn of the Brooks House at 310 N. Kalamazoo.

Just sign here please

❖ Life is full of lessons. One is to read the fine print before you sign on the dotted line. In 1938, many students at the University of Michigan had not yet learned such a lesson. It seems a petition was circulated by a group of freshmen, asking that a psychology lecture held on Saturday afternoons be changed to Wednesday so students could attend football games.

The next day, those who signed the petition read in the newspaper what they actually signed: "We, the undersigned, hereby petition that the lecture in Psychology 2 be changed from Saturday to Wednesday afternoon. By signing this document, without reading it, we cheerfully disqualify ourselves as candidates for any degree conferred by this university. We furthermore declare that the freshmen are our superiors in wit and wisdom, and that our stupidity is surpassed only by the mental lethargy of the underpaid faculty that teaches us."

Who got stiffed?

Herman W. Mudgett was a medical student at Ann Arbor when he got the bright idea of taking out insurance on cadavers and then collecting when he demonstrated that they were dead! He finally got caught and, needless to say, there went his medical career. However, he went to Chicago and became one of the most infamous murderers in American history.

◆ Bloomfield Hills, the site of Cranbrook Institute, had a very simple beginning in 1819. Judge Amasa Bagley picked the spot for a tavern and farm. Soon it was a bustling agricultural center. Then, at the turn of the century, upscale city folks from Detroit started buying up property to construct private estates. Among the newcomers was the publisher of the *Detroit News*, George G. Booth, and his wife, Ellen Scripps Booth, who built an estate called Cranbrook. The couple established a school on the estate to accommodate their own children as well as others in the area. Today, the estate is part of Cranbrook Institute of Science and is part of the 315-acre complex making up the Cranbrook Educational Community. There is an art museum; science institute (which boasts a laser show and 60 hands-on exhibits); graduate art school; lower, middle, and upper schools; and a manor house. Forty acres of gardens surround the manor.

From a simple beginning

◆ The University of Michigan was founded in 1817 in Detroit, after Indians offered 1,920 acres for "a college at Detroit." The Michigan territorial legislature accepted the land, then chartered the "Catholepistemiad or University of Michigania." In 1837, the college was renamed the University of Michigan and moved to Ann Arbor as a preparatory school. No college curriculum was offered until 1841.

The talent cradle

The U. of M. is the oldest state university in the country created directly by voters through their state constitution. It is known as the "Mother of State Universities." The first professorship in education and the first course in forestry at any American university were both established there. It also had the first hospital operated by a state university. Lucinda Hinsdale Stone was instrumental in persuading the university in 1870 to open its doors to women, the first state university to do so.

The U. of M. has produced some amazing graduates, including one president—football standout, Gerald R. Ford; three supreme court justices; six Nobel Prize winners; and seven NASA astronauts. As of 1992 there were over 330,000 alumni. One in every 750 Americans has a Michigan degree.

◆ Betty Smith, author of the 1943 novel *A Tree Grows in Brooklyn*, attended the University of Michigan from 1927 to 1930. The school inadvertently served as a springboard to the creation of her famous book. As a 23-year-old mother of two, Smith enrolled in courses that did not conflict with her children's schedule. The only ones available to her were creative writing classes! Other famous literary types who spent time at the university include Arthur Miller. Notables on staff have included Robert Frost, Donald Hall, and novelist Allan Seager. The Reverend Lloyd C. Douglas, who served as pastor of the First Congregational Church in Ann Arbor, wrote *Magnificent Obsession* in 1929.

U. of M. planted seeds

The first land-grant college

◈ Michigan State University (of Agricultural and Applied Science) was authorized in 1855 and opened in East Lansing in 1857 as Michigan Agricultural College, the first agricultural school in the nation. When the land-grant colleges were established by the federal government in 1862 for the development of schools to teach "agriculture and the mechanic arts" (which is why most of them are called "A & M" schools), the funds gained from selling the granted land were used to improve and expand the school.

As of 1992, 42,088 students from every county in Michigan, every state in the nation, and 108 foreign countries were pursuing education in the 14 academic colleges there.

WHO WAS FIRST?

Wired!

◈ Debi Horn, a Gibraltar housewife, became the first American to have her mouth wired shut to lose weight. When Debi's 229 pounds melted away to 156 in just seven months, her oral surgeon, Dr. Daniel M. Laskin, D.D.S., wired an additional 100 mouths shut.

Long-distance love affair

◈ Detroit played host to the first transatlantic telephone wedding ever. It took place December 2, 1933. Bertil Hjalmar Clason was in Detroit and Sigrid Sophia Margarete Carlson was in Stockholm, Sweden, when Judge John Dennis Watts of Wayne County performed the rites. The ceremony was relayed from Detroit through New York to a Maine radio station and from there to Scotland to London and finally, to Stockholm!

They were first

The following are more Michigan firsts:

- In 1945, Grand Rapids became the first city to add fluoride to its drinking water in an effort to prevent cavities in its citizens' teeth!
- Marie Owen has the distinction of being the very first woman appointed as a police officer. A patrolman's widow, she was appointed to the Detroit Bureau of Police by Morgan A. Collins, Superintendent of Police, in 1893.
- Michigan Bell introduced the first trimline phone to Jackson customers on August 2, 1965. The dial (push-button phones were still a concept) was located in the receiver, between the earpiece and mouthpiece. Customers could rent this modern piece of equipment for $1 per month!
- Three Rivers was the home of a Jesuit mission in the 17th century and today is home to Chet Shafer, a homespun philosopher and columnist. He formed the Guild of Former Pipe Organ Pumpers in 1940, an organization that boasts a membership of 2,500. The group claims to be the first and only non-essential organization in the world.

SPIRITUAL LIVING

◆ Religion isn't far from the minds of the good residents of Indian River, and with good reason: the world's largest crucifix is located there. Constructed of California redwood and bronze, the cross is 55 feet high and 22 feet wide, weighing in at seven tons. Nestled in a rustic setting at the Catholic Shrine, on each side of the crucifix are the Holy Stairs, for those who wish to approach the cross on their knees. Each star contains a First Class Relic. There are rows of pews in front of the cross for worshipers attending daily masses. Also on display is a statue of Our Lady of the Highway, carved from Carrera marble, and a collection of dolls representing nuns of 217 religious orders, all dressed with meticulous detail.

God's country

◆ Elijah Poole joined the Temple of Islam and renamed himself Elijah Muhammad. He established Temple No. 1 in 1934 in Detroit. The religion teaches African-Americans to be self-sufficient and to take pride in their African heritage. Elijah Muhammad gave all his followers an "X" for a last name to represent the slave name they would never know. Malcolm X (see p. 43) was a powerful leader in the sect, but when he began to move away and change his teachings, he was assassinated by three members of the temple.

Temple of Islam

◆ Voters in Michigan elected Father Gabriel Richard as a nonvoting delegate to Congress on September 4, 1823. He was the first Roman Catholic priest to sit in Congress, and served until 1825.

The collar and Congress

◆ Jim Bakker of Muskegon and his wife, Tammy Faye, saw their multimillion-dollar PTL (Praise the Lord) TV ministry crumble after church secretary Jessica Hahn came forward with tales of a sex scandal. Her revelations came at a time when newspapers were scrutinizing the Bakkers' vacation complex and theme park, Heritage Village, which was supported by donations and based in Charlotte, North Carolina.

Jim, Tammy, and Jessica

Investigation unearthed the unbelievable life-style the Bakkers had been enjoying on their congregation's donations. During an auction held to pay off their sky-high debts, among items sold was an elegantly decorated, air-conditioned doghouse, valued at $8,000. Bakker was eventually convicted of fraud and sentenced to 45 years in prison. His wife, Tammy Faye, whose heavy makeup was consistently satirized by the press, was granted a divorce in 1992 and currently serves a small church in Florida.

Jessica Hahn, the church secretary who was done wrong, went to lick her wounds at Hugh Hefner's Playboy mansion. While there she had her nose fixed and got breast implants. She later appeared in a sleazy music video, "Wild Thing," with the late shock-comedian Sam Kinison.

A lot of faith

◆ Ohio minister George Bennard was an evangelical minister who preached in every state in the union except Utah and Louisiana. That alone is quite a feat. But the Reverend Bennard continues to bring happiness to thousands more today with his 1913 song, "The Old Rugged Cross." So popular is his song that when NBC polled viewers on their favorite song, it was voted the most popular hymn in the country. Reverend Bennard lived in Reed City for several years and in 1954 the Chamber of Commerce erected a cross in his honor. He was also invited to ride in the Rose Bowl Parade on an "Old Rugged Cross" float, which was 35 feet long and covered with flowers. Both events, he said, were among the greatest thrills of his life.

Churches played important role

◆ The **Second Baptist Church of Beaubien** is one of the oldest Baptist churches in the North. It was organized in 1836, but the congregation was poor and could not afford to construct a church until 1857. The first celebration of the Emancipation Proclamation in Detroit was held at the church January 6, 1863. The following October, black volunteers met at the Second Baptist Church to form the First Michigan Colored Infantry.

The oldest **Bethel African Methodist Episcopal Church** in Michigan was formed in 1839 in Detroit. The church also housed the very first public school for African-American children, and in the early 1900s it assisted migrants from the South to find jobs and housing.

The **Chain Lakes Missionary Baptist Church** was founded in 1838, with core members meeting in homes. In 1848 it was formally organized. In 1853 representatives from churches in the surrounding area gathered to form the Michigan Anti-Slavery Baptist Association in the building belonging to the Chain Lakes Missionary Baptist Church.

Pastor helps found Holland

◆ Dr. A.C. Van Raalte, secessionist pastor, and a group of 53 Dutch people seeking religious freedom, bought government land in Michigan. He discovered that the land on the Black River on Lake Macatawa had rich loam ideal for farming. Over the course of the following years, thousands of Dutch immigrants arrived. His group founded Holland in 1869. Two years later, much of the Michigan city was destroyed by fire.

Today, Holland is a popular tourist destination, thanks in part to the Tulpen Feest (Tulip Festival). Dutch food, clothes, shops, and customs are displayed and thousands of tulips planted throughout the city bloom on cue for the event held every May.

Return to sender

◆ The first Amish community in the state is believed to have been founded in 1847, when five Ohio families moved to the Sturgis district. Living and dressing plainly, private and proud, the Amish keep to themselves. When disaster strikes, they rally around and immediately repair or rebuild what has been destroyed. So it was in 1937, when the Amish learned they would be receiving some WPA (Works Progress Administration) funds to rebuild schools in their district. They filed a formal protest in Washington, saying that the acceptance of loans is forbidden by the tenets of their religion. If the schools needed rebuilding, they would do it themselves. And they did.

❖ After Mormon leader Joseph Smith was murdered in Illinois in 1844, New Yorker James Jesse Strang tried to claim that both Smith and God had meant him to be the next head of the Church of Jesus Christ of Latter-Day Saints. Brigham Young and others disagreed, and excommunicated Strang. Strang took his followers to Voree (now Burlington), Wisconsin, where he began to establish his own secret sect. Looking for some place safer to settle, a scouting party explored Michigan's Big Beaver Island in 1847. Strang began to move his people there at once.

The American king

In 1849, Strang built a tabernacle and laid out the town of St. James. Once the Strangites were firmly entrenched on Big Beaver, their leaders granted personal property rights and incorporated the island into a kingdom. On July 8, 1850, Strang was crowned king in a pageant of great pomp and ceremony.

The rule of King Strang was supreme and his authority complete. He forbade the use of tea, tobacco, and liquor. Followers were required to pay a tithe of all they earned, produced, or received. This money was used for improvements, care of the aged and poor, and payment of state and township taxes.

When Strang took several wives and ordered his followers to do likewise, public opinion turned against the colony. Internal dissension began to build when Strang decreed that the women must wear bloomers or knee-length skirts instead of long dresses. Husbands were whipped when their wives didn't comply. Strang represented his "kingdom" in the state legislature for two terms. But on June 16, 1856, Strang was shot by two men who had left his community. He died in Voree 23 days later. His Michigan kingdom did not survive his death.

A novel about the Mormon period on Big Beaver Island is *The Strangers on the Island* by Brand Whitlock, written in 1933.

❖ Alphadelphia, a utopian community located on 3,000 acres near Kalamazoo, was founded in the 1840s by a German, H. R. Schetterly. The members, who numbered about 300 in the community's heyday, did their own work but shared the results of that work with the others. They all lived together in one large house. The group began to disintegrate fairly rapidly, however, and by 1848, the members split the land up among them and went their separate ways.

Utopia at Kalamazoo

PIONEERS OF THE FINAL FRONTIER

Astronauts who perished

◆ Tragically, Michigan has lost two astronauts to space disasters. In a ground test of the new Apollo spacecraft in 1967, Roger B. Chaffee perished with fellow crew members Gus Grissom and Edward White during a fire on the launching pad. As a result of the fire, the Apollo was completely redesigned before it was sent to the moon. Chaffee was a native of Grand Rapids, born in 1935.

Gregory Jarvis, born in Detroit, was an employee of Hughes Aircraft Company when he was chosen to fly on the space shuttle *Challenger.* Jarvis was the payload specialist but was not a NASA astronaut on the spacecraft which exploded just after launch, in 1986, killing all crew members including schoolteacher Christa McAuliff.

Other astronauts

• **Alfred M. Worden** was born in Jackson. Selected for the space program in 1966, he flew on one mission, *Apollo 15,* in July of 1971. He is currently president of Jet Electronics and Technology, Inc., in Grand Rapids.

• From Cass City, astronaut **Brewster H. Shaw, Jr.,** was selected for the space program in 1978. He flew on three shuttle missions, November 1983, November 1985, and August 1989. He is currently Deputy Director, Space Shuttle, NASA Headquarters, stationed at NASA JFK Space Center in Florida.

• **Jack R. Lousma**, born in Grand Rapids, was selected for the space program in 1966. He flew on two missions, *Skylab 3,* in 1973 and one shuttle mission in March 1982. He is currently president of the Consortium for International Earth Science Information Network (CIESIN), Ann Arbor.

• Flint-born **Donald R. McMonagle** became an astronaut in 1987 and has piloted one mission, in April 1991.

• **David C. Leestma** was selected for the space program in 1980. Born in Muskegon, he was a mission specialist on two missions, in October 1984, and August 1989.

• Astronaut **Richard A. Searfoss**, born in Mount Clemens, was selected for the space program in 1991. Searfoss, a pilot, hasn't had a chance to fly any missions, yet!

Advancing knowledge of the heavens

•LeRoy-born astronomer **Forest Moulton** was the first to suggest the now accepted theory that the many smaller satellites of the planet Jupiter are actually captured asteroids.

• Another Michigan-born astronomer, **Heber Curtis** of Muskegon, theorized that nebulae were "island universes" far out in space, instead of within our own Milky Way, as most astronomers believed at the time. He was found to be right.

• Solar physicist **Eugene Parker**, a native of Houghton, made predictions about solar winds that were confirmed by the flyby of the Mariner Venus probe several years later.

◆ On October 23, 1934, at Ford Airport in Dearborn, preparations were finally completed for a very special balloon flight. Swiss-born scientist Jean Felix Piccard (brother to Auguste Piccard and uncle to Jacques) and his American wife, Jeannette Ridlong Piccard, were ready to rise into the stratosphere in a balloon. Auguste had developed sealed gondolas, which could carry people to altitudes far beyond the point where breathing was possible. The goal was to carry instruments to altitudes where they had never been before, especially to measure cosmic rays that don't penetrate the atmosphere.

Out of sight!

On the flight at Dearborn, Jean Felix was busy with the instruments, so the hydrogen-filled balloon was piloted by his wife. They reached an altitude of 57,579 feet—11 miles!—becoming the first balloonists to reach the stratosphere (and allowing Jeannette to legitimately be referred to as the first woman in space). After Jean's death in 1963, Jeannette became a consultant to NASA, and ten years later she achieved another lifelong dream by becoming one of the first group of women ordained as Episcopal priests.

◆ U.S. astronauts are honored in the Michigan Space Center located in Jackson. The space center is filled with unique exhibits about the space program, including the *Apollo 9* Command Module, a *Challenger* shuttle exhibit, space suits, satellites, a Lunar Surveyor probe, and moon rock number 15555.

Beam me up, Scottie!

Visitors are given a chance to climb into a capsule and there's an excellent display of astronaut suits, right down to the undies they wore in space and the bio-harness they used. You can also try on helmets or use the glove box scientists used to handle lunar specimens. There's a scale that will compare your earth weight to what you would weigh on Mars, Venus, Jupiter and the moon. Outside the center is a gold geodesic dome with an 85-foot Mercury Redstone Rocket at its doorstep!

SCIENTIFIC MICHIGAN

◆ "Dr. Death", the "Terminator", the "Suicide Doctor" are all names given to Dr. Jack Kevorkian, a Michigan pathologist. His name hit the headlines in 1990 after he created a "mercy machine" and assisted Janet Adkins in taking her life. Kevorkian gave Adkins his machine, which allows a terminally ill person to take his or her own life by breathing carbon monoxide through a mask. He considers it "medicide." The state of Michigan considers it a crime. A ban on assisted suicides, scheduled to go into effect on March 30, 1993, was activated on February 26—the House voted 92-10, Senate took 90 minutes to approve, 28-6, and Gov. John Engler signed it immediately. The governor and congress feared Kevorkian patients were trying to beat the ban. He had already assisted 15 suicides—three taking place during the week of February 15. If Kevorkian assists any more, he is committing a crime.

Dr. Death and his mercy machine

**Not so scientific . . .
just magical**

◆ Harry Blackstone, one of the nation's most famous magicians, bought a summer place in Colon. There he met an Australian magician, Percy Abbott, and formed a partnership. The partnership failed, but Abbott went on to establish Abbott's Magic Manufacturing Company in 1933. It's the world's largest "magic" firm today.

Harry Houdini died in a Detroit hospital October 31,1926, of peritonitis. The body was shipped to New York City for burial, which Sir Arthur Conan Doyle attended. When illusionist and magician Kreskin attempted to communicate with Harry Houdini's spirit in 1990, he selected the town of Marshall because of its American Museum of Magic. Housed in a 130-year-old building, it contains 250,000 magic-related items from the world's most famous magicians. (Kreskin had no luck.)

Nobel Prize winners

◆ Ann Arbor-born microbiologist **Thomas Weller** won the Nobel Prize for physiology and medicine in 1954 for cultivating the polio virus in a laboratory. This allowed scientists to study the viruses in a controlled "test tube" situation and eventually led to the development of the polio vaccine. He shared the prize with John Enders and Frederick Robbins. Weller was the first to grow the rubella virus in a laboratory and isolate the chicken pox virus.

Microbiologist **Alfred Hershey** was born in Owosso. His work on genetic mutations was important in the understanding of nucleic acids and gained him the 1969 Nobel Prize for physiology and medicine, shared with Salvador Luria and Max Delbrück.

Ishpeming-born chemist **Glenn Seaborg** was among the first team of scientists who worked on the early atomic bomb project at the University of Chicago. He received the Nobel Prize in 1951 for chemistry and the Enrico Fermi award in 1959 for his discovery of nine important chemical elements. Appointed by John F. Kennedy in 1961, he was the first scientist to serve as head of the Atomic Energy Commission.

Samuel Chao Chung Ting is an Ann Arbor-born physicist who was raised in China and then returned to Michigan. At Brookhaven National Laboratory he discovered subatomic particles, making the idea that matter is made up of "quarks" much more likely. He and Burton Richter shared the Nobel Prize for physics in 1976.

Did "ja" know?

Michigan has produced five Miss Americas. Detroit's **Patricia Donnelly** (1939) entered on a dare. Her singing and fiddling helped her win the crown. She went on to sing professionally and performed in two broadway plays. **Marilyn Buferd** (1946) was from Detroit, but entered as Miss California. Montague-native **Nancy Fleming** (1961) was just out of high school when she wore the Miss America crown. **Pamela Eldred** of Birmingham received her crown in 1970. In 1988, **Kaye Lani Ray Rafko**, the 1988 Miss America, encouraged people to become volunteers in cleaning up rundown schools.

MICHIGAN ORIGINALS

Each state, every region, has its own personal style of folk art. The Michigan Territory offered early artists an unbelievable palette of colors and materials from which to choose. And so it was that early Michigan art was born from the great timbers that once blanketed the territory.

Follow along as we take you on an awesome journey of Michigan's artists, artisans, craftsmen, and writers.

- From the Timbers
- Of Paints, Pottery & Printer's Ink
- From the Ground Floor Up
- Of Bricks and Stone, Wood and Glass
- Wolverine Writers
- Author, Author! Wolverine Winners
- The Cartoonists
- Michigan Residents of Note
- Thespians Take Center Stage

FROM THE TIMBERS

Lumberjacks spent idle hours whittling on small pieces of wood they picked up in the forest. From a friendly pastime emerged some truly talented woodcarvers. Many found jobs carving the majestic figureheads to grace the early Great Lakes schooners that no longer exist today. However, one prized figurehead, an Indian, which graced the bow of the *Forest Queen* (her home port was Marine City), is now on display at the Edison Institute in Dearborn.

Still others left us a collection of whimsical handiwork, such as carved spring fans and pinwheels. The lumberjack's equivalent of a ship in a bottle is the intriguing wooden ball inside a wooden cage, carved from a single piece of wood!

Then there were the puppets and marionettes. Michigan is home to a surprising number of early puppets. The Detroit Federal Theater at one time used 20 puppets carved by the Lano family between 1800 and 1860. Carved entirely of walnut, they represented traditional Italian marionette characters.

Shrine of Pines

Years after the great lumber boom, yet another artisan would see the beauty in the mighty Michigan forests. Ohio-born Oberholzer, whose name means "Upper Wood," moved to Lake County in the 1920s. He served as a hunting and fishing guide and dabbled in taxidermy. One day while searching for some pine to use as a mounting board, Oberholzer instead discovered the beauty of pine.

Locals say he could look at a stump or root and visualize the completed piece. A self-taught master woodworker, Oberholzer hand-chiseled furniture from virgin white pine stumps and roots. Scraping them with pieces of broken glass and wire brushes, he carefully rubbed each piece by hand with natural resin and pitch. He would sun-dry pieces, sometimes for years, before using them. Among his more impressive works is a table and drawers carved from a 700-pound pine tree stump, which can be seen at the Shrine of Pines Museum in Baldwin.

Indians and art schools

Julius Melchers was a German immigrant whose woodshop produced hundreds of Indian carvings in the 1870s. A gifted stonecutter, he later cut the sandstone blocks that graced Detroit City Hall and carved the figures of LaSalle, Cadillac, and Father Marquette.

Melchers opened an art school that acted as a pipeline to Europe, bringing in a variety of artists, and with them, the influence of the Barbizon School. Alumni from the school included A.B. Wenzell, a nationally known illustrator; landscape artist Joseph Gies; and Myron Barlow, who painted the Jewish history murals in Temple Beth El in Detroit. The paintings of Frederick Carl Frieseke, an Owosso resident, were featured in museums, and Ezra Winters, who grew up in Manistee, gained national prominence with his murals.

Detroit Industry **by Diego Rivera**

OF PAINTS, POTTERY & PRINTER'S INK

He was a Communist and a political activist who supported the Mexican Revolution. Before arriving in Detroit in 1932, one of Diego Rivera's most famous works was a one-wall mural entitled *Capitalist Dinner*. It depicted John D. Rockefeller, J.P. Morgan, and Henry Ford, gathered around a table dining on a ticker-tape meal.

Muralist's detail impresses Ford

Detroit's Institute of Art hired Rivera to create murals on the walls of the museum's Roman Baroque courtyard. He toured Detroit's industrial center, but it was the massive Ford River Rouge plant that seduced Rivera's imagination. He ferociously sketched for a solid month, studying each phase of the auto assembly operation. When his preliminary work for *Detroit Industry* was unveiled, the Fords were overwhelmed. Henry Ford said he was amazed the artist had managed to combine in accurate detail every aspect of his auto operation.

Gwen Frostic is one of Michigan's leading artists and conservationists. In the 1940s she began writing poetry and carving woodblocks for prints. Soon after, she established a 285-acre wildlife sanctuary and a huge gallery in Wyandotte. Visitors can watch 15 original Heidelberg presses in operation as printers prepare Frostic's prints. Michigan's governor set aside Gwen Frostic Day in honor of her many contributions to art and nature.

Woodblock prints

**Artist records
early Indians**

Artists played a very important part in recording the early history of the Michigan Territory. Artist James Otto Lewis documented the territory's early Indian life when he accompanied Governor Lewis Cass on a treaty-making tour and sketched many great Indian chiefs of the day, including Black Hawk.

Lewis's work was sent to the Smithsonian, where it was lost to fire in 1865. Luckily, lithograph copies had been made in color, making them doubly important and rare. Lewis received the grand sum of $5 for designing the seal of the City of Detroit in the mid-1850s. The same basic design is still used, although it has gone through several revisions.

Gotcha!

Terry Fugate of Kalamazoo traveled a long way to play a practical joke on art fans in the Big Apple. Fugate tacked up posters all over New York City, announcing the opening of the Jean Freeman Gallery, located at 26 West 57th Street in Manhattan. All the popular art magazines carried announcements that artist Justine Dane would be featured.

Art lovers flocked to the location only to find that it didn't exist. There was no gallery, no artist, not even any property at that address. Fugate claimed that the hoax was an authentic work of conceptual art. *The New York Times* called it a "non-gallery of non-art."

FROM THE GROUND FLOOR UP

Like father, like son

The Finnish father-and-son architect team of Saarinen and Saarinen used Michigan as their headquarters to make a great impact on American architecture. The senior Saarinen, Eliel, immigrated in 1923, after placing second in a contest to build an office building for the *Chicago Tribune*. Starting in 1932, he worked at Cranbrook Academy of Art in Bloomfield Hills, teaching architecture and designing buildings and their interiors, which played an important role in the Art Deco period. He also served as Cranbrook president.

Eero joined his father in 1936 and together they won a national design competition for the National Gallery of Art in Washington, D.C. Then they designed the Cranbrook Academy of Art and later the North Christian Church in Columbus, Indiana, famous for its 192-foot needle-thin spire.

After the 1950 death of his father, Eero continued on and designed the General Motors Technical Center at Warren, MIT's Kresge Auditorium, the TWA Passenger Terminal at Kennedy International Airport, the CBS Tower in New York, the John Deere Building in Moline, Illinois, and the Dulles International Airport terminal.

Humor in building

Architect Minoru Yamasaki has left a great impression on downtown Detroit design by using humor as a main ingredient. In 1960 his Reynolds Metal Company building was surrounded by steel mesh, a tongue-in-cheek reflection of the company's main industry. In 1962 he designed the Michigan Consolidated Gas Company skyscraper. The long, narrow windows give a rippling effect, as if one were looking through natural gas fumes! He was one of the principal designers of New York City's World Trade Center and also designed the McGregor Memorial Conference Center located at Wayne University.

One long porch

Mackinac Island started as a frontier outpost in 1780s, later becoming the fur trade hub. As civilization moved west, the rough-hewn edges of early camps were smoothed away by more refined settlers. So it was that Mackinac Island became a summer play-ground for the rich.

In 1887 a remarkable hotel was constructed on the island. The grand old lady of hotels still holds court on the island and boosts 260 rooms. Her three-story veranda overlooking the Mackinac Straits gives a spectacular view. The Grand Hotel's front porch is perhaps its most famous feature. Extending 800 feet, it is believed to be the longest porch in the world, and many consider it rocking-chair heaven.

OF BRICK AND STONE, WOOD AND GLASS

Henry Ford's interest in creative technology ran to more than his automobiles. In 1915, he constructed Fairland, a 56-room mansion, at a cost of $1.8 million, an unbelievable sum for any building at that time.

House of Ford

Henry and such friends as Thomas Edison combined their imaginations to create a functional home of the future. Underneath the home was a six-level powerhouse with massive turbines and generators. Composed of marble and brass, it was Henry's pride and joy. This made the estate self-sufficient, supplying its own power, heat, light, and even ice. A 14-foot waterfall built on the Rouge River rushing outside produced the power for the plant, which was connected to the house through a tunnel. The power plant could generate enough power to light all of Dearborn.

In the house itself each bathroom had four faucets, two for well water, and two for rainwater, both hot and cold, and, also hot air for drying hands. The marble benches poolside were heated and heating pipes were extended outside to keep the 500 birdbaths located around the estate from freezing. Other features included a central vacuum cleaner, a 65-extension telephone system, and a one-lane bowling alley.

The Dodge mansion

In Rochester, the castle-like mansion called Meadow Brook Hall was built between 1926 and 1929 by Alfred Wilson and Matilda (Dodge) Wilson, widow of the auto pioneer John Dodge. The Tudor-style mansion boasts 110 rooms patterned after the great houses of England, with 35 fireplaces, a massive great hall, solariums, a large library with hand-carved paneling, hidden staircases, antique needle-point draperies, sculptured ceilings, art works, courtyards, and gardens. It even has its own pipe organ! Some 80 percent of the original furnishings remain intact.

A three-way foot bridge?

How many directions do you need to take on a bridge, anyway? Apparently bridge makers in Midland thought three was a good number. The unique bridge, constructed in 1981, is located in Chippewassee Park. The bridge spans the Tittabawassee and Chippewa rivers and connects three different shorelines. The three walkways meet in the middle where they form a hub of benches overlooking the merging rivers.

Fence made of bottles

In Waters, once known as Bradford Lakes, there was a great fence made of bottles. Contructed by logger Henry Stephens, the fence measured 2 feet high by 200 feet long and was made of 15,000 whisky and beer bottles. Stephens also lined his entire basement with bottle caps, creating a mosaic pattern with the names of his lumbering buddies hidden in the design.

The RenCen has its own zip!

The Renaissance Center was constructed in downtown Detroit in the 1970s and is so massive that the U.S. Postal Service has even assigned it a personal zip code! Nicknamed "RenCen" by locals, who don't like to spend a lot of time chitchatting, the center was backed by 51 businessmen such as Henry Ford II, who hoped to pump new life into the downtown area. It worked.

The RenCen is actually four, 39-story semi-octagonal, steel-framed office towers that surround the 73-story, 1,400-room Detroit Plaza Hotel (reportedly the tallest hotel in the world). Made of glass and concrete, it is home to over 70 shops, four movie theaters, and a parking area that can take care of 6,000 cars. (Don't forget where you park in this place!)

There are two glass-encased elevators offering a spectacular view of either the Detroit River or Windsor, Ontario, depending which side you choose. If you get tired of shopping and walking, take a break in one of the revolving lounges on the top floor.

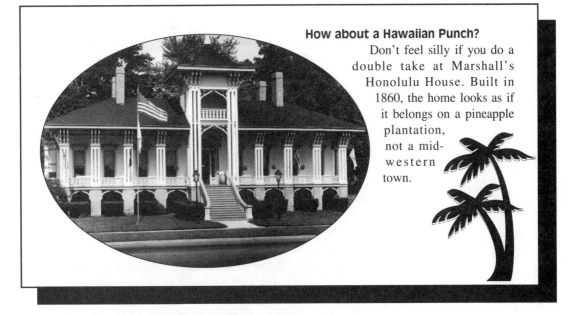

How about a Hawaiian Punch?
Don't feel silly if you do a double take at Marshall's Honolulu House. Built in 1860, the home looks as if it belongs on a pineapple plantation, not a mid-western town.

WOLVERINE WRITERS

To each his own

Author James Fenimore Cooper wrote *Oak Openings*, a story set in the wilderness during the War of 1812. With it Cooper became one of the first authors to pen a story using the Michigan Territory as a setting. Describing the forests that towered into the clouds, Cooper wrote, "But God created the woods and the themes bestowed by His bounty are inexhaustible."

Another early author was not as enthralled with the rough new country. Caroline Kirkland had emigrated from New York and settled in Pinckney. She is said to have considered her neighbors coarse and shallow, going public with those thoughts in an 1839 collection of stories called *A New Home*.

Fiction with frostbite

Atwood is a world away from the Klondike, but that territory became the topic of some of Michigan author Rex Beach's best works. He wrote *The Spoilers* in 1906 and, in 1913, *The Iron Trail*. He also wrote novels set in New York City and Florida but is best remembered for his stories about life on the frozen tundra.

History does not repeat itself

Indiana author Ross Lockridge and his family rented a cottage on Lake Shore Drive in Manistee, in August of 1945. It was during this stay that Lockridge revised the final version of his monumental novel *Raintree County*.

Twenty years earlier another member of the literary community had selected the same location for a family vacation. Stuart Pratt Sherman, editor of the *Cambridge History of American Literature*, had stayed at the same cottage with his wife. Unfortunately, on August 20, 1926, their canoe capsized and, while they were swimming to shore, Sherman, only 44, had a heart attack and died on the beach.

Author can't escape mischievous past

Ringold Wilmer Lardner, Sr., better known as "Ring" Lardner, continues to be a local hero in Niles years after his death. Lardner started his writing career by covering sports for the *Niles Sun*. Among his best-known works is *You Know Me, Al: A Busher's Letters*. Published in 1916, it is considered among the finest fictional stories about baseball. He later took a tongue-in-cheek look at the literary world in *How to Write Short Stories*.

Fond of his hometown, he is quoted as having said, ". . . we didn't have no telephones and neither did anybody else and those was the happiest days of my life." A plaque designates his childhood home and Niles has a Ring Lardner Junior High School. The Trinity Episcopal Church is the proud owner of a piece of wood, once part of the church organ, which bears the initials "RL" carved by the author himself during his more mischievous days.

The apple doesn't fall far from the tree. Lardner's son and namesake, Chicago-born Ring Wilmer Lardner, Jr., made his own mark as a screenwriter. In 1942, he won an Oscar for *Woman of the Year* and another in 1970 for the hit movie *M*A*S*H*.

Guest did a heap o' living in Detroit

Although not born in Detroit, Edgar Guest emigrated with his family from England to the Motor City as a young boy. Often criticized for his sentimental verse, his rhymes became popular nationally through his syndicated newspaper column. *A Heap o' Livin'*, published in 1916, was a best-seller. A popular Detroit radio host, Guest was on the air from 1931 to 1942.

Eat, drink, and be Mary

Most people love to eat food, and some even like to write about it. Albion-born author Mary Frances Kennedy excelled in the latter and published *Serve It Forth* in 1937. The book began a career writing "about eating, and about what to eat, and about people who eat." During her lifetime, Kennedy published 26 works including her famous translation of an important French publication, *Physiology of Taste*.

Scattergood Baines had Michigan roots

Clarence Budington Kelland is better known as "Bud" Kelland to his readers. The story *Mark Tidd* earned him great recognition; however, it was the Portland native's creation of Scattergood Baines that made him a success. The character was a Yankee promoter who was the subject of hundreds of short stories and one novel.

Kelland's serials were favorites of *Saturday Evening Post* readers. (So popular, indeed, that the publication depended on Kelland's stories to boost sagging summer circulation.) However, Kelland's stories were so similar it is said that even he mixed up the characters! His popular novel *Mr. Deeds Goes To Town* was made into a movie in 1936. Other serials that were expanded into books include, *Arizona, Valley of the Sun, Sugar Foot Appearance, Dangerous Angel*, and *Murder Makes an Entrance*.

Medical community gets bad diagnosis

Paul Henry DeKruif's first book, *Our Medicine Man*, was published in 1922 and scolded the medical profession for what DeKruif considered its ignorant flaws. The book claimed the medical profession had turned commercial, and even featured characters who resembled medical leaders of the time. It was a personal crusade which would surface in many of the Zeeland native's later works.

In 1926, the Ph.D. from the University of Michigan published *Microbe Hunters*, a book that challenged the gap between medical discovery and practical applications of some cures and preventions. It became a major best-seller. Other works by DeKruif include *Hunger Fighters, Life Among the Doctors*, and *A Man Against Insanity*.

From Mackinac Island to Rome

Author Constance Woolson grew up in a prominent New Hampshire family and enjoyed all the trappings of wealth. Her summers were spent at Mackinac Island and her mother's uncle, James Fenimore Cooper, helped fan the flames of her imagination. She based her most famous book, *Anne*, on the resort island. Written in 1879, the story was a featured series in *Harper's Weekly* and eventually sold 57,000 copies.

Woolson traveled throughout her life, and in 1880, while in Florence, Italy, she became acquainted with author Henry James. It was a friendship that lasted for the rest of her life. In 1894, after fighting influenza for an extended period and battling depression, Woolson either jumped or fell to her death from the second-story of a building in Venice, Italy. She is buried in Rome.

Horses snooze during speech practice

Will Carleton is known as the "Balladeer of the Simple Life." He is best known for "Over the Hill to the Poor House," published in 1873. The Hudson resident said he often practiced his speeches on farm animals and at times put the horses to sleep! It is not known what those speeches did to human audiences. You be the judge:

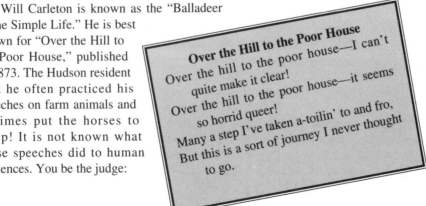

Over the Hill to the Poor House

Over the hill to the poor house—I can't quite make it clear!
Over the hill to the poor house—it seems so horrid queer!
Many a step I've taken a-toilin' to and fro,
But this is a sort of journey I never thought to go.

Poet of the Chicago slums

❧ Following the publication of *The Man With the Golden Arm*, Detroit author Nelson Algren was better known as the "Poet of the Chicago Slums." The realistic novel about drug addiction in Chicago was turned into a 1955 movie starring Frank Sinatra. In 1956, Algren wrote *A Walk on the Wild Side*.

No royalties for popular child author

❧ In 1865, Litchfield grammar-school student Rose Hartwick Thorpe happened upon a story in *Peterson's Magazine* entitled *Love and Loyalty*. Set in the English Civil War, it tells the story of a young Cavalier sentenced by the Puritans to be shot as a spy when the evening curfew bell is rung. He is saved by a young woman who runs to the belfry and wraps herself around the bell clapper so that it cannot ring.

Thorpe turned the story into a poem, "Curfew Must Not Ring Tonight," which became an immediate favorite. Although it was an international success, Thorpe received no more than her original payment for her effort. As an adult, Rose Thorpe continued to write and later moved with her family to San Antonio, Texas. There she was inspired to produce another favorite, "Remember the Alamo." She died on her 89th birthday in 1939.

Michigan's biggest bookstore

Detroit's John K. King bookstore is a bookworm's paradise. There's four floors filled with over one million used and rare books, prints and paintings, making it the biggest bookstore in the state. The store once possessed the original deed to Mackinac Island. The deed is long gone, but the bookstore maintains its uniqueness. The store manager is nuts about anything to do with moose, and the store is guarded by Sparky, the awesome attack dog.

Priest-turned-author

❧ William X. Kienzle, after twenty years as a parish priest and 12 years as the editor of *Michigan Catholic*, left the priesthood and became a mystery writer. His primary character is the thoughtful priest Father Koesler, first featured in *The Rosary Murders*, which became a film starring Donald Sutherland in 1987. Each year a new Father Koesler novel is published.

A study on violence

❧ Joyce Carol Oates's work often presents a look at violence in contemporary American society. A professor of English at the University of Detroit, she used Detroit as the setting for many of her stories. She produced the novels *Them* in 1969 and *Wonderland*, in 1971. The title of her 1990 book, *Because It Is Bitter and Because It Is My Heart*, takes its title from a Stephen Crane poem of the same name. Oates has written nonfiction and poetry under the pen name Rosemond Smith.

The author was a murderer

❧ Jack Abbott, who also wrote as Jack Eastman, was at one time the toast of the New York literary world. Led by controversial author Norman Mailer, Abbott was touted as an important new literary force. He was, in fact, a cold-blooded murderer and con artist.

Born in Oscoda in 1944, Abbott spent all but nine months of his adult life in prison. After a violence-filled youth he was arrested at 18 and placed in the Utah State Penitentiary, where he killed an inmate in 1966. He escaped in 1971 and was free for six weeks, during which time he robbed a Denver bank.

Once recaptured he was placed in maximum security where he filled the hours by reading. In 1977, he read about Norman Mailer's current book, *The Executioner's Song*, a true story about death-row inmate Gary Gilmore. Abbott began writing Mailer long letters detailing the torture and abuse he was suffering as an inmate. Mailer pushed Abbott's letters to publishers, claiming they were works of literary genius. Random House placed Abbott under contract to write a book called *In the Belly of the Beast*.

Eventually Mailer and others successfully campaigned for Abbott's early release because of his status as "an important new writer." In June 1981, Abbott was transferred to a halfway house. At once he was embraced by New York's literary world.

Abbott's true personality raised its ugly head just one month later on July 18, 1981, when he got into an argument with a young waiter. Abbott viciously stabbed him to death, then fled. He was apprehended working in an oil field in Louisiana. Norman Mailer (who still hadn't gotten the message or more likely refused to believe he had been duped) appeared at Abbott's trial, calling for a light sentence and saying, "Culture is worth a little risk." Abbott was sentenced to 15 years to life, after finishing the remaining eight years of his previous sentence in Utah. Unfortunately, the trial pushed Abbott's book to best-seller status.

AUTHOR, AUTHOR! WOLVERINE WINNERS

Jay Norwood "Ding" Darling was a man ahead of his time and is known as the "Father of Conservation." He won two Pulitzer Prizes for editorial cartoons. The cartoonist grew up in Norwood before going to work for the *Des Moines Register*. He stayed with the Iowa paper for almost his entire career, 1906 to 1949.

Ding and the Pulitzers

In 1917, his cartoons went into syndication, with 135 papers featuring the strip. He chose national events and human weaknesses as topics for his work. His concern for conservation led him to help establish wildlife preservation laws, migratory waterfowl refuges and soil conservation.

Hemingway did more than write in Michigan

Soon-to-be author Ernest Hemingway as a young man spent the summer of 1919 in Petoskey, often going fishing with friends. That activity in itself is innocent enough, but one day the trip home got Hemingway and his buddies in trouble. While heading back to Petoskey at the day's end, the group decide to shoot out the streetlights in little Boyne City! Little did the angry residents know that someday they would figure in biographies of the Illinois-born Nobel Prize novelist.

More Michigan Pulitzer Prize winners

Poet **Theodore Huebner Roethke** used the cycles of nature as the base for many of his works. Saginaw-born, he won a Pulitzer Prize in 1954 for *The Waking: Poems 1933-53* and later won a Bollingen Award for *Words for the Wind*. His wife published a sensuous collection of poems posthumously, including "The Far Fields."

Ray Stannard Baker was a Pulitzer Prize-winning author who was published under two names. As Baker, *Woodrow Wilson: Life and Letters* earned him a Pulitzer in 1940. The Lansing-born writer was friends with Wilson and had served as his assistant. As David Grayson, he wrote seven volumes of essays, of which the best known is the 1907 volume entitled *Adventures of Contentment*.

Pulitzer-Prize winning author **Bruce Catton** served as senior editor of the *American Heritage Magazine*, but his forte is the Civil War. He wrote 13 books on the topic, on which he is considered an expert. In 1953, he was awarded the Pulitzer for *A Stillness at Appomattox*. Other works include *Grant Takes Command* and *Waiting for the Morning Train*. Catton, raised in Benzonia, became fascinated as a child with the town's Civil War memorial.

Award winners children love

The two top awards in children's literature are the Caldecott Medal, for a picture book, and the John Newbery Award for a young adult book.

Chris VanAllsburg, both author and illustrator, was born in Grand Rapids. He won Caldecott Medals for two best picture books in four years—*Jumanji* and *The Polar Express*.

Why Mosquitoes Buzz in People's Ears earned New Era author **Verna Norberg Aardema Vugteveen** a 1976 Caldecott Medal.

A Door in the Wall is author **Marguerite Loft DeAngeli's** best-known work, earning her a Newbery Award in 1950. Born in Lapeer on March 14, 1889, she died almost 100 years later.

Ann Arbor resident **Nancy Willard** received the Newbery Award in 1982 for her work *A Visit to William Blake's Inn: Poems for Innocent and Experienced Travelers*.

THE CARTOONISTS

Father of motion picture cartoons

Spring Lake-born cartoonist Winsor McCay was a pioneer of motion picture animation. After spending 15 years as a cartoonist for the *Cincinnati Commercial Tribune*, he introduced to the New York newspaper audience two early comic strips, "Dreams of Rarebit Fiend" and, his most famous, "Little Nemo in Slumberland."

In the early 1900s, McCay hand-colored over 4,000 drawings on 35-mm film for Little Nemo. Touring the vaudeville circuit, he presented the animated film, illustrating his monologues by hastily sketching as the story unfolded. Between 1912 and 1914 he created *The Story of the Mosquito* and *Gertie the Dinosaur*, then prepared between 6,000 and 10,000 sketches each, on transparent rice paper! Although lasting only minutes, the films were perfectly timed to respond to McCay's on-stage presentation. After documenting the sinking of the *Lusitania* in the same fashion, McCay returned to his first love, cartooning.

Grand Rapids cartoonist Dick Calkins was dreaming of space travel when automobiles were still a novelty. Born in 1895, he had an imagination ahead of his time. Calkins created "Buck Rogers," one of the first intergalactic heroes and all-round good guys. Calkins drew the cartoon strip, which soon became a series of novels, from 1929 through 1947. He later wrote stories for those great *Red Ryder Comic Books* in the 1950s. Even in the 1990s, Buck Rogers still appears in games, novels, and syndicated TV shows.

Dreams of space travel

Capone's antics drove artist to create "Dick Tracy"

Cartoonist Chester Gould's anger toward Prohibition gangsters such as the notorious Al Capone lead to the creation of the invincible comic-strip detective, "Dick Tracy." The sharp-nosed detective came to life while Gould was living in Chicago in 1931. But Tracy was introduced to the reading public by way of the *Detroit Daily Mirror* on October 4, 1931, in the strip shown here.

Eventually the strip was carried by almost 1,000 newspapers and read by an estimated 65 million people. Gould retired in 1977, but Dick Tracy lives on in the pen of a new cartoonist. Warren Beatty brought Tracy to the big screen in the colorful 1991 movie that also starred Detroit-born Madonna as Breathless Mahoney.

MICHIGAN RESIDENTS OF NOTE

Edgar Lee Masters came to Spring Lake while still practicing law in Chicago. Allegedly Masters worked on his masterpiece, *Spoon River Anthology*, while sitting on a cement bench on the lakefront. The work was published in 1915 and two years later he purchased a large farm house on Fruitport Road. It was there Masters penned *Toward the Gulf*, another collection of poetry.

A masterpiece while sitting on a bench

Arts center just for kids

Dr. Joseph Maddy, an accomplished musician, and professor at the University of Michigan, set out to show educators that school-age children could become outstanding musicians. In 1927, he organized two concerts for school administrator conventions in Detroit and Dallas that were extremely well received. Vowing to establish a place where students could gather in the summer to play music, he and Thaddeus Giddings purchased an old hunting lodge south of Traverse City and opened the National High School Orchestra Camp in 1928. It was

the nation's first music-oriented summer camp, and is still the best-known, biggest, and most successful in the nation. Today it's known as Interlochen Arts Camp, a part of the Interlochen Center for the Arts. Each summer over 1,400 students gather from all over the world to immerse themselves in every facet of the arts from music and dance to creative writing.

Interlochen Arts Academy

In 1962, Dr. Maddy finally achieved his goal of total education, art plus academics, when he established the Interlochen Arts Academy. Today, this unique, full-time boarding school is the best of its kind in the nation. Tuition runs about $14,500 per school year for the 430 students who come from every state and 13 countries. With 260 on the faculty, it's no wonder that there have been 23 Presidential Scholars at the academy since the award was established by President Carter in 1979—more than at any other high school in the nation. The schools 50,000 alumni include such well-known performers as Meredith Baxter, Sean Young, Linda Hunt, Tovah Felshuh, Jessye Norman, Peter Erskine, and Tom Hulce. Music alumni play in all the nation's major symphonies, and writing students have won over 250 awards in the last ten years. If Dr. Maddy were alive today, he'd be more than pleased with his world-class creation.

THESPIANS TAKE CENTER STAGE

Life in Michigan began with the Indians and later the soldiers. It was the officers at Fort Detroit who are credited with organizing the first amateur troupe to perform in the state. In 1798 they produced *The Rivals*, *The Mock Duke*, and other favorites for their wives. These homemade productions were presented until about 1830.

Places, please

The first professional theater opened in Detroit about 1849. It was later called the Metropolitan and then the Comique. As they say, the show must go on, and when the building was destroyed by fire in 1853, another was built on the spot. It was used later as a livery stable.

Early actors grace Michigan stage

Lawrence Barrett, a tragedian, received his first role at the age of 15 with a stock company playing at the Metropolitan. Barrett, whose real name was Brannigan, quit his clerking job at Sheldon's Dry Goods to join the troupe. He developed into one of America's finest actors.

The Temple Theatre was constructed by a joint effort of the Shriners of Saginaw Valley and the W.S. Butterfield Theaters in 1926. Called the showplace of northeastern Michigan, it seated 2,196, the largest theater outside of Detroit. It boasted plush carpets, red velvet seats, and a huge domed ceiling. There was even a huge crystal chandelier in the lobby.

Theater was a showplace

An original Barton organ, purchased for $15,000 in 1927, filled the theater with music and, in more recent years, the only 70-mm screen in the state hung over the arched stage. In 1977 the theater closed, only to be reopened in 1980 dressed in its original splendor, thanks to efforts by local civic organizations.

Special effects thrill audiences

Michigan theaters offered everything from blood-and-thunder "dramas" to light-hearted comedies. One such production, *One of the Bravest*, had several people rescued from a burning building, using real horses and fire engines. In another play, a real steam train, "steam hissing from the boiler, sparks flyin' " crossed a stage! Not to be outdone, another production featured an explosion of a Mississippi steamboat. It was considered the greatest special effects feat of its day.

In a local schoolhouse, the rituals for the Order of Knights of Pythias (which was later founded in Washington, D.C.) were written by Justus H. Rathbone, a schoolteacher, between 1858-61. The idea for the order developed during long winters on Lake Superior shore, when, to pass away idle hours, the teacher presented theatricals in the school building, among them a dramatization of the friendship of Damon and Pythias. The school has been preserved as a Knights of Pythias Shrine.

Knights of Phythias

Bonstelle helps theater grow

Although she was christened Laura Justine Bonstelle, as the story goes, a typesetter's error changed her name to Jessie. Born in 1871, her mother transferred her dreams of life on stage to her daughter, who proved to be a natural performer. By the time she was two, Bonstelle began reciting temperance verses at church. She appeared on stage in Howell in 1886, under the auspices of family friend Dr. Edward D. Stair.

Bonstelle moved into theater management and was soon hiring and firing actors, staging productions, directing, and acting. She proved to be a hard-nosed business woman with a flair for picking out talent. On her stages many now-famous actors got their start, such as William Powell, Frank Morgan, and Katherine Cornell. In 1925, with backing from Detroit businessmen, she opened the Bonstelle Playhouse.

America's first professional playwright

Detroit playwright, Howard Bronson Crocker, has the distinction of being American's first professional playwright. Born in 1842, he wrote 20 plays, many of them portraying the life-styles and customs of the upper class. His most famous play—*Shenandoah*—was written in 1888.

Music House offers something for everyone

Even those with a tin ear should enjoy the Music House in Acme, with a song in their heart. Housed in a granary constructed in 1905, the Music House contains a collection of music boxes, nickelodeons, and organs. Considered a showcase for automatic musical instruments dating from the 1880s, it includes one of the largest pipe organs ever built. The 1922 Amaryllis organ (shown here), built in Antwerp, Belgium, is 30 feet wide. It's one of the few organs of this type to survive the world wars.

CALENDAR OF EVENTS DAY BY DAY

If there is an asterisk (*) after an item, check the index in this AWESOME ALMANAC for more information.

JANUARY

1 C.W. Post created first batch of Postum 1895 Battle Creek *

Awesome Michigan Wolverines won first Rose Bowl ever played, 49-0 1902

Jazz musician Milt Jackson born 1923 in Detroit

Poet-essayist Louis Edward Sissman born in Detroit 1928

No-fault divorce went into effect in Michigan 1972

2 Jim Bakker, TV evangelist imprisoned for fraud, born in Muskegon 1939 *

C. R. Wharton, Jr., became the first African-American to be president of a major, predominantly white university when he took charge of Michigan State 1970

4 Stevens T. Mason, Michigan's "Boy Governor," died at age 31, in New York 1843*

Actor Richard Stahl born in Detroit 1932

6 Entertainer/actor/TV producer Danny Thomas born in Deerfield 1914 *

Auto executive/author John Zachery DeLorean born in Detroit 1925 *

7 Orchard Lake Scotsmen formed the first curling club and played their first match 1832

8 "Okie" Johnson declared winningest high school coach

9 Sportscaster Dick Enberg born in Mt. Clemens 1935

10 Author-poet Philip Levine (pseud: Edgar Poe) born in Detroit

11 Territory of Michigan formed with Detroit as capital, 1805

13 Supreme Court Justice Potter Stewart born in Jackson 1915

14 Ford introduced moving assembly line. What previously took $12\frac{1}{2}$ hours will take 93 minutes in one year *

15 Industry uproar when Henry Ford gives workers wage of $5 for an 8-hour day. Average was $2.34 for 9 hours *

16 Screenwriter/producer Stirling Silliphant born in Detroit 1918

17 Auto executive Harry Herbert Bennett born in Ann Arbor 1892

Durant (for Buick), Ford, Briscoe (for Maxwell), and Olds meet to discuss merger *

19 Baseball professional Christopher Andrew Sabo born 1962 in Detroit

20 Baseball executive Walter Owen Briggs, Jr., born in Detroit 1912

Comedian Arte Johnson of "Laugh In" fame born in Benton Harbor 1934

21 Author-murderer Jack (Rufus Jack Henry) Abbott born 1944 in Oscoda *

Motown singer Aretha Franklin became first female inducted into the Rock and Roll Hall of Fame, 1987 *

22 Actress Piper Laurie born Rosetta Jacobs in Detroit 1932

24 Football coach Jerry Burns born in Detroit 1927

Fashion designer Dominic Rompollo born in Detroit 1935

25 Ann Arbor, a 13-year-old city, won the bid for the location of the University of Michigan 1827 *

Grand Rapids became the first city in the nation to add fluoride to its drinking water 1945 *

Detroit Tigers' Hank Greenberg is first Jewish player elected to Hall of Fame 1956 *

26 Michigan, the 26th state, joins the Union as a free state, 1837 *

Kalamazoo dentist invented electric drill 1875, but it's too heavy for commercial use *

Actress Joan Leslie born in Detroit 1925

Religious leader Thomas J. Gumbleton born 1930 in Detroit

27 Nobel Prize physicist Samuel Chao Chung Ting born in Ann Arbor 1936 *

29 American Baseball League is formed; it includes a Detroit team, 1900*

Actor Tom Selleck, star of "Magnum, P.I.," born 1945 in Detroit

Golf professional Donna Marie Caponi born 1945 in Detroit

30 Actor David Wayne born in Traverse City 1914 *

Comedian Dick Martin of "Rowan and Martin's Laugh-In" born in Battle Creek 1922 *

Great Wallendas fell in Detroit Coliseum killing two and paralyzing one 1962

31 Baseball player Al Buckenberger was born 1861 in Detroit

31 Engineer Harold Louis Humes born in Marquette 1900

FEBRUARY

2 Actress Elaine Stritch born 1928 in Detroit

Supermodel Christie Brinkley (Mrs. Billy Joel) born 1953 in Monroe

3 Thomas Alva Edison printed first newspaper on a train, while traveling between Port Huron and Detroit 1862 *

Baseball Hall of Famer Larry MacPhail born in Cass City 1890 *

4 Aviation hero Charles Lindbergh born in Detroit 1902 *

Actor William Talman, the DA or "Perry Mason" from 1957-66, born 1915 in Detroit

U.S. Senator Donald Wayne Riegle, Jr., born 1938 in Flint

Rock star Alice Cooper (real name: Vincent Furnier) born in Detroit 1948 *

5   Football player Craig Morton born in Flint 1941
6   Author/educator Walter Boughton Pitkin born 1878 in Ypsilanti
7   Astronaut Alfred M. Worden born in Jackson 1932 *
    Boxer Milton McCrory born in Detroit 1962
8   Light heavyweight boxing champ Ad Wolgast born in Cadillac 1888
    Fire erupted in State Building in Lansing and burned for two days, 1951
9   Attorney/hockey executive John Augustus Ziegler, Jr., born in Grosse Pointe 1934
    Coldest day ever recorded in Michigan occurred 1934 at Vanderbilt. It was a frigid minus 51° Fahrenheit
    Singer Barbara Lewis born in South Lyon 1944
10 Actor Robert Wagner born in Detroit 1930 *
    Actor Richard P. Anderson born in Midland 1946
11 Kathleen DuRoss Ford (third wife of Henry Ford II) born in Belding 1940
    3-cent Land-Grant Colleges stamp issued at East Lansing 1955 *
12 Fort St. Joseph under Spanish flag for a day in 1781 *
14 Teacher/historian/author Edmund George Love born in Flushing 1912
    Michigan governor declares 8-day bank holiday to keep banks from folding 1932
    Union Trust lacked funds to reopen, so banks were closed to prevent run 1933
15 Football coach/businessman Earl H. "Red" Blaik born in Detroit 1897
    Astronaut Roger B. Chaffee born in Grand Rapids 1935 *
    Motown songwriter Brian Holland of Dozier and Holland born in Detroit 1941
16 Director Robert Joseph Flaherty born 1884 in Iron Mountain
    Singer and Palm Springs, California, Mayor Sono Bono of Sonny and Cher born in Detroit 1935 *
17 Actress Martha Henry born in Detroit 1938
18 The Detroit Boat Club, oldest existing yacht club, in US, formed 1839
    Private Eddie Slovik, executed for desertion in WWII, born in Detroit 1920 *
19 Singer/composer Smokey Robinson born in Detroit 1940 *
21 Hall of Fame owner for 44 years of the Boston Red Sox, Tom Yawkey, born in Detroit 1903
    Black Nationalist leader Malcolm X who grew up in Lansing, assassinated 1965 *
22 National Ski Association of America founded in Ishpeming 1904 *
    Cadillac-born boxer Ad Wolgast won lightweight boxing title 1910
23 Government official/manufacturer Roy Dikeman Chapin born in Lansing 1880 *
    Governor G. Mennen "Soapy" Williams born 1911 in Detroit *
25 Actor Christopher George born in Royal Oak 1929
26 A law was passed in 1809 to establish school districts for the poor, but nothing was done.

Pair of draft horses pulled the greatest load ever, 47 tons, near Ewen, 1893
Actress Betty Hutton born in Battle Creek 1921 *
Singer Mitch Ryder (William S. Levise, Jr.) born 1945 in Detroit
27 Famed aircraft designer Clarence Leonard Johnson born in Ishpeming 1910
    Actor Guy Mitchell born in Detroit 1927
    James Leo Herlihy, author of *Midnight Cowboy,* born in Detroit 1927
28 Author Robert Allen Cromie born in Detroit 1909
    Architect/engineer John Gerard Dinkeloo born in Holland 1918
29 Astronaut Jack R. Lousma born in Grand Rapids 1936 *

MARCH

1   Congressman Albin M. Bentley shot in U.S. House of Representatives 1954
2   Writer Paul Henry DeKruif born in Zeeland 1890*
    First teach-in held, at University of Michigan, 1965
3   Author/journalist Ringold Wilmer "Ring" Lardner born 1885 in Niles *
    Isle Royale National Park authorized by Congress 1931 *
    Automotive journalist Robert W. Irvin born 1933 in Highland Park
4   Co-founder of Amway, Richard Martin DeVos, born 1926 in Grand Rapids
    Supremes singer Mary Wilson born in Detroit 1944 *
6   Football/wrestling star Gustave Sonnenberg born 1889 in Ewen *
    Entertainer, TV announcer, and major advertising image Ed McMahon born 1923 in Detroit *
    Imprisoned banker Ivan Boesky, who paid $50-million fine, born in Detroit 1937
7   Unemployed stage Hunger March riot at Detroit Ford plant, 4 killed, 1932
8   Secretary of the Treasury George Humphrey born in Cheboygan 1890
    Musician Sam Koontz Donahue born 1918 in Detroit
9   Symphony conductor Thomas Schippers born in Kalamazoo 1930
    Comedian Marty Ingels born in Brooklyn 1936
10 Musician Bunny DeBarge of the DeBarge family born in Grand Rapids 1955
12 Western novelist Stewart Edward White born in Grand Rapids 1873
    Broadway producer Roger Stevens born in Detroit 1910
13 First agricultural college in nation opens at East Lansing 1857 *
14 John Newbery Medal winner Marguerite DeAngeli, born in Lapeer 1889 *
    William Clay Ford, son of Edsel, born in Detroit 1925 *
15 Famed botanist Liberty Hyde Bailey born in South Haven 1858

Track athlete and *Chariots of Fire* author Jackson Volney Scholz born 1897 in Buchanan *

17 Postmaster General Arthur Summerfield born in Pinconning 1899 *

20 CBS executive Frank Stanton born in Muskegon 1908

U. of Michigan beat Dartmouth to win first NCAA hockey championship 1948

21 Producer/theater owner James Morton Nederlander born 1922 in Detroit

22 The nation's first regional shopping mall opened in Southfield 1954

24 New York governor and presidential candidate Thomas Dewey born in Owosso 1902 *

Viola Liuzzo of Detroit, white civil rights activist, was murdered in Selma, Alabama, 1965 *

26 Political leader William Grawn Milliken born 1922 in Traverse City

Former Supremes lead and solo singer Diana Ross born in Detroit 1944 *

Michigan State won 1979 NCAA basketball title defeating Indiana State 75-64

28 Novelist Nelson Algren (real name: Nelson Algren Abraham) born 1909 in Detroit *

Musician Thaddeus Joseph Jones born 1923 in Pontiac

29 Michigan enacted fireworks legislation in 1929 allowing cities to buy them but not individuals

30 Floyd Odlum, founder of Atlas Investment Corp. and husband of aviator Jacqueline Cochran, born 1892 in Union City *

31 Novelist Marge Pierce was born in Detriot 1936

APRIL

1 University administrator/diplomat James Burrill Angell born in Ann Arbor 1916

Ferndale incorporated with restrictions against non-English-speaking races 1918

Golfer Dan Pohl born in Mount Pleasant 1955

Voters approved, by a very narrow margin, the new constitution 1963 *

2 Political leader Orville Liscum Hubbard born 1903 in Union City

3 Grand Funk Railroad musician Mel Schacher born in Owosso 1951*

4 Actress Elizabeth Wilson born 1925 in Grand Rapids

Actress Christine Lahti born in Detroit 1950

5 B-horror film producer Roger William Corman born 1926 in Detroit

Actor Michael Moriarity born in Detroit 1941

Actor Max Gail born in Detroit 1943

6 A heavyweight prize fight in Detroit was won by James J. Jeffries when he knocked out Finnegan in the first round, 1900

GM bought Oakland Motors in 1909; it became part of the Pontiac Division in 1932 *

7 A cooking mishap led Kellogg Brothers to invent new breakfast food 1894 *

Botanist David Grandison Fairchild born in Lansing 1869

Oscar-winning film director Francis Ford Coppola born in Detroit 1939 *

Henry Ford died by candlelight 1947, the night the Rouge River flooded *

8 Author Elizabeth Bacon Custer, wife of the general, was born in Monroe 1842 *

Author Glendon Swarthout born 1918 in Pinckney *

10 Western actor Tim McCoy born in Saginaw 1891

Actor Harry Morgan, who played Col. Sherman T. Potter in "M*A*S*H," born in Detroit 1915 *

Last run of horse-drawn fire engine in Detroit 1922 *

11 Michigan infantry regiments mustered into the U.S. Army for the Spanish-American War 1898

12 First international billiards championship match held in Detroit 1859 *

Baseball player and coach Charlie Lau born in Romulus 1933

13 Henry Ford started commercial airline service from Chicago to Detroit 1925 *

14 Former President Gerald Ford's birthday celebrated though he was born in Nebraska 1913 *

Ford Motor Company produced 20 millionth auto 1931*

16 The call went out for volunteers to serve 90-day enlistments in the Civil War 1861

Author Howard Mumford Jones born in Saginaw 1892

17 Pulitzer Prize biographer Ray Stannard Baker, who also wrote under pseudonym David Grayson, born in Lansing 1870 *

Albert S. Howell of Bell and Howell born in West Branch 1879

Lions' defensive tackle Alex Karras suspended by Pete Rozelle for gambling 1963*

18 Author Rose Hartwick Thorpe born in Litchfield 1850 *

19 Nobel Prize physicist and head of the U.S. Atomic Energy Commission Glenn T. Seaborg born in Ishpeming 1912

20 UAW Union leader Walter Reuther shot through window of his Detroit home 1948 *

21 "Godfather of Punk," Iggy Pop (real name: James Newell Osterberg) born 1947 in Ann Arbor

22 Baseball player Neal Ball, born in Grand Haven 1881 *

Designer Kenneth Jay Lane born in Detroit 1932

Comedian Byron Allen born 1961 in Detroit

23 Supreme Court Justice Frank Murphy born in Harbor Beach 1890 *

Actor/producer Lee Majors born in Wyandotte 1940

24 423 Michigan soldiers leaving the South after the Battle of Vicksburg, drowned when steamer *Sultana* exploded near Memphis 1865

Basketball player Rudy Tomjanovich born in Hamtramck 1948

26 Famed golfer Leo Diegel, twice PGA champ, born in Detroit 1899

27 Director Norman Bel Geddes, father of actress Barbara Bel Geddes, born in Adrian 1893

The Rev. Tim LaHaye born in Detroit 1926

Basketball player George Gervin born in Detroit 1952

29 Congress passed law giving the right to trade with Indians only to U.S. citizens, thus leaving Michigan fur trade to John Jacob Astor, 1816*

Astronomer Forest Moulton born in LeRoy 1872 *

Football coach George Allen born in Detroit 1918*

MAY

1 Organist/composer Leo Sowerby born in Grand Rapids 1895

Michigan voted in favor of prohibition a year before it became a national mandate 1918

Psychologist/self-help author Wayne Walter Dyer born 1940 in Detroit

Songwriter Ray Parker, Jr., composer of *Ghostbusters* theme, born in Detroit 1954

2 Edgar-winning mystery novelist Charlotte Armstrong born 1905 in Vulcan

3 Five-time middleweight boxing champ Sugar Ray Robinson born in Detroit 1921 *

4 Baseball player Rick Leach born in Ann Arbor 1957

6 Rocker Bob Seger born in Ann Arbor 1945 *

Astronaut David C. Leestma born in Muskegon 1949 *

7 Attorney Marvin M. Mitchelson, famed for his "palimony" cases, born in Detroit 1928

9 Richard Byrd became first person to fly over North Pole, in plane named for Edsel Ford's daughter, 1926

Union leader Walter Reuther and wife killed in plane crash 1970 *

10 4th Michigan Cavalry captured confederate leader Jefferson Davis 1865

11 Constitutional convention heading toward statehood held at Detroit 1835

Baseball Hall of Famer Charles Leonard Gehringer born 1903 in Fowlerville *

Artificial heart inventor/surgeon Robert Jarvik born in Midland 1946

12 Auto executive Lynn Alfred Townsend born in Flint 1919

13 Teddy Roosevelt sued Marquette newspaper editor and received 6 cents in damages 1913 *

Singer/musician/songwriter Stevie Wonder born 1951 in Saginaw*

Tornadoes flattened parts of Kalamazoo 1980 *

14 Detroit citizens paraded for 10 hours to show support for the legalization of beer 1932

Astronaut Donald R. McMonagle born in Flint 1952 *

15 Golden State Warriors basketball coach Don Nelson born in Muskegon 1940

16 Hostage in Iran John Earl Graves born 1927 in Detroit

Congressman John Conyers, Jr., born in Detroit 1929

Jazz singer Betty Carter (real name: Lillie Mae Jones) born 1930 in Flint

Indiana Senator Dan Coats born in Jackson 1943

Astronaut Brewster H. Shaw, Jr., born in Cass City 1945 *

17 Louis Jolliet and Père Marquette set out from St. Ignace to hunt for "Great River" (the Mississippi) 1673 *

Evangelist Carl McIntire born 1906 in Ypsilanti

Football player Earl E. Morrall born in Muskegon 1934

18 Explorer and missionary Père Marquette, age 38, died near Ludington in 1675*

Michigan became first state to abolish death penalty in 1847 after an innocent man was hanged

19 Pneumatic hammer was invented by Detroiter Charles Brady King 1892

20 Christopher Columbus Smith, founder of Chris Craft boats, born in St. Clair 1861

Parapsychologist Edmund P. Gibson born in Grand Rapids 1898

Businessman William Hewlett of Hewlett-Packard born in Ann Arbor 1913

Baseball player Harold "Prince Hal" Newhouser born in Detroit 1921 *

Golfer Dave Hill born in Jackson 1937

Southfield native Gilda Radner, a Prime Time Player, died of ovarian cancer at 42, 1989 *

23 Radical reformer Rennie Davis of the "Chicago 7" born 1941 in Lansing

25 Forty-seven died when tornado struck Oakland County, 1896 *

Poet Theodore H. Roethke born 1908 in Saginaw*

Jesse Owens broke 3 world records and tied another at a Big Ten Conference track meet in Ann Arbor 1929

26 Baseball manager Joe Altobelli born in Detroit 1932

Baseball player Dan Roundfield born in Detroit 1953

27 Caryl Chessman, rapist, robber, and murderer who spent twelve years making his execution a public cause, born 1921 in Saint Joseph

28 Auto racer Eddy Sachs born in Detroit 1917

Actress Martha Vickers (real name: MacVicar) born 1925 in Ann Arbor

Hockey player Mark Steven Howe born in Detroit 1955 *

Baseball player Kirk Gibson born in Pontiac 1957

31 Soo Canal connecting Lakes Superior and Huron officially opened 1855 *

Lt. Col. M.V. Parker named first woman to a command a recruiting center, at Detroit 1975 *

JUNE

3 Amway co-founder Jay Van Andel born in Grand Rapids 1924*

Singer Suzi Quatro (Leather Tuscadero on TV series "Happy Days") born 1950 in Detroit

4 Massacre at Fort Michilimackinac achieved through a trick by Indians playing lacrosse 1763 *

Broadcast journalist Charles Collingwood born in 1917 in Three Rivers

Eldra "El" DeBarge of the DeBarge family born in Grand Rapids 1961

6 Fur trader Alexis St. Martin accidentally shot in abdomen on Mackinac Island, leading to important discoveries about digestion 1822

Children's author Verna Norberg Aardema born 1911 in New Era

Astronaut Richard A. Searfoss born in Mount Clemens 1956 *

8 Père Marquette reburied at St. Ignace after Indians found his grave 1677 *

Grand Rapids hosted first night ballgame 1901 *

Deadly tornadoes struck 1953, leaving 142 dead *

9 Singer Jackie Wilson born 1932 in Detroit *

10 Michigan, Illinois, and Wisconsin ratified the 19th amendment, giving women the right to vote — the first states to do so, 1919

Eugene Parker, solar wind physicist, born in Houghton, 1927 *

Football coach Chuck Fairbanks born in Detroit 1933

11 Newly named capital of territory, Detroit, burned down 1805 *

Journalist Richard Maney born in Chinook 1892

Lawyer/politician Jerry Cavanagh born in Detroit 1928

12 Author James Oliver Curwood born in Owosso 1878

Henry Ford organized Ford Motor Company with 13 stockholders; he owned 25.5 percent *

Actor Timothy Busfield born Lansing 1957

14 Michigan and adjoining lands claimed by French at a village near Sault Ste. Marie 1671

15 Thomas Well, Nobel Prize-winning immunologist, born in Ann Arbor 1915 *

16 James J. Strang, leader of a Mormon offshoot group on Beaver Islands, was murdered 1856 *

Award-winning novelist Joyce Carol Oates born 1938, in Detroit *

Outfielder Ron LeFlore born in Detroit 1952

18 Steamer *Illinois* became first ship to go through Soo Locks 1855 *

Children's author-illustrator Chris Van Allsburg born 1949 in Grand Rapids *

19 Baseball player Eddie Cicotte, a participant in the Black Sox Scandal, born in Detroit 1894 *

First movie of the sun taken 1934 at U. of M. *

Instrumentalist Mark DeBarge of the DeBarge Family born in Grand Rapids 1959

20 First wedding performed over the radio: Detroit to the USS *Birmingham*! *

Detroit race riots leave 34 dead and 700 injured 1943

22 The first Chinese woman to ever receive a medical degree, Mary Stone, granted degree at Ann Arbor 1896

Olympic Gold Medal wrestler Russell Vis born in Grand Rapids 1900 *

23 Ford sold first automobile in Detroit 1903 *

24 Chrysler Corporation received first installment of $1.5-billion loan guarantee that helped to revive the company 1980

25 Screenwriter John Richard Briley born in Kalamazoo 1925

3-cent Mackinac Bridge stamp issued at Mackinac 1958

17-cent electric auto stamp issued at Greenfield Village 1981

26 Two-time Civil War Congressional medal of Honor winner, Frank Baldwin, born in Manchester 1842

Newbery Medal-winning children's author Nancy Willard born 1936 in Ann Arbor *

27 Astronomer Heber Doust Curtis born in Muskegon 1872 *

28 Political leader Carl Milton Levin born 1934 in Detroit

Comedienne/actress Gilda Radner (Mrs. Gene Wilder) born 1946 in Detroit *

3-cent Soo Locks stamp issued at Sault Ste. Marie 1955

29 Michigan territory extended to Missouri River and up to Canada 1834

Emma Azalia Smith Hackely, musical genius at age 3, born in Detroit 1867 *

Judge-author John Donaldson Voelker born 1903 in Ishpeming *

18-cent Year of the Disabled stamp issued at Milford 1981

30 Michigan Territory organized from the northeastern section of Indiana Territory 1805

Arthur Hendrick Vandenberg, Jr., U.S. senator for 33 years and prime mover in foreign aid after World War II, born in Grand Rapids 1907

Lions football team are named through radio show 1934 *

Magician Harry Blackstone, Jr., born in Three Rivers 1934 *

Florence Ballard, an original member of the Supremes, born in Detroit 1943 *

GM unveiled first Corvette, the first plastic laminated car, 1953 *

"In Living Color" actor David Alan Grier born in Detroit 1958

JULY

3 Author Mary Frances Kennedy Fisher born in Albion 1908

Baseball player Frank Tanana born in Detroit 1953

4 Soldiers headed for Black Hawk War brought Asiatic cholera epidemic to Detroit, 1832 *

6 Michigan abolitionists join Republican Party, demanding repeal of slavery laws, 1854

Singer Della Reese born in Detroit 1932 *

7 Architect Grosvenor Atterbury born in Detroit 1869

Old-age assistance, like Social Security, approved for Michiganians 1933

8 First league baseball game held "under the lights," at Grand Rapids 1909

11 British surrender Detroit and the Stars and Stripes are raised 1796

Novelist and *Saturday Evening Post* mainstay Clarence Budington Kelland born in Portland 1881 *

Presidential aide/journalist Jerald Franklin Terhorst born 1922 in Grand Rapids

12 Actress Denise Nicholas born 1944 in Detroit

13 Hottest day ever recorded occurred in 1936 at Mio. It was a sweltering 112° Fahrenheit!

8.4-cent bulk-mail stamp featuring Steinway grand piano issued at Interlochen 1978

15 Construction began on Camp Custer (later Fort Custer) 1917

17 Fort Michilimackinac taken without a shot being fired in War of 1812 *

18 Golfer Calvin Peete born in Detroit 1942

19 Grand Haven-born shortstop for Cleveland, Neal Ball, made first unassisted triple play in major league history 1909 *

Actor Dennis Cole born in Detroit 1943

20 Misunderstood orders result in head-on railway crash at Salem, killing 30, 1907

Military leader/author George A. Lincoln born in Harbor Beach 1907

21 The First Michigan regiment fought in the Battle of Bull Run, with 6 deaths, 1861

Publisher Ralph Lane Polk born in Detroit 1911

22 Strike of copper workers seeking 8-hour day began 1913, lasted 9 months

Singer Margaret Whiting born in Detroit 1924

Director/writer Paul Joseph Schrader born 1946 in Grand Rapids

23 William A. Burt of Washington patented an early version of the typewriter 1829 *

Rioting erupts, after Detroit police raid a west side after-hours drinking club, leaving 39 dead, 1967

24 Antoine de la Mothe Cadillac, in service to Louis XIV, lands at site of Detroit and starts to build Fort Ponchartrain, 1701 *

Jockey Julie Krone, first woman to win five races in one day, born Benton Harbor 1963

3-cent Landing of Cadillac stamp issued at Detroit 1951

26 1929 Ford Roadster is driven coast to coast—backward 1930

Motown singer Mary Wells died in Los Angeles 1992 *

27 Detroit *Gazette* began publication 1817; it lasted until 1830.

Business executive Rick Inatome born in Detroit 1953

30 Automotive pioneer Henry Ford, son of Irish immigrants, born 1863 in Wayne County *

12-cent Henry Ford stamp issued at Greenfield Village 1968

Missing Teamster leader Jimmy Hoffa declared dead by Oakland County judge 1982 *

31 First railroad chartered in old Northwest Territory, granted to Pontiac and Detroit Railway, 1830. It was never built.

Last Playboy Club in U.S. shut in Lansing, ending an era 1988 *

AUGUST

2 Author/naturalist Holling Holling from Holling Corners born 1900

The first trimline phones offered to Michigan Bell customers 1965 *

Tennis player Aaron Krickstein born in Detroit 1967

3 Treaty of Greenville between Indians and General Anthony Wayne opened Michigan to settlement 1795 *

Roman Catholic Archdiocese of Detroit created 1937

4 Poet Robert Hayden, first black named Poet Laureate by Congress, born in Detroit 1913

5 Baseball player Dave Rozema born in Grand Rapids 1956

6 Musician Randy DeBarge of the DeBarge family born in Grand Rapids 1958

State of emergency canceled after two-week race riot in Detroit 1967

7 Wallace circus train collision, attributed to brake failure, in Durand 1903

Nobel Peace Prize-winning U.N. official Ralph Bunche born in Detroit 1904 *

8 Songwriter Gene Buck born 1886 in Detroit

Political leader Jim Blanchard born 1942 in Detroit

9 Congressman-then-Vice President Gerald R. Ford became first president from Michigan and first not to have been elected in the normal fashion 1974 *

11 Artist Gari Melchers, whose work was commissioned by Congress, born 1860 Detroit *

Author William Brasler born in Grand Rapids 1947

13 Organist Dave "Baby" Cortez, who had a #1 hit in 1959 with "The Whistling Organ," born in Detroit 1938

14 Nebula-winning science fiction writer Alexei Panshin born in Lansing 1940

Basketball star and HIV infected Earvin "Magic" Johnson born in East Lansing 1959 *

22-cent lacemaking stamp issued at Ypsilanti 1987

15 Pulitzer Prize novelist Edna Ferber born in Kalamazoo 1887 *

Harlow H Curtice, former president of General Motors, born in Petrieville 1893

16 First territorial governor William Hull surrendered Detroit to the British in War of 1812. Accused of cowardice and sentenced to be shot, his sentence was commuted

Sexsational singer Madonna born Bay City 1958 *

Northwest Airlines flight crashed on takeoff from Detroit, killing 156 with 1 survivor, 1987

17 *Columbia* became the first ore carrier to pass through the Soo Locks, 1855 *

Boxing promoter Jack Kearns born in Waterloo 1882

Educator Harrison Chase born in Big Rapids 1913

Henry Ford took his first airplane ride, with Lindbergh in the *Spirit of St. Louis* over Detroit 1927 *

19 Actress Colleen Moore (Kathleen Morrison) born 1902 in Port Huron

Actor Gerald McRaney of "Major Dad" born in Collins 1948

20 Radio station WWJ, owned by the *Detroit News*, began first scheduled broadcast 1920 *

21 Ransom Olds exported the first auto 1893 *

Historian/author Constance Windsor Green born in Ann Arbor 1897

22 Explorer/educator Laurence McKinley Gould born in Lacota 1896

Cadillac Company, named after the French explorer, founded in Detroit 1901 *

Musician James DeBarge of the DeBarge Family born in Grand Rapids 1963

Author George Plimpton played against the Lions in a real preseason game 1971 *

24 Gregory Jarvis, civilian astronaut killed on space shuttle *Challenger,* born in Detroit 1944 *

25 The first seeding machine was patented by Joseph Gibbons of Adrian 1840

Actor Tom Skerritt of "Picket Fences" born in Detroit 1933

26 Territorial government voted to establish the University of Michigan 1817 *

Building of the Soo Canal approved by Congress and President Fillmore 1852

27 Steamboat *Walk-in-the-Water* arrived in Detroit from Buffalo, becoming the first ship in the upper Great Lakes, 1818 *

Jazz trombonist Rayburn Wright, director at Radio City Music Hall, born in Alma 1922

29 Football player Carl Banks born in Flint 1962

30 Baseball Hall of Famer "Kiki" Cuyler born 1899 in Harrisville *

31 Michigan's first newspaper was printed 1809. It folded after the first issue

First Roman Catholic periodical in English published in Detroit 1809

SEPTEMBER

1 Novelist Rex Beach, who wrote about the Klondike, born 1877 in Atwood *

Noah would have felt at home on this day in 1914 in Bloomington—it rained 9.78" in one day!

Comedianne/actress Lily Tomlin born in Detroit 1939 *

3 Ernest Hemingway married at Horton Bay 1921 *

4 First Roman Catholic priest, Father Gabriel Richard, is elected to Congress 1823 *

U.S. Bank of Pennsylvania defaulted on payments, leaving Michigan with $5,000,000 bond debt in 1841

Henry Ford II, oldest son of Edsel, born Detroit 1917 *

Hockey player John Vanbiesbrouck born in Detroit 1963

5 Baseball player Edward Stein was born in Detroit 1869

The UP's Great Fire of 1881 became the first major disaster handled by Red Cross *

Educator Glenn Blough born in Edmore 1907

John Mitchell, President Nixon's attorney general and defender in Watergate, born in Detroit 1913 *

6 Detroit-born Leon Czolgosz assassinated President William McKinley in Buffalo, New York, 1901 *

9 English refuse to supply Indians with ammunition and lower-priced goods, at Detroit 1761

Lions move home games to Briggs Stadium 1938 *

Basketball player Daniel Majerlee born in Traverse City 1965

Basketball player B. J. Armstrong born in Detroit 1967

10 Football player Gary Danielson born in Detroit 1951

11 Former priest-turned-mystery writer William X. Kienzle born in Detroit 1928 *

13 Actress Ruth McDevitt born in Coldwater 1895

Former vice president of NBC, Emmy-winner Lester M. Crystal born 1934 in Duluth

Actor Richard Kiel (Jaws in the James Bond movies) born 1939 in Redford *

14 Boxer Stanley Ketchel born in Grand Rapids 1887

Religious leader Edmund Casimir Cardinal Szoka born 1927 in Grand Rapids

15 Michigan's first woman in Congress, Ruth Thompson, born in Whitehall 1887 *

"World's Largest Weather Vane" dedicated in Montague 1984 *

16 More than 1.5 million gallons of oil spilled into the Saginaw River 1990

19 Sgt. John Clem, age 12, served with Michigan's 22nd; was at Chickamauga 1863 *

Melvin R. Bissell of Grand Rapids patented the first practical carpet sweeper 1876 *

Military leader Hugh A. Drum born in Fort Brady 1879

First rail tunnel to go beneath water to a foreign country opened in 1891 between Port Huron and Canada

Singer Freda Payne born 1945 in Detroit

California Angel baseball player Jim Abbott born in Flint 1967

20 6-cent Père Marquette stamp issued at Sault Ste. Marie 1968

21 Auto executive Preston Thomas Tucker born in Capac 1903

Auto executive Roy Dikeman Chapin born in Detroit 1915 *

Baseball player/executive John Joseph McHale born in Detroit 1921

24 Producer Gene Corman born in Detroit 1927

26 Convention meeting at Ann Arbor rejected compromise of taking UP and giving up Toledo Strip, 1836; then promptly started to change minds

Cartoonist Winsor McCay, pioneer of motion picture animation, born 1869 in Spring *

27 Manufacturer Joy Morton born in Detroit 1855
28 1912 Olympian and international Olympics organizer Avery Brundage born in Detroit 1887
29 Detroit retaken by American General William Henry Harrison after the British evacuate, burning it in their wake, 1813 *
   Author Hal Bennett born in Detroit 1936
   Grand Funk Railroad musician, Donald Brewer, born in Flint 1948 *
30 Educator/author Paul Frederick Voelker born in Evart 1875

OCTOBER

1 Airplane manufacturer William Edward Boeing born in Detroit 1881 *
   Buick became first company to be swallowed up by GM. Olds Motors Works will follow *
   World's first mass-produced tractor made at Dearborn 1917
   Actor George Peppard born 1933 in Detroit *
4 Chester Gould's "Dick Tracy" first appeared in *Detroit Daily Mirror* 1931 *
5 Michigan's first state constitution approved by voters 1835
   Close call when nuclear accident occurs at Fermi reactor in Detroit 1966
6 Author of *Teahouse of the August Moon,* Vernon John Sneider born 1916 in Monroe
7 Show biz reporter James St. James born in Saginaw 1945
8 1871 fires sweep Midwest on same day. Chicago; Peshtigo, Wisconsin; and Holland destroyed *
9 Pulitzer Prize historian Bruce Catton born in Petoskey 1899 *
11 Religious leader James Aloysius Cardinal Hickey born 1920 in Midland
14 Speed skating and cycling champ Sheila Young born in Birmingham 1950 *
   Presidential candidate John F. Kennedy publicly proposed Peace Corps in U. of Michigan speech 1960 *
15 The passenger steamer *Alpena* sank in Lake Michigan en route to Chicago 1880 *
   Longest tow on record—4,759 miles with a Ford Model T—started this date, 1927
   4-cent Wheels of Freedom stamp issued at Detroit 1960
   Pictured Rocks National Lakeshore, Munising, became first national lakeshore 1966 *
16 Military leader William Rufus Shafter born 1835 in Kalamazoo County
   Basketball player/executive Dave DeBusschere born in Detroit 1940 *
17 First Cadillac car completed in Detroit and sold in New York 1902
   Olympic Gold Medal hockey player Ken Morrow born in Flint 1956
   Oldest twin cats of Diane Phelps of Dearborn, born this day in 1963, both died 1985
18 Actress Pam Dawber (Mrs. Mark Harmon) born 1951 in Farmington *

Boxer Tommy Hearns born in Detroit 1958
Detroit resident Sebastian Spering Kresge, founder of Kmart, died 1966 *
Chester Marcol of Hillsdale College in Michigan kicked 62-yard field goal 1969
19 Music critic/author Pitts Sanborn born in Port Huron 1878
   Journalist Russell Kirk born 1918 in Plymouth
   Lawyer and Watergate participant Herbert Warren Kalmbach born 1921 in Port Huron
21 Poet Will Carleton, creator of "Over the Hill to the Poor-House," born 1845 in Hudson *
   Double Pulitzer Prize-winning cartoonist "Ding" Darling born 1876 in Norwood *
   Advertising executive Leo Burnett born in Saint John's 1891
   Actress Joyce Randolph born in Detroit 1925
   Sleeping Bear Dunes became a national lakeshore 1970
23 Balloon altitude record set by Jean & Jeannette Piccard at Dearborn 1934 *
24 Detroit was incorporated as a city 1815
   Lions player Chuck Hughes died on field during game at Chicago 1971
27 Musician Garry Wayne Tallent of the E Street Band born 1949 in Detroit
   Earl Anthony of Battle Creek became the first bowler to earn $100,000 in one year in tournaments 1975
31 Company of Colony of Canada granted exclusive right to trade at Detroit in 1701
   Magician and escape aritist Harry Houdini, died of peritonitis in Detroit 1926 *

NOVEMBER

1 State legislature (though Michigan wasn't yet a state) met for the first time, for one day only, 1835
2 Actor Robert Armstrong of *King Kong* fame born 1896 in Saginaw
   3-cent Michigan Centenary stamp issued at Lansing 1935
   Concert pianist Ruth Laredo born in Detroit 1937
   Baseball player Tom Paciorek born in Detroit 1946
3 State's worst mine disaster occurred at Barnes-Hecker Mine, 52 men killed, 1926
   World's first car tunnel to a foreign country, between Windsor, Canada and Detroit, opened 1930 *
   Baseball player Bob Welch born in Detroit 1956
4 Retailer Sewell Avery born in Saginaw 1874
5 New constitution ratified by the voters, with many restrictions on the legislature, 1850
6 Edsel Bryant Ford, only son of Henry, born in Detroit 1893 *
   Senator Bob Griffin born in Detroit 1923
   Guitarist Glenn Frey born in Detroit 1948 *
7 Treaty with four Indian nations signed, giving U.S. right to lower eastern quarter of Michigan, 1807

Baseball player Jim Kaat, who played ball in four decades, born Zeeland 1938
9 A huge windstorm, called the Freshwater Fury, killed 270 and sank ten ore ships 1913
Football player Eugene Lipscomb born in Detroit 1931
10 Actor "Sinbad" born Benton Harbor
11 Ambassador Bridge, connecting Detroit and Windsor, Canada, dedicated 1929 *
Two-day Armistice Day Blizzard centered over Michigan begins, killing 73, 1940
12 Actor/director Richard Quine born in Detroit 1920
Actress Kim Hunter (real name: Janet Cole) born in Detroit 1922 *
Boat racer Bill Muncey born in Royal Oak 1928
14 The Dodge Brothers produced first car 1914 *
Singer/entertainer/composer Johnny Desmond born in Detroit 1921 *
16 Tony-winning dancer/actress Donna McKechnie born 1942 in Pontiac
17 American Newspaper Publishers Association organizes in Detroit 1886
18 Banker/government official Joseph Morrell Dodge born in Detroit 1890
Singer Hank Ballard born 1936 in Detroit
20 Poet John Frederick Nims born in Muskegon 1913
21 Actress Marlo Thomas, daughter of Danny Thomas and wife of Phil Donahue, born in Detroit 1943 *
26 J. B. Sutherland of Detroit received a patent for a refrigerated railway car 1867
Abolitionist and former slave Sojourner Truth died at Battle Creek 1883 *
27 No. 3 was unlucky number on Wabash Line near Seneca—20 killed in head-on collision, 1901
28 Motown founder and record producer Berry Gordy, Jr., born in Detroit 1929 *
29 French at Detroit surrender to British Roger's Rangers in 1760
Baseball player Bill Freehan born in Detroit 1941
30 Telegraph was used for first time in Michigan, between Detroit and Ypsilanti 1847

DECEMBER

1 Poet Julia A. Moore, called Sweet Singer of Michigan, born 1847
2 Elizabeth Chandler organized the first antislavery society in state, 1830
Political leader Charles Coles Diggs, Jr., born in Detroit 1922
Emmy- and Tony-winning actress Julie Harris born Grosse Pointe Park 1925 *
First transatlantic telephone wedding took place in Detroit 1933
3 Educator/editor/author/priest Francis X. Canfield born in Detroit 1920
Syd Howe becoms first pro hockey player to score six goals in one game 1944
Plane crash at Metropolitan Airport killed 8, 1990

4 Baseball player Ed Reulbach born in Detroit 1882
Author Dorothy Lyons born in Fenton 1907
Nobel Prize microbiologist Alfred Hershey born Owosso 1908 *
Financier Robert Lee Vesco born in Detroit 1935
Philanthropist Stewart Rawlings Mott born in Flint 1937
5 Catcher Frank E. "Mike" Bowerman born in Romeo 1868
Founder/publisher of *Esquire,* Arnold Gingrich born in Grand Rapids 1903
6 Boxer George "Kid" Lavigne born in Saginaw 1869
Comedian Wally Cox, best known for TV show "Mr. Peepers," born in Detroit 1924
7 Actress Ellen Burstyn born in Detroit 1932 *
8 Singer/songwriter Bernie (Bernard Leo) Krause of The Weavers born 1938 in Detroit
9 Jazz musician Donald Byrd born 1932 in Detroit.
11 Fire at Lansing's Hotel Kerns kills 34, 1934
Political activist /California congressman and ex-husband of Jane Fonda,Tom Hayden born 1939 in Royal Oak
Author of "Ninety-two in the Shade," Thomas Francis McGuane born in Wyandotte 1939
13 Singer Ted Nugent born in Detroit 1949 *
14 Second meeting at Ann Arbor chose to accept the compromise of accepting the UP in exchange for the Toledo Strip, opening the way to statehood, 1836 *
Attorney Mark Edward Schlussel born in Detroit 1940
Singer Joyce Vincent born in Detroit 1946
15 Manufacturer of semi-trailers Harvey Charles Fruehauf born in Grosse Pointe 1893
16 Poet Faye Kicknosway born 1936 in Detroit
17 Musician Sy (Melvin James) Oliver born 1920 in Battle Creek
18 Chairman of Stroh Brewery, Peter W. Stroh born in Detroit 1927 *
20 Children's author Carol McDole born in Ludington 1936
Grammy-winning R & B singer Anita Baker born in Detroit 1957
21 Attorney Alan Earl Schwartz born in Detroit 1925
23 M.P.Lowrie of Adrian received the first music degree presented in the state, 1873
25 False "Fire!" alarm kills 72 during Christmas Eve service in Italian Hall in Calumet during long miners' strike in 1913
28 Actor Martin Milner, of "Adam-12," born in Detroit 1927
Labor union official Owen Frederick Bieber born in North Dorr 1929
30 UAW sit-down strikes 1936 earns workers a 5-cent raise at GM's Flint plant and turns Flint into union town
31 Actor Jason Robards, Sr., father of actor Jason Robards, Jr., born 1892 in Hillsdale
Helen Richey, first woman to fly airmail, lands in Detroit 1934 *

INDEX OF PEOPLE, PLACES, AND ORGANIZATIONS

AWESOME ALMANACS™

The AWESOME ALMANACS of the 50 States are created by encyclopedia editor Jean F. Blashfield and the staff of B&B Publishing, Inc. Each AWESOME ALMANAC contains comprehensive coverage of the best, the worst, the most, the least, of each state, as well as essential and fun information. Fun for browsing and useful for reference, the Awesome Almanacs are great for the traveler, students, and information buffs.

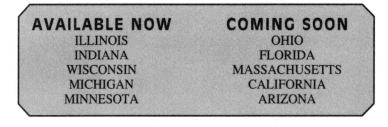

AVAILABLE NOW	COMING SOON
ILLINOIS	OHIO
INDIANA	FLORIDA
WISCONSIN	MASSACHUSETTS
MICHIGAN	CALIFORNIA
MINNESOTA	ARIZONA

152-200 pages each, all AWESOME ALMANACS are profusely illustrated with black and white photographs, art, and maps. They contain a calendar of historical events and births of famous people. Indexed.

Paperback – $12.95
(20% discount to schools and libraries)
You will find AWESOME ALMANACS in your favorite bookstore, or order from:

B&B PUBLISHING, INC.
P.O. BOX 393
FONTANA, WI 53125

FOR CREDIT CARD OR SCHOOL AND LIBRARY ORDERS,
call 1-800-325-6125